Wordsworth and the Critics

John L. Mahoney

Wordsworth and the Critics

The Development of a Critical Reputation

CAMDEN HOUSE

First published 2001
by Camden House

Camden House is an imprint of Boydell & Brewer Inc.
PO Box 41026, Rochester, NY 14604–4126 USA
and of Boydell & Brewer Limited
PO Box 9, Woodbridge, Suffolk IP12 3DF, UK

ISBN: 1–57113–090–x

Library of Congress Cataloging-in-Publication Data

Wordsworth and the critics : the development of a reputation / John L. Mahoney
    p.   cm. (Studies in English and American literature, linguistics, and culture.
    Literary criticism in perspective)
    Includes bibliographical references and index.
    ISBN 1–57113– 090–x (alk. paper)
        1. Wordsworth, William, 1770–1850—Criticism and interpretation—
History. I. Title. II. Studies in English and American literature, linguistics,
and culture (Unnumbered).

PR5887.3 .M34 2000
821'.7—dc21

                                            00-064201

A catalogue record for this title is available from the British Library.

This publication is printed on acid-free paper.
Printed in the United States of America.

For Ann, as always

But where will Europe's latter hour
Again find Wordsworth's healing power?
Others will teach us how to dare,
And against fear our breast to steel;
Others will strengthen us how to bear
But who, ah! who, will make us feel?
The cloud of mortal destiny,
Others will front it fearlessly —
But who, like him, will put it by?

Keep fresh the grass upon his grave
O Rotha, with thy living wave!
Sing him thy best! for few or none
Hears thy voice right, now he is gone.

—Matthew Arnold
Memorial Verses

Contents

Acknowledgments

WHILE IT MAY NOT TAKE A VILLAGE TO MAKE A BOOK, it clearly took the hard work, devotion, and helpful advice of many to write this modest history of a literary reputation, especially the reputation of such a formidable and long-lived poet as William Wordsworth. Following the course of his critical reception from early journal, review, and magazine notices to the most recent scholarship on the life and work is a great challenge.

I would be remiss indeed if I neglected to offer thanks to the many scholars who have been there before me in this task of studying Wordsworth's critical reception. N. S. Bauer, Dan Crosby, Marilyn Gaull, John Hayden, James Logan, David Perkins, Thomas Philbin, Thomas Raysor, Steven Sharp, Donald Reiman, David Stam, and Nathaniel Teich have done major work in the field, and I am in their debt. At the same time I must not neglect the painstaking tracing of Wordsworth reviews in the M. A. theses, Ph.D. dissertations, and essays of Olive Paralee Burchfiel, Robert Stone Christian, Thomas J. Gavagan, Elton Henly, and Essie Scott Liggins. They have been truly laborers in a fertile and complex vineyard, and I have reaped many benefits from their work.

Elaine Tarutis, my continuing Editorial Assistant, is that rare example of someone who combines excellent research skills with the fine art of manuscript editing and preparation, and this study could not have reached fruition without her steady and cheery support. Dr. Brendan Rapple, Reference Librarian of the O'Neill Library of Boston College, is every scholar's model of guide, philosopher, and friend. Not far behind in commitment to the project and special talents required for its completion are Heather Lynch, Kristina Reader, Teri Torchia, Anne Halli, and Patrick Coombs, whose remarkable tracking down of key materials was matched by their ability to isolate crucial sections of these materials for my perusal. All five were winners of Faculty Undergraduate Research Assistantships, and I'm grateful to Boston College for affording me the opportunity to participate in the program. I'm also grateful to the Boston College Thomas F. Rattigan Research Fund for strong support of my work. Special thanks also for many services provided by both the O'Neill Library of Boston College and by the British Library.

Especially supportive and helpful in the course of a long project have been Rosemarie Bodenheimer, Judith Wilt, Richard Schrader, J. Robert Barth, S.J., Alan Richardson, Dayton Haskin, Paul Lewis, and Kevin Van Anglen. Professor Schrader's continuing readiness to render bibliographical and editorial advice has again been a model of scholarly collegiality.

As always, Ann Dowd Mahoney has been a quiet but never-failing supporter. Mary Lou and Neil Hegarty, Margaret Mahoney, and Dot and Ray Angelone as well as John and Lenor, Pat and Jim, Bill and El-vie were always cheering from the stands. And Alison, Emma, Emily, and Erin were nearby. And once again my special thanks for the special gifts of Harry Locke and of Jackie Cain and Roy Kral.

J. L. M.
Chestnut Hill, MA
May 2000

Introduction

TRACING THE HISTORY of any writer's critical reputation, of a writer's reception both by fellow writers and by those who ply the crafts of reviewing, critiquing, or, especially nowadays, theorizing, is a daunting but important task. There is the obvious problem of time: the farther removed the writer from the present, the more massive the body of material responding to the author's work. There is the added factor of the length of the writer's career. Wordsworth, for example, wrote steadily from his earliest schoolboy days in the 1780s almost to the end of his life in 1850. The better known the writer in his lifetime, the closer to a circle of literary friends and colleagues, the fuller the correspondence and the commentary. Then there is the matter of availability of print material, of books, journals, magazines, newspapers, and a well-established body of literary reviews. The greater the availability of such material, the more formidable the challenge to the contemporary scholar to insure that he or she is in touch with a large and representative body of such material.

Shakespeare is removed from us by almost four hundred years, and yet, considering a number of factors such as technology, manuscript preservation, cultural priorities, indeed the very ideas of authorship itself, nothing like a literary reputation and a continuing tradition of critical response to *his* work really developed until the late seventeenth or early eighteenth century.

The coming of the printing press and of Gutenberg's movable type in the mid-fifteenth century were to provide the engines of criticism, although the first printed books were Bibles, religious treatises, and some of the humanistic writings recovered in the Renaissance revival of learning. The early sixteenth century witnessed the rise of a vernacular language after the dominance of Latin, the competing claims of science and religion, the growth of literacy (however slow) and the accompanying development of public and private libraries. These phenomena certainly paved the way for a widening reading audience, interested in news and, eventually, in literary news. J. A. Downie and Thomas Corns, noting the end of pre-publication censorship with the expiration of the Licensing Act in 1695, contend that "the most striking periods of growth in newspaper and periodical publishing in England happened during years of political unrest" (1–2).

The years following the Restoration of 1660 saw an evolution from "crude newsbooks" and "two-page essay papers and simple miscellanies" (Hurd 5) to a full-blown development of the periodical, foreshadowed perhaps by publications such as L'Estrange's *Observator.* Papers such as Defoe's *Review* (1704) and Steele's *Tatler* (1709) appeared, with the *Tatler* becoming a regular publication geared for a coffee-house audience of both men and women. And even though *The Tatler* ceased publication in 1711, Steele remained an important presence and influence, launching with his friend and colleague Joseph Addison the enormously successful *Spectator* which reached an impressive daily circulation of three thousand copies.

What followed amounted to a torrent of publication: Oliver Goldsmith's *Citizen of the World*, Henry Fielding's *The Patriot*, Tobias Smollett's *Critical Review*, Samuel Johnson's papers (the *Idler, Adventurer*, and *Rambler*) and Edmund Cave's *Gentleman's Magazine*, for which Johnson did Parliamentary reports. Much of this ranged beyond literary criticism to include essays on politics, religion, manners, and morals. Daily, monthly, and yearly literary reviewing will be the first concern of this study. Well before Wordsworth's entrance into the literary scene, such reviewing was alive and indeed flourishing, often taking on a savage tone. One need only remember Pope's *Dunciad* and *Epistle to Dr. Arbuthnot* to see a poet taking sharp umbrage at what he could only regard as the most vicious *ad hominem* criticism.

The eighteenth century also saw the development and flourishing of reviews such as the *Monthly Review*, the *Critical Review*, the *Analytical Review*, the *British Critic*, the *Anti-Jacobin Review and Magazine*, the *Christian Observer*, the *Eclectic Review*, the *Annual Review* and many others, each with a particular political or religious slant. All of these kept an ever-widening audience abreast of news and information of all kinds. When one Ralph Griffiths brought out the *Monthly* in 1749, there was hardly any other journal of its kind, dealing as it did not only with the usual material, but also with commentary on scholarly works and on a variety of literary forms previously ignored. Like the modern literary editor of *The New York Times Book Review*, the *New York Review of Books* or many local literary pages, Griffiths tried to provide full reviews of major publications, but also brief notices of less notable works with the modest disclaimer, cited by Derek Roper, that his ambitions were "to enter no farther into the province of criticism, than just so far as may be indispensably necessary to give some idea of such books as come under our consideration." Modesty aside, *The Monthly* succeeded impressively, and with a number of able reviewers such as Smollett, competitors soon spied a market, with Smollett himself founding the *Critical Review* in 1756. As Roper puts it, in the period before the coming of the *Edinburgh Review*, "these Reviews stood at the height of their power and prestige. The 'cultural explosion' of the eighteenth century had meant a vast increase in the number of persons eager to learn about books. The rising not only brought prosperity to the *Monthly* and *Critical*, but supported other successful Reviews: between 1793 and 1796 five notable Reviews were being published" (19–21).

All of the above notwithstanding, in 1802, as Marilyn Gaull notes, "periodical criticism entered a new era with the founding of the *Edinburgh Review*" (17). Published in Scotland at the height of an intellectual renaissance, it was handsomely funded by Archibald Constable the bookseller, attracted the most talented writers and reviewers, and provided them with the kind of freedom that good criticism requires. The *dramatis personae* of the founding and early development were truly impressive, some of them leaving their mark on literary history and literary reputations from the beginning. Most notable, especially in a study of the making of Wordsworth's reputation, were the renowned Francis Jeffrey, editor for 26 years, and later a judge and a Lord; Henry Brougham, a longstanding member of Parliament who led the movement for the abolition of the slave trade and later became Lord Chancellor; and Sidney Smith, the noted Anglican minister who eventually became Canon of St. Paul's. With decidedly liberal, progressive leanings, the *Edinburgh Review* seemed bound to encourage rivals, and rivals were forthcoming. As Gaull argues, "it was so liberal, so intellectually audacious and politically uncommitted that, following a review in October 1808, that appeared opposing the war against France, the Tories, led by Sir Walter Scott, defected to start the London based *Quarterly Review*" (18–19). Its conservative bent is immediately apparent as one finds a new cast of characters on its staff: William Gifford, editor of the politically conservative *Anti-Jacobin* and a critic unhappy with the state of contemporary literature; John Wilson Croker, First Secretary of the Admiralty; George Canning, who was to become Prime Minister in 1827; card-carrying conservatives such as Southey and Scott; and the patron and good angel of the *Quarterly*, the publisher John Murray. John Hayden, a distinguished student of nineteenth-century British reviewing, regards the *Edinburgh* and *Quarterly* as quite simply "the two greatest periodicals in the history of English journalism and the two greatest critical influences on English Romantic literature" (38).

Magazine publication was at the same time exploding, and according to Gaull, it had become "the dominant form of periodical publication by 1815" (9). Here was the perfect medium for an increasingly aware and demanding middle-class reading public eager for news and amusement. The *London Magazine,* with its great array of talent including Lamb, Hazlitt, Clare, and DeQuincey; *Tait's Edinburgh Magazine*; and *Blackwood's Edinburgh Magazine* — these are just a few examples of many such publications.

Add to these media the daily newspapers, especially those of the editor Daniel Stuart and his *Morning Post,* which included Coleridge, Wordsworth, Southey and Lamb among its contributors, and one gets the sense of the vitality of the print medium in Wordsworth's early writing years. Coleridge, of course, had two papers of his own — *The Watchman* and *The Friend: A Literary, Moral, and Political Paper. The Times,* according to Gaull, had a daily circulation of 5,000, and Stuart's *Evening Courier* "ran from 10,000 to 16,000 as the public awaited news of war" during the years between 1793 and 1815 (43). Leigh Hunt, who along with Keats had suffered the slings of outrageous labeling when dubbed the leader of the Cockney School of Poetry in *Blackwood's Edinburgh Magazine,* proceeded to launch in 1808, with his brother John, what Gaull describes as the most influential London paper, the *Examiner: A New Sunday Paper upon Politics, Domestic Economy, and Theatricals* (31). Hayden sums up the flourishing of journals and suggests the intertwining of literature and politics in his comment that "the early nineteenth century was in fact the heyday of political reviewing; never before or since has it been so energetic and widespread" (1).

Such was the situation in which the young William Wordsworth, or for that matter any young writer, found himself as he began to ply his wares in the early 1790s, a situation that needs to be fully understood and appreciated by any student of the poet and his work. This book will, however, not simply attempt to follow the course of a life and career, as many admirable standard and recent biographies have done, but rather the course of a reputation as it evolved from the poet's earliest probes to his first celebrity, to notable critical attacks, to his position as a recognized major poet in the first half of the nineteenth century. T. M. Raysor makes the interesting point that "the study of Wordsworth's early reputation has attracted a great deal of attention not only as part of his life, but as a chapter in literary criticism to which

Coleridge, Hazlitt, Lamb, Leigh Hunt, DeQuincey, Jeffrey, Wilson, and almost every famous or infamous literary critic of the early nineteenth century has contributed" (61).

The words "fifty years" of a century sound ominous: the sheer volume of Wordsworth's work and the length of his writing career present the late twentieth-century scholar with a formidable task. Almost from the beginning his work attracted the attention of the journals, magazines, and newspapers, which focused on a broad range of themes. These included the experimental nature of his earliest poetry and poetic theory; the development of a new kind of self-centered and challenging autobiographical/philosophical poetry; his political and religious leanings as they developed over a lifetime of eighty years; and finally his established status as Squire of Rydal Mount, receiver of honorary degrees from Oxford and Durham, and his crowning as Poet Laureate. The sheer volume of materials surrounding the reception of his work during his lifetime is in many ways quite enough for a volume such as this one. Indeed another volume — Stephen Gill's brilliant new study *Wordsworth and the Victorians* comes to mind — might be devoted to the responses of his fellow nineteenth-century poets, critics, and philosophers. The curious windings of twentieth-century criticism from the early literary and intellectual history to the New Criticism to more recent developments such as Deconstruction, Feminism, New Historicism, and Cultural Studies already have the potential, for anyone so brave to consider it, for a formidable critical anthology. Wordsworth has been loved and despised, canonized and questioned, yet he remains part of the much maligned Pantheon, the Literary Canon. He is still very much with us — in the Academy and beyond — as readers of poetry, poets, teachers, philosophers and cultural critics. And this is a strategic time for one of the company of Wordsworthians to study how his work has been, is, and — possibly — will be received.

There are, of course, a number of ways of proceeding, many of which, I suspect, would be helpful in coming to terms with the evolution of Wordsworth's reputation as a writer. But in keeping with the purpose of the Camden House Series, the present writer has chosen to follow a narrative route rather than constructing a descriptive bibliography of reviews or a chronology or a summary of critical viewpoints. The following pages will, to be sure, suggest the sheer volume of publications in the hustle and bustle of the literary world, from a time when newspapers, reviews, and magazines were the key vehicles for reaching audiences, to a later era that favored more formal essays, to the twentieth century with its early phenomenon of books on Wordsworth and its later lodging of critical opinion in the large enterprises of university and commercial presses as well as the enormous variety of journals devoted to British Romantic poetry in general and to William Wordsworth in particular.

I have already suggested the folly of attempting a definitive study of Wordsworth's reputation in a volume this size, in a series of this kind. Anyone close to Wordsworth studies can attest to the fact that the scholarship of even one year is a major challenge. So, with proper, indeed unavoidable, humility I propose to be as comprehensive as possible in presenting a representative sample of important critiques of Wordsworth from the beginning. But, more important and I hope more useful, I want to look for large themes and trends, the ups and downs of attitudes towards the poet's work from that wide audience that includes professional academic critics, journalistic critics with special literary interests and competence, and those more general readers and their personal responses to poetry as part of the experience of an educated man or woman.

Such an approach is in keeping with the spirit of the Camden House *Literary Criticism in Perspective* series which traces literary scholarship and criticism on major and neglected writers alike, or on a single major work, a group of writers, a literary school or movement. In so doing the authors, authorities in their fields, address a readership of scholars, students of literature at the graduate and undergraduate level, and the general reader. One of the key purposes of the series is to illuminate the nature of literary criticism itself and to reveal the impact of social and historical contexts on aesthetic judgments once considered objective and definitive.

Works Consulted

Downie, J. A. and Thomas N. Corns, eds. *Telling People What To Think: Early Eighteenth-Century Periodicals from "The Review" to "The Rambler."* London and Portland, OR: Frank Cass & Co., Ltd., 1993.

Gaull, Marilyn. *Romanticism: The Human Context.* New York and London: W. W. Norton, 1988.

Gill, Stephen. *Wordsworth and the Victorians.* Oxford: Clarendon P, 1998.

Hayden, John O. *The Romantic Reviewers, 1802–1824.* Chicago: U of Chicago P, 1968.

Hurd, Harold. *The March of Journalism: The Story of the British Press from 1622 to the Present Day.* Westport, CT: Greenwood Press Publishers, 1970.

Raysor, Thomas M. "The Establishment of Wordsworth's Reputation." *Journal of English and German Philology.* 54 (1965): 61–71.

Roper, Derek. *Reviewing Before the Edinburgh, 1788–1802.* Newark: U of Delaware P, 1978.

1: Early Responses

WORDSWORTH'S WORK WAS NOTED almost from the beginning. No sudden wonder, no unrecognized laborer in literary vineyards was he. He was associated early on with poets and critics who, praise him or blame him, kept his name fairly prominent in contemporary discussions of literature. Elsie Smith contends that it was "chiefly due to Coleridge, too, that Wordsworth achieved any contemporary fame" (13). Coleridge writes to John Thelwall in 1796 that Wordsworth was "the best poet of the age" (1.215–216). And looking back on Wordsworth's earliest work, Coleridge notes in his *Biographia Literaria* that "year after year increased the numbers of Wordsworth admirers. They were found too not in the lower classes of the reading public, but chiefly among young men of strong sensibility and meditative minds; and their admiration (inflamed perhaps in some degree by opposition) was distinguished by its intensity, I might almost say, by its *religious* fervour" (2.9).

While Wordsworth wrote poems as early as his schoolboy days at Hawkshead School, his first poems of note were *An Evening Walk Addressed to a Young Lady* and *Descriptive Sketches Taken During a Pedestrian Tour Among the Alps*. Kenneth Johnston most recently has said that by the end of 1793 "the poems were well enough regarded to be discussed at avant-garde student literary groups at Cambridge" (332). The first poem, with his sister Dorothy as listener, is very much in the tradition of Sensibility. Composed at Cambridge and during his first two vacations from the university in 1788 and 1789, it moves geographically from his Cockermouth birthplace and Keswick to his true homes in Windermere and Grasmere, catching the sights and sounds, the lights and shades of the walk. Yet it is in many ways more than the standard poem of Sensibility, associated with writers like Thomson, Beattie, and Collins, as the visual is touched by a certain meditativeness and awe in the presence of nature.

Descriptive Sketches, composed in 1791 and 1792 and published in 1793 after his experiences in Revolutionary France, recounts a summer journey to the Continent with his friend and fellow walker Robert Jones. This poem, too, is richly descriptive and strongly emotional, with its spectacular scenes from Switzerland — the crossing of the Alps in particular — and its reflection on the power, politics, and violence of the events in France.

It is important in a study such as this one to attend, however briefly, to what might be considered lesser poems of Wordsworth. While written about less often by later critics, these poems received a fair amount of attention, much of it favorable, in their time, and a brief overview of positive and negative responses in journals and magazines provides valuable insights into dimensions of Wordsworth's writing that continue to be objects of critical attention in the years ahead. Some reviewers are quick to associate the poems with the picturesque conventions of eighteenth-century poetry. The *Critical Review* for July 1793 praises the new and picturesque imagery of *An Evening Walk* (347–48). Later in the same *Review*, the critic is harsh on *Descriptive Sketches*, saying that the poet has caught "few sparks from these glowing scenes," that Wordsworth's "lines are often harsh and prosaic; his images ill-chosen, and his descriptions feeble and insipid" (472–74). Thomas Holcroft in the *Monthly Review*, irritated by the self-consciousness he detects, is sarcastic in his "How often shall we in vain advise those, who are so delighted with their own thoughts that they cannot forbear putting them into rhyme, to examine those thoughts till they understand them." Or, even more sharply expressed, "More descriptive poetry? Have we not yet enough? Must eternal changes be rung on uplands and lowlands and nodding forests and brooding clouds, and cells, and dells, and dingles? Yes; more and yet more: so it is decreed" (216–18).

The *Analytical Review* offers a mixed but significant review, praising *Descriptive Sketches* thus: "The diversified pictures of nature which are sketched in this poem could only have been produced by actual and attentive observation with an abundant store of materials." Yet the poem "has a certain laboured obscurity and artificial cast of expression which often involves the poet's meaning in obscurity." One detects a certain pattern already emerging in this earliest criticism. Wordsworth, we hear, is a reasonably good descriptive poet whose work is often weakened by "obscurity," an increasingly used word, along with "metaphysical," more often than not suggesting excessive philosophizing. In a word, he is successful to the extent that he tempers his self-centeredness and his tendency to ruminate even in poems such as *An Evening Walk* and *Descriptive Sketches* and continues in the descriptive vein of the Poetry of Sensibility (294–96).

The "Peregrinator" in the *Gentleman's Magazine* has strong praise for *An Evening Walk* in what he regards as the first full review of the poem. He finds a very practical value in the pleasure he has received from the tour described and wishes the same for "others who shall have to make, or who have already made, the same tour." A reader of the poem will find added pleasure in the "general imagery of the country enumerated and described with a spirit of elegance which prove that the author has viewed nature with the attentive and warm regard of a true poet." Though not without faults, there is much to anticipate from this "first production of Mr. W.'s name," says the reviewer, noting the poet's mention of the forthcoming *Descriptive Sketches* (253).

But Wordsworth, like fortunate young writers in any age, had a major rooter, a fellow poet with strong philosophical leanings and a growing reputation, who took a measured approach to *Descriptive Sketches* but ultimately offered the kind of praise that was bound to catch the attention of readers. It was Coleridge, and in the "Notes" to his own *Poems on Various Subjects* he calls attention to problems with the rhythm of the poem and, here is the word again, a diction that is "too frequently obscure," but, saving the best for last, offers praise for the poem as superior in "manly sentiment, novel imagery, and vivid colouring" (185). More impressive is his retrospective look at *Descriptive Sketches* in his *Biographia Literaria*. Recalling that he had become acquainted with the poem in his last year of residence at Cambridge (December 1794), he recalls that for him "seldom, if ever, was the emergence of an original poetic genius above the literary horizon more evidently announced." With the same critical rigor Coleridge expresses some reservations about the language and imagery and about a certain notable "obscurity," but he nevertheless concludes that "it is remarkable how soon genius clears and purifies itself from the faults and errors of its earliest products" (1.77–78).

A New Kind of Poetry: Theory and Practice

It is Coleridge who also recounts in his *Biographia Literaria* Wordsworth's and, to some extent, his own plan for the first major literary effort of Wordsworth's career, the *Lyrical Ballads* project. Here was the plan for a new kind of poetry, one that was to move beyond philosophical description and meditative sensibility to deal with men and women living close to the land, away from the drawing room and salon, and to represent them in a language free of conventional poetic diction and closer to the language of their daily lives. "In this idea," writes Coleridge, "originated the plan of the 'Lyrical Ballads'; in which it was agreed, that my endeavours should be directed to persons and characters supernatural, or at least romantic, yet so as to transfer from our inward nature a human interest and a semblance of truth sufficient to procure for these shadows of imagination that willing suspension of disbelief that constitutes poetic faith" (2.6).

Wordsworth, the real master spirit of what reviewers will quickly come to call, for better or worse, a new "system" of poetry, was to have a different aim, "to give the charm of novelty to things of everyday, and to excite a feeling analogous to the supernatural by awakening the mind's attention from the lethargy of custom, and directing it to the loveliness of the world before us" (2.7). Such was the plan resulting in a 1798 edition with a brief "Advertisement," followed two years later by a second edition, with additional poems and with the celebrated "Preface" that became for many the manifesto of the new experiment or system.

The "Preface" announces a poetry truer to the people, with settings, language, and characters he knew best: mendicants who drew their sustenance from the kindness of others and who in turn evoke the generosity of others; abandoned women and their plight; and children alert and alive, and untouched by the corruptions of the world. "It was," as John Jordan puts it, "a much more sophisticated kind of description based on an almost mystical awareness of an interaction in observation between the scene and the observer, so that the quality of the experience became the significant thing, and the feeling gave importance to the action" (163–64).

There is, as I've noted in my *Wordsworth: A Poetic Life* (67–68), a quite classical-neoclassical dimension to the developing version of the "Preface" although, as Kenneth Johnston has noted, Wordsworth is ultimately trying to reconcile the mimetic and expressive dimensions. Johnston's crisp sentence is most perceptive: "What had been hypothesized in 1798 was theorized in 1800, and now retheorized for 1802" (765). As Wordsworth retheorizes, he would have poetry be faithful to nature, but he views nature as a living and organic process and emphasizes the importance of mind in shaping the materials of experience and the need for a freer, more direct, and more natural expression.

Poetry for Wordsworth is "the most philosophic of all writing . . . its object is truth, not individual and local, but general, and operative." Taking his place with the great apologists for poets, he contends that, unlike the biographer and the historian, the poet "writes under one restriction only, namely, the necessity of giving pleasure to a human being possessed of that information which may be expected of him, not as a lawyer, a physician, a mariner, an astronomer, or a natural philosopher, but as a Man" (1.139). Yes, he has been more narrowly mimetic in some of his rustic ballads, presenting men and women close to nature with genuine emotions and forceful expression. At the same time, however, he has been responsive to the need for poet-reader engagement, hoping to "gratify certain known habits of association" (1.122) with his "spontaneous overflow of powerful feeling" and his "emotion recollected in tranquillity." And he will avoid naked realism by throwing over his rustic scenario "a certain colouring of imagination, whereby ordinary things should be presented to the mind in an unusual aspect" (1.123).

Interestingly enough, Wordsworth's "Preface," often regarded not only as his manifesto, but as a manifesto for Romantic, even Modern poetry, evoked a wide range of response from critics and from fellow writers of the time. For some it was a pioneering experiment, for others a notable but failed system, for almost all something dramatically different. Coleridge praised the analysis of the low state of contemporary taste and the proposal for remedying the serious problem of eighteenth-century poetic diction. The reviewer in the "General View of Literature, 1808" for the *Edinburgh Annual Register* (1810) offers a useful overview and response in an essay entitled "Of the Living Poets of Great Britain." Connecting Wordsworth, Coleridge, and Southey as "Lakers," he sees them not as some "vulgar" readers do, as "ingenious and accomplished men" committed "to overthrow the ancient landmarks of our poetry." Yet "their peculiarities do not by any means seem to us the most valuable properties of their productions." They are linked by their emphasis on "natural feeling" and "simplified" language as found in "ordinary life." Wordsworth in particular adds a doubtful dimension, indeed a "radical error" in his idea that "the language of low and rustic life ought to be preferred, because, in his opinion, the essential passions of the heart find a better soil in which they can attain their maturity, and because in that condition of life our elementary feelings co-exist in a state of greater simplicity" (426–27). Anna Seward, among the first to appreciate *An Evening Walk* and *Descriptive Sketches*, praising Wordsworth's "genius" and "charming passages," writes that he "is right in observing that the use of common life language in verse is frequently a beauty, but not right in extending that use to all modes of phraseology within the limits of the immodest, the disgusting and the ungrammatic" (6. 258, 280).

William Lyall in the *Quarterly Review* would separate admiration for the poems from "entertaining all the tenets of his poetical system." On the one hand, the earlier poems "exhibit a mind richly stored with all the materials from which poetry is formed; — elevation of sentiment —

tenderness of heart — the truest sensibility for the beauties of nature — combined with extraordinary fervour of imagination, and a most praiseworthy love of simplicity both in thought and language." Yet "he has by no means turned these valuable endowments to their greatest advantage," and his works "have hitherto not met with the most flattering success" (201). Taking to task Wordsworth's impatience with dissenting readers, the reviewer nevertheless contends that "though Wordsworth is, we think, occasionally somewhat unlucky in the topics . . . yet we know not any writer who, upon the whole, has painted them with more pathos and fidelity." As far as the poet's speaking of purifying the language of "low and rustic life, the truth is, if the language of low life be purified from what *we* should call its *real defects*, it will differ only in copiousness from the language of high life" (204–5).

James Montgomery, in a generally favorable review of the later 1807 poems, begins with comments on the ballads by citing Wordsworth as distinguishing himself "in this age of poetical experiment" as "one of the boldest and most fortunate adventurers in the field of innovation." Citing Wordsworth's comments in the "Preface" on rustic life and common language favorably, he does add that "however we might agree with him, so far as his system would restrict the multitude of epithets that frequently render verse too heavy for endurance — we would certainly protest against the unqualified rejection of those embellishments of diction, suited to the elevation of enthusiastic thoughts equally above ordinary discourse and ordinary capacities, which essentially distinguish Poetry from Prose." Remembering Wordsworth's remarks in the "Preface" about there being no essential difference between the language of poetry and prose, he reinforces his key point that the "poetical sensibility" will generally "suggest language more lively, affecting, and fervent, than passion itself can inspire in minds less tremblingly alive to every touch of pain or pleasure" (35–37).

So Wordsworth receives what amounts to qualified praise although the negatives underline sharply specific reservations. Rudeness, writes an anonymous reviewer in the *New London Review*, is not the same as simplicity, and Wordsworth at times does not follow his own principles for superior poetic diction (33–35). And Charles Burney, a critic of some importance, bemoans in the *Monthly Review* a return to the vulgar practices of the past (202–10).

Interestingly enough, the poems themselves receive a fair amount of praise even when the theory or system is questioned. James Montgomery, already cited, is a good example. For him some of the ballads — he singles out *The Old Cumberland Beggar*, "Verses on the Naming of Places," and, with long quotations, *Tintern Abbey* — "have taught us new sympathies, the existence of which in our nature had scarcely been intimated to us by any preceding poet." It is this emphasis on Wordsworth's power to read the human heart, to engage the feelings that begins to be noted even when there are still reservations about the poet's system. Montgomery gives new meaning to the power of poetry when he describes Wordsworth as "himself a living example of the power a man of genius possesses, of awakening unknown and ineffable sensations in the hearts of his fellow-creatures." Granted the puerility of some of the ballads, the poetry on occasion has a "pleasing effect." And when the poet presents "*ordinary* things in an *unusual* way by casting over them a certain colouring of imagination, he is compelled very frequently to resort to splendid, figurative, and amplifying language" (37–38).

Thomas Stoddart in the *British Critic*, negative on the obscurity and inflated language of *An Evening Walk* and *Descriptive Sketches*, responds positively to the *Lyrical Ballads* where Wordsworth has adopted a purity of expression that transcends the merely rustic and "is infinitely more correspondent with true feeling than what by the courtesy of the day, is usually called poetic language." He declares himself the poet "chiefly of humble and rustic life . . . and he portrays it . . . with the beautiful and permanent forms of nature" (125–26).

The responses of Wordsworth's friends and fellow writers are also instructive. DeQuincey writes to Wordsworth a long letter of admiration for the *Lyrical Ballads* which gave him more than "the whole aggregate of pleasure I have received from some eight or nine other poets that I have been able to find since the world began . . . and that not yourself only but that each place and object you have mentioned . . . and all the souls in that delightful community of yours — to me are dearer than the sun" (95). Unpredictable as usual, Byron, while savaging the 1807 *Poems*, feels that the *Lyrical Ballads* received proper praise in the reviews (65–66).

Robert Southey, a fellow Laker, has reservations not so much with the idea of Wordsworth's experiment, but with his choice of subject. In his somewhat mixed notice in the *Critical Review* he writes: "The 'experiment,' we think has failed, not because the language of conversation is little adapted to the purposes of poetic pleasure but because it has been tried upon uninteresting subjects" in poems like *The Thorn*, *The Idiot Boy*, and "Goody Blake and Harry Gill." He strikes a more positive note in his remarks that "every piece discovers genius; and, ill as the author has frequently employed his talents, they certainly rank him with the best of living poets" (204). Southey waxes rhapsodical in a March 30, 1804 letter to John Rickman: "Wordsworth," he writes, "will do better, and leave behind him a name, unique in his way; he will rank among the very first poets, and probably possesses a mass of merits superior to all, except only Shakespeare" (2.278).

Returning to Coleridge, Wordsworth's close friend and original collaborator, we notice a mild distancing, not so much from Wordsworth, the poet of strong feeling and lively and engaging imagination, but from the poet of humble and rustic life, the sponsor of the language of real men, and the advocate of the idea that there is no essential difference between the language of prose and poetry. Coleridge, as much as anyone, was responsible for Wordsworth achieving contemporary fame.

Coleridge begins his *Lyrical Ballads* commentary in the *Biographia Literaria* with a tracing of the background of his own involvement, especially his contribution of *The Rime of the Ancient Mariner*. And he is remarkably candid and fair in his evaluation although challenging Wordsworth's premises about life close to the soil. Basing his reservations on Aristotle's "poetry as poetry, is essentially ideal, it avoids and excludes all accident," he feels that rustics "offer scanty vocabulary for educated reflection, and if you refine it, how is it any different from the language of the ordinary man of common sense." He, in fact, argues against the essential nobility of such a life, pointing out that for him characters like Michael and Ruth are hardly low. And he is straightforward in pointing up the gap between some of the rustic pieces and the greatness of a poem like *Tintern Abbey*. His tone is basically sympathetic as he argues that "the omission of less than a hundred lines would have precluded nine-tenths of the criticism on the work" (1.69). Wordsworth, he says, "in a comparatively small number of poems . . . chose to try an experiment; and this experiment we will suppose to have failed" (2.119).

On the one hand, he comments, there are the "austere purity and appropriateness of language"; the "weight and sanity of the sentiments gained not from books but from meditative observation"; "the sinewy strength and originality of single lines and paragraphs"; "the perfect truth of nature in his images and descriptions"; "meditative pathos"; "the gift of IMAGINATION in the highest and strictest sense of the word," a gift that puts Wordsworth next only to Shakespeare and Milton (2.142–51). On the other hand, he wonders about what he calls the "matter-of-factness," the too frequent use of the dramatic form, the tendency toward using images and emotions too great for the subject.

Wordsworth's preoccupation with the particular, even with the accidental as ways of achieving credibility for his theory is counterproductive since full, literal explanation is not the point of poetry. And his piecemeal imagery is a product of the inferior faculty of fancy when his wonderfully strong imaginative power "would have flashed the whole picture at once upon the eye." Coleridge will later use the same criteria in his critique of the Wordsworthian desire for verisimilitude in *The Excursion*. "Is there," he questions, "one word for instance, attributed to the pedlar in THE EXCURSION, characteristic of a *pedlar?* One sentiment, that might not more plausibly, even without the aid of any previous explanation, have proceeded from any wise and beneficent old man, of a rank and profession in which the language of learning and refinement are natural and to be expected?" As a matter of fact, he continues, so many, if not all "the admirable passages interposed on this narration, might, with trifling alterations, have been far more appropriately, and with far greater verisimilitude, told of a poet in the character of a poet" (2.134–35).

Yet, all of the above having been said, Coleridge can stand back and "reflect with delight, how little a mere theory, though of his own workmanship, interferes with the processes of genuine imagination in a man of true poetic genius, who possesses, as Mr. Wordsworth, if ever a man did, most assuredly does possess 'The Vision and The Faculty Divine'" (2.59–60).

William Hazlitt, certainly a major critical voice in the Romantic era whose comments will be heard again in this study, is specific in his likes and dislikes and in his particular political biases. With typical flair he places Wordsworth "at the head of that which has been denominated the Lake School of poetry; a school which, with all my respect for it, I do not think sacred from criticism or exempt from faults, of some of which faults I shall speak with becoming frankness" (5.161).

For Hazlitt "Mr. Wordsworth's genius is a pure emanation of the Spirit of the Age" (11.86). He connects the "Lake School" with the beginnings of the French Revolution, or rather with "those sentiments and opinions which produced that revolution." His strong anti-eighteenth-century feelings are evident in his anger at the "mechanical" poetry of the age, especially the work of "the followers of Pope and the old French school of poetry." For Hazlitt the Revolution provided an "impulse that moved poetry from the most servile imitation and tamest common-place, to the utmost pitch of singularity and paradox" (5.161).

Yet, admire Wordsworth as much as he did, Hazlitt could not respond with any real enthusiasm to most of the poet's ventures into humble and rustic life. To be sure, Wordsworth "is the most original poet now living. He is the reverse of Walter Scott in his defects and excellences. He has nearly all that the other wants; and wants all that the other possesses. His poetry is not external, but internal; it does not depend upon tradition or story, or old song; he furnishes it from his own mind, and is his own subject . . . . Of many of the Lyrical Ballads, it is not possible to speak in terms of too high praise" (5.156). As we shall see later, however, Hazlitt's admiration is tempered when he says that "we cannot extend the same admiration to . . . the manners of country life in general. We go along with him while he is the subject of his own narrative, but we take leave of him when he makes pedlars and ploughmen his heroes and the interpreters of his sentiments" (19.20).

Although Francis Jeffrey eventually turned out to be the most sharply negative of Wordsworth's reviewers, he did have some relatively kind words for the ballads in his reviews of the 1807 poems. They were in his judgment "deservedly popular" with a "strong spirit of originality, of pathos, and natural feeling" in spite of their "occasional vulgarity, affectation, and silliness." Yet Jeffrey feels it "necessary to set ourselves against this alarming innovation." "Childishness, conceit, and affectation, are not of themselves very popular or attractive; and though *mere* novelty has sometimes been found sufficient to give them a temporary currency, we should have had no fear of their prevailing to any dangerous extent, if they had not been graced with no more seductive accompaniments" (214–15).

Thomas Raysor sums up nicely the general sales reception of the *Lyrical Ballads*, a reception more than favorable even when reviewers and general readers questioned his theory of poetry, his "system" as they liked to call it. "After a slow start in 1798," he writes, "largely caused by the malice of Southey against Coleridge, the first edition sold as well as could be expected for a volume so revolutionary in its originality; and the successive editions of 1800, 1802, and 1805, though small, came in fairly rapid succession, and gave clear evidence of a growing reputation." But this reputation was soon to be subverted, mysteriously it would seem given later developments in this history as the two volumes of poems published in 1807, poems like the songs and sonnets so valued by readers today, found hardly a kind word.

"The debacle," Raysor notes, "came in the reception of the *Poems in Two Volumes of 1807*, for Wordsworth's name was certainly trampled under foot, not only by Jeffrey, but by the whole body of critics; and the reading public seems to have accepted their adverse judgment" (71). Briefly, the *Critical Review*, speaking of the poetic genius revealed in the *Lyrical Ballads*, laments his wasting of his gifts on the trivial subjects of the two volumes. The recurring word "obscure" is again summoned, and again, it would seem, with the connotation of difficult or philosophical. The reviewer in *Le Beau Monde* regards the poems as inferior to the *Lyrical Ballads*, more childish and unintelligible (138–142). Byron, as already mentioned, after praising the *Ballads*, attacks the 1807 poems in *Monthly Literary Recreations*, feeling that Wordsworth was wasting his talents on "trifling subjects," "abandoning his mind to quite ordinary ideas in quite silly language" (65–66).

The Critical Review connects Wordsworth with a tribe of egotistical writers (399–403). Jeffrey, fully armed for critical attack in the *Edinburgh Review*, while noticing a continuation of Wordsworth's vulgar subjects, now begins to inject his dissatisfaction with the poet's self-centeredness, his coloring with his own emotion what might be worthy subjects: "It is possible enough, we allow, that the sight of a friend's garden-spade, or a sparrow's nest, or a man gathering leeches, might really have suggested to such a mind a train of powerful impressions and interesting reflections; but it is certain that, to most minds, such association will always appear forced, strained, and unnatural" (218). Judith Page notes Jeffrey's negative gendered critique with his description of the poems and his charge about Wordsworth's feminization of poetry with his "namby pamby," his "prettyisms," his "babyish" manner (38). Jeffrey limits his praise to the poet's "Character of the Happy Warrior," a "manly" work inspired at least in part by Horatio Nelson as well as Wordsworth's beloved brother John, drowned in a shipwreck in 1805 (220). Even the *Immortality Ode* is ridiculed, with only the sonnets escaping the full wrath of Jeffrey's criticism (227).

The essay "Of the Living Poets of Great Britain" in the *Edinburgh Annual Register's* "General View of Literature" for 1808 focuses more sharply on the inwardness or interiority of Wordsworth's life and work. "Hitherto an unsuccessful competitor for poetic fame, as far as it depends upon the general voice of the public, no man has ever considered the character of the poet as more honourable, or his pursuits as more important." The reviewer sees the poet as believing he could reform an age, "which we devoutly believe can be reformed by nothing short of a miracle." In his retreat from the world to the bliss of solitude, "this very state of secluded study seems to have produced effects upon Mr. Wordsworth's genius unfavourable to its popularity." Solitude, argues the essayist, brings its own special dangers to the poet as he loses touch with the great world beyond and becomes too enmeshed in common and uninteresting subjects. Yet, responding to a unique Wordsworthian quality, "his power of interesting the feelings is exquisite, and we do not envy the self-possession of those who can read his beautiful pastorals, 'The Brothers' and 'Michael,' without shedding tears" (428–30).

James Montgomery, after his strong words of support for the great innovation of the *Lyrical Ballads*, turns surprisingly negative on some of the 1807 poems, complaining about the heaviness of the sonnets and the philosophical preaching. He praises the descriptive beauties of *Resolution and Independence* but speaks harshly of the *Immortality Ode* in which "the reader is turned loose into a wilderness of sublimity, tenderness, bombast, and absurdity, to find out the subject as well as he can" (35–42).

Anna Seward, who had mixed reactions to the ballads, continues her general critique in remarks about the 1807 poems. Here Wordsworth is "an egotistic manufacturer of metaphysic importance upon trivial themes" in poems such as "I wandered lonely as a cloud." The poet succeeds for her only when he writes naturally (6.366–367).

In an important general review of both *Lyrical Ballads* and 1807 *Poems* in the *Quarterly Review* for October 1815, William Lyall picks up on a key and continuing theme in the criticism of Wordsworth's early poems. Writing on the several Prefaces, he speaks of the "raciness about his language, and an occasional eloquence in his manner, which serve to keep the reader's attention alive." Yet all of this is counteracted by that same ineffectual straining after something beyond plain good sense, which is so unpleasant in much of his poetry (202). The public, he contends, can just as surely dislike the poet's taste as he can berate theirs.

Ironically, given the later Victorian focus on the philosophy of Wordsworth's poetry, Lyall, apparently with the *Immortality Ode* in mind, sees the poet's flights soar beyond truth into some unknown land in which the reader is lost. "When we are called upon to *feel emotions which lie too deep for tears even with respect to the meanest flower that blows, to cry for nothing, like Diana in the fountain*, over every ordinary object and every common-place occurrence that may happen to cross our way, all communion of feeling between the poet and those who know no more of poetry than their own experience and an acquaintance with the best model is necessarily broken off" (208). Coleridge, however, enters the most resounding rejoinder to complaints about the *Ode*, and in so doing takes a major critical step forward in dealing with the early and continuing complaint about the poet's obscurity. And not only does he deal with the complaint; he provides what seems to be a new way of dealing with the large challenge of the difficulty of poetry, of a poet's attempts to render what are essentially the subtle nuances of human feeling, of the symbol's power to catch some of these nuances. "A poem," he argues, "is not necessarily obscure because it does not aim to be popular. It is enough if the work be perspicuous to those for whom it is written." With not a trace of snobbery he makes the case for high art, for audiences ready and able to meet the challenges of poetry instead of being bogged down in the "savage torpor" that Wordsworth describes in the *Lyrical Ballads* "Preface." "The ode," he contends with great confidence and insight, "was intended for such readers only as had been accustomed to watch the flux and reflux of their inmost being, to which they know that the attributes of time and space are inapplicable and alien, but which yet cannot be conveyed save in symbols of time and space" (2.147). For Coleridge Wordsworth is behind only Shakespeare and Milton in imaginative power.

Despite his disclaimers and self-defenses, Wordsworth was clearly shaken by the reviews. Many students of the poet would attribute the relatively long fallow period after the 1807 *Poems* to a certain malaise if not depression. He had said in the 1800 "Preface" that the reception of his ballads "has differed from my expectations in this only, that I have pleased a greater number than I ventured to hope I should please" (1.118). In his celebrated letter to Lady Beaumont he expresses his conviction that the 1807 *Poems* were geared not for some least common denominator audience, but for serious readers, yet "their imagination has slept; and the voice which is the voice of my Poetry without Imagination cannot be heard" (2.1:146). He speaks also of his "calm confidence that these Poems will live" despite the condemnation of incompetent judges. And he reasserts his faith that his writings "will, in their degree, be efficacious in making men wiser, better, and happier," (2.1:150) a faith underlined by his nephew Christopher in his confidence that "since he did not write for earthly fame, he maintained his equanimity in all weathers" (2.331).

Yet Wordsworth was not unaware of the importance of audience, however limited it might be. Sharp criticism such as Jeffrey's meant poor sales, considerably poorer than those of the *Lyrical Ballads*. Jeffrey had created the image of a cult of poetry, the "Lake School, silly, sentimental, and increasingly reactionary." Young voices such as John Wilson, later to be an important advocate, had the courage to praise in Wordsworth's poems "such marks of delicate feeling, such benevolence of disposition, and such knowledge of human nature, as made an impression on my mind that nothing ever will efface," but for both artistic and financial reasons Wordsworth was deeply hurt by the latest reception of his work.

Actually, although there was a long publication silence after the 1807 reviews, the next major poetic venture, *The White Doe of Rylstone*, had been completed by January 1808. Again the matter of obscurity came to the fore. Wordsworth was concerned about being misunderstood by a "public" — quite a different grouping from the "people" for Wordsworth — who were looking for the kind of action and adventure found in Byron's tales or Scott's romances. What Wordsworth had in mind was a spiritual work set in a particular historical setting.

The central action is a border uprising against loyalists to Queen Elizabeth in which the entire Norton family, with the exception of a daughter Emily, perishes. But the event provides only a setting for the bereft Emily and her search for and discovery of spiritual consolation in her relationship with a mysterious doe who, after the death of Emily, visits Bolton Priory and the gravesite of the Norton family weekly. Despite the pleas of his sister Dorothy and others, Wordsworth held the poem back for seven years before he brought it out in an expensive quarto volume, beautifully illustrated with an engraving of the doe after the painting of Sir George Beaumont. He felt strongly about the poem, both for its moral and for its potential sale, and he wanted it to be presented most attractively.

The reception of the poem was mixed, to be sure. Jeffrey's one-sentence exclamation is a worthy rival of his other, and more often quoted, one sentence dismissal of *The Excursion*, to be discussed below. "This," he says of *The White Doe*, "has the merit of being the very worst poem we ever saw imprinted in a quarto volume." But this is only the beginning as he launches into his comment that the poem is "a happy union of all the faults, without any of the beauties, which belong to his school of poetry" (355). The poet "appears in a state of low and maudlin imbecility" (355–56).

William Lyall is more temperate in his notice in the *Quarterly Review*. "As a mere narrative," he says, "it does not possess much interest; the story is told, as it were, in scraps; a few prominent scenes are selected, and the circumstances which connect them left pretty much to the imagination." In a word, the poem lacks closure; again there is "obscurity and flatness" and a kind of artificial "simplicity." The reader is too often left with a vagueness in the language — "dream," "vision," "phantom," "transport ever higher" — when what is needed is precision (224–25), a complaint that continues to reveal the kind of poet

Wordsworth has become and the kind of reader he has consistently expected. At the same time Lyall takes time to point to "that true feeling of poetry with which the poem is pervaded" (225). Wordsworth, he feels, must learn to profit from "sincere criticism," and if he doesn't, "he can have nobody to blame but himself" (225).

There are several positive reviews. the *British Review* recognizes the challenge Wordsworth faces in readers unhappy with his extreme simplicity, yet the reviewer praises his naturalness and his power to communicate sadness in *The White Doe* (370–77). The *Gentleman's Magazine* likewise sees the poem as rising above the merely rustic and simple to catch a certain kind of tender feeling (524–25).

Two Josiah Conder notices in the *Eclectic Review* reveal a growing critical attention to the pensive, ruminative, philosophical Wordsworth, more attentive to his own responses than the particular setting of the poem. Often Wordsworth is placed in the company of Milton as a philosophical poet who challenges the minds of readers but who lacks the power of story and setting in Sir Walter Scott. In the midst of positives and negatives comes the friendly and reverential voice of John Hamilton Reynolds in a sonnet contributed to *Champion*, a poem praising Wordsworth for the peace his poetry has brought to a troubled heart (54). It is a tribute to the continuing power of the many moods of the poet's mind and a strong rejoinder to the attacks of the *Edinburgh Review*.

Wordsworth himself thought the poem should have received more critical attention. He remained a poet known chiefly to other poets rather than the wider audience he envisioned. And the pattern continued into his next venture, the long poem *The Excursion*, his first new poetry after a long silence. I say "new" with the understanding, of course, that the poem was part of the master plan he had envisioned as early as 1798 and that the first book, *The Ruined Cottage*, was completed in that year with drafts of what were to be second and third books originally written in 1806. He had planned, we know, an epic of the poet, *The Recluse*, and the "Preface" to *The Excursion* returns in detail to that plan for a three-part work that would be "a review of his own mind . . . and how far Nature and Education had qualified him for such employment." He further describes how as preparation for his epic venture, "he undertook to record, in verse, the origin and progress of his own powers, as far as he was acquainted with them." But that preparatory poem — *The Prelude* — was not to be published in his lifetime, and the masterwork, despite the constant prodding of Coleridge, was to remain a great but uncompleted dream.

Only *The Excursion* became a reality at this time, an interesting and engaging work in the poet's literary life, with a cast of characters embodying the spectrum of Wordsworth's attitudes toward a range of subjects — the workings of the individual mind in its quest for meaning; the social, political, and religious situation; the celebration of a Christian faith that nourishes, guides, and brings wisdom.

It also evoked a wealth of critical response, mixed to be sure, but clearly representing a new attitude and approach to the poet of the *Lyrical Ballads* and the lyric poems of consciousness like *Tintern Abbey*, the sonnets, the *Immortality Ode*, and others. *The Prelude* was unpublished and unknown except to a select few, so *The Excursion* tended to take on the trappings of a major long poem, the work of a more mature poet now increasingly conservative in politics and religion.

Robert Stone Christian, an important student of Wordsworth's reputation, takes a measured view of the eclipse and resurgence of that reputation and advances an illuminating summary and judgment. "Wordsworth's literary reputation," he states, "had suffered for nearly twenty years following his publication, with Coleridge, of *Lyrical Ballads* in 1798." Understanding and appreciation were slow to come "due in large part to the abrupt break with the literature of Neoclassicism, enunciated by that epoch-making little volume, which clearly indicated that English poetry was moving out in a new direction — a direction for which reading public and critics alike were unprepared and toward which many were hostile" (11).

The *New Monthly Magazine* reviewer describes the poem as "medieval mysticism" (57). A *British Critic* review describes *The Excursion* as "metaphysical poetry in the tradition of Donne and Cowley which instructs through the imagination and the passions, taking something material and temporary and associating it with something spiritual and eternal, thus ennobling and purifying the heart" (449). Often, however, "Wordsworth is obscure, prosaic, and difficult to understand" (465). The *British Review* regards the poem as not suited for readers without "poetic enthusiasm" or "devotional warmth" (64), but rather for those with a "meditative disposition," "reverential feeling," and "philosophical habits" (51).

Many of the reviews strike a retrospective note with their sense of Wordsworth as a now mature poet, a major literary figure. Thomas Noon Talfourd's essays "On the Genius and Writings of Wordsworth" criticize those who judge only the poet's theories instead of examining the poems themselves. It is in the poems that his most impressive gifts appear — "his power of description, his capturing the interplay of mind and nature, his perception of moral beauty, his contemplation of the grand abstractions of humanity" as in the *Immortality Ode*, his power of rendering strong individual characters as in *The White Doe* (498– 506, 648–655).

Francis Jeffrey, a key player in the drama of Wordsworth's evolving reputation, plays a major role in the assault on the poet, and his sharp attacks over nearly two decades in the *Edinburgh Review* proved to be a major problem for Wordsworth's literary reputation. Jeffrey clearly led the charge against *The Excursion* in his November, 1814 review, his oft-quoted "This will never do. It bears no doubt the stamp of the author's heart and fancy; but not half so visibly as that of his peculiar system" (1) serving a little facilely as a summary of his full judgment about the poem. Too tied and dependent upon the Wordsworthian "humble and rustic" system, he contends, it is long, wordy, obscure, and tedious, "a tissue of moral and devotional ravings," without any real action. And, sounding a lot like Coleridge, he regrets the choice of the pedlar as moral guide: "For, after he has thus wilfully debased his moral teacher by a low occupation, is there one word that he puts into his mouth, or one sentiment of which he makes him the organ, that has the most remote reference to that occupation?" (30).

Not completely negative, Jeffrey sees Wordsworth succeeding at least in his "forceful moral declarations, pathetic negatives, perception of the springs of emotion, energetic description and elegant single images," and he finds his strong opposition to industrialism and his support for lower class education admirable. And while he notes the poem's commitment to the religious "belief in the providence of a wise and beneficent Being" as "our great stay and support under all afflictions and perplexities upon earth," all of this is simply "too drawn out" (1–30).

James Montgomery, in the *Eclectic Review*, has some mild theological reservations, but generally writes favorably about what he regards as evidence of grace in the poem, the sense that man is regenerated by the natural world, that characters, especially the Wanderer, take on a certain epic stature, and that, unlike Crabbe and Cowper, Wordsworth casts "the pensive hue of thought over his delineations of the poor. He loves nature with a passion amounting almost to devotion," writes Montgomery, and "he discovers throughout her work an omnipresent spirit which so nearly resembles God in power and goodness that it is sometimes difficult to distinguish the reverence which he pays it, from the homage due to the Supreme alone" (13–39).

This emphasis on a kind of religious note, however theologically unorthodox it might be, is an increasingly important dimension of the critical reception of *The Excursion*. John Wilson, whose early *Black-wood's* review was sharply negative, writes later in his "Essay on the Lake School of Poetry, No. II, On the Habits of Thought, inculcated by Wordsworth" that the poet has the power "to awaken readers to the workings of the moral law and the beauties of the human affections." For Wilson, who clearly becomes a champion of Wordsworth, the poems are "more exalted than Milton's." Wordsworth is the new Rousseau, presenting not just the beauties of the external world, but those beauties as touched by the power of his mind (257–63).

On this same religious dimension as a positive feature of *The Excursion*, the reviewer for the *British Review* assures his readers that the poem will survive its negative reviews. And it "will live because it has a vital principle within it, . . . because the poet has looked abroad on the immortal form of beauty and goodness, moulding and influencing the moral man and spreading through the grandeur of creation, the visibility of God, because he has descended into the most private recesses of the mind and shown to man the depth of intellectual knowledge, the mystery of himself" (56).

Two reviews of some length, while they have sharp disagreements, nevertheless recognize Wordsworth's poetic gifts and the special power of *The Excursion*. Charles Lamb and William Gifford in the *Quarterly Review*, after offering a sketch of the poem, recognize it as "of a didactic nature, and not a fable or story; yet it is not wanting in stories of the most interesting kind, — such as the lovers of Cowper and Goldsmith will recognize as something familiar and congenial to them." Yet "the prevailing charm of the poem is, perhaps, that, conversational as it is in its plan, the dialogue throughout is carried on in the very heart of the most romantic scenery which the poet's native hills could supply" (101). Continuing the strong critical emphasis on the religious dimension of both poem and poet, the reviewers contend that "to a mind constituted like that of Mr. Wordsworth, the stream, the torrent, and the stirring leaf — seem not merely to suggest association of deity, but to be a kind of speaking communication with it" (102).

Other lines are for the reviewers "high poetry; though (as we have ventured to lay the basis of the author's sentiments in a sort of liberal Quakerism) from some parts of it, others may, with more plausibility, object to the appearance of a kind of Natural Methodism: we could have wished that the tale of Margaret had been postponed, till the reader had been strengthened by some previous acquaintance with the author's theory, and not placed in front of the poem, with a kind of ominous aspect, beautifully tender as it is" (105).

Addressing the reasons for Wordsworth's failure to achieve great popularity, they contend that the source is "the boldness and originality of his genius." It is, the argument goes, an age in which a poet cannot securely follow "the direction of his own mind into whatever tracts it might lead .... He must not think or feel too deeply" (110). In a powerful critique of those who have censured Wordsworth for his poetry about children as silly and sentimental, they can only associate them with those who "never having possessed the tenderness and docility of that age, know not what the soul of a child is — how apprehensive! how imaginative! how religious!" And for those — Jeffrey comes to mind — who complain about philosophy from the mouth of a pedlar, "Mr. Wordsworth's plan required a character in humble life to be the organ of his philosophy" (111).

The *British Review* focuses sharply on the audience needed to appreciate *The Excursion* fully. Recognizing the poem as "a sealed book" to many readers, to those attracted to "the wonders of romance," the reviewer agrees that the profound moral sentiments of the poem "will appear only like metaphysical homilies." And with what clearly seems like a dig at Jeffrey, he says that a reader must bring to the poem "a portion of the same meditative disposition, innocent tastes, calm affections, reverential feelings, philosophic habits, which characterize the poet himself; for readers of another kind we greatly fear, (and we deeply sympathize in the author's shame and mortification,) that this poem 'will never do.'" The poem needs good readers (50–51).

Few loom larger as critics of Wordsworth in the early nineteenth century than the already mentioned William Hazlitt. Often respected as a familiar essayist and author of a sensational autobiography, *Liber Amoris*, it is only in the twentieth century that his power as a critic and theorist has been fully recognized. His approach can best be understood in the light of his recurring praise for emotional strength in a work of art. Gusto, his famous synonym for emotional excitement, is "power or passion defining any object." What makes this emphasis unusual is the special dimension he brings to it, a dimension that helps to explain his interest in and writing about Wordsworth.

Hazlitt was quick to separate true emotion from mere egocentricity and sentimentality. Such emotion is rooted in the larger reality beyond the self and is proportionate to that which evokes it. Shakespeare, Hazlitt's great hero, was "all that others were, or that they could become," "the least of an egotist that it was possible to be" (5.47). A contemporary of Wordsworth, his approach to the poet is nonetheless not sharply negative.

His criticism nicely locates the poet in his time, pointing up both strengths and weaknesses and underlining his contributions.

As a poet of the Lake School with a strong anti-Enlightenment bias, Wordsworth's genius is "a pure emanation of the Spirit of the Age. Had he lived in any other period of the world he would never have been heard of . . . . He sees nothing loftier than human hopes; nothing deeper than the human heart . . . . In a word his poetry is founded on setting up an opposition (and pushing it to the utmost length) between the natural and the artificial; between the spirit of humanity, and the spirit of fashion and of the world" (11.86–87).

Hazlitt, perhaps unexpectedly for some, has, despite notable reservations about the larger project, words of praise for some of the *Lyrical Ballads* — *Tintern Abbey* and "The Reverie of Poor Susan" — parts of *Resolution and Independence* and some of the short lyrics and sonnets of the 1807 volumes. He recalls in his essay "My First Acquaintance with Poets" how he responded to Coleridge's reading aloud of some of the ballads. "I felt," he says, "that deeper power and pathos which has been since acknowledged . . . as the characteristics of this author; and the sense of a new style and new spirit of poetry came over me. It had to me something of the effect that arises from the turning up of fresh soil" (17.117). The *Lyrical Ballads*, despite a good deal of contemporary satire, are the kind of poetry which "takes commonest events and objects, as evidence that nature has an intrinsic truth and beauty that needs no ornament to show it off."

Hazlitt's most notable complaint concerned Wordsworth's egotism, his "faculty of making something out of nothing, that is, out of himself, by the medium through which he sees and with which he clothes the barrenest subject. . . . He is the greatest, that is the most original poet of the present day, only because he is the greatest egotist" (8.43).

Unlike Jeffrey, Hazlitt has a more balanced view of Wordsworth's "later philosophical productions," most notably *The Excursion*. It would be difficult to find more lavish general praise of *The Excursion* than in the opening of his review in the *Examiner* for August 21, 1814: "In power of intellect, in lofty conception, in the depth of feeling, at once simple and sublime, which pervades every *part* of it and which gives to every object an almost preternatural and preterhuman interest, this work has seldom been surpassed" (19.10). The question is whether the subject of the poem is equal to the genius of the poet. The execution fails despite the noblest of subjects and sentiments. "He has chosen to encumber himself with a load of narrative and description, which, instead of assisting, hinders the progress and effect of the general reasoning" (19.11–12). And "however we may sympathize with Mr. Wordsworth in his attachment to groves and fields, we cannot extend the same admiration to their inhabitants, or to the manners of country life in general" (19.20).

Sharpest of all Hazlitt's comments, especially as it gets at the roots of a strain of criticism we've noted almost from the beginning, is his observation that "Mr. Wordsworth's mind is obtuse, except as it is the organ and the receptacle of accumulated feelings." His mind, to put it another way, "is not analytic, but synthetic; it is reflecting, rather than theoretical. *The Excursion*, we believe, fell still-born from the press. There was something abortive, and clumsy, and ill-judged in the attempt" (11.91).

To use Robert Stone Christian's words, Wordsworth's reputation went into partial eclipse in the years following *Lyrical Ballads*, the 1807 *Poems*, and *The Excursion*. 1819 saw the publication of *Peter Bell* and *Benjamin the Waggoner*, and sharply negative reviews followed. Wordsworth was seen as representing too sharp a break with the tradition — in his settings, his focus on rustic life, and his use of what was regarded as something less than appropriate poetic diction. As we try to understand the eclipse, a continuing undertone of criticism of what we've been noticing as his obscurity, his philosophical preoccupations, his metaphysical tendencies becomes even more interesting. This latter critique is linked with Wordsworthian inwardness, a concern with the workings of the inner life, especially as it is linked intimately with a spiritual force in nature and revealed in poems like *Tintern Abbey* or as it is reflected in the poet's characters through whom he speaks so often — from Simon Lee, to the child of "We Are Seven," to Lucy, to the Wanderer and the Solitary of *The Excursion*. Few critics of the time seem aware that the poetry was moving away from system and toward what has come to be known as a poetry of consciousness, that Wordsworth was, long before the actual publication of *The Prelude* after his death in 1850, probing the inner life as it developed from moments of youthful ecstasy, to school days, to revolutionary fervor for France, to first passionate love, to disillusionment and final hope in nature's saving power.

Even though some critics who wrote for periodicals could note and discuss, often impatiently, this personal dimension, their attention was directed more toward the new poet with the new poetic theory. The critical response to the 1815 *Poems*, with its elaborate division into poems of fancy, imagination, moods of his own mind and others, clearly illustrates the problem. The *Monthly Review* critic, after noting the strong admiration for nature rooted in the poet's reclusive life, sees genius wasted in the poetry. The poems are silly, unmusical, without any real intellectual foundation, and dedicated to an "obscure" system. Even worse is the extravagant rhetoric of the various versions of the *Lyrical Ballads* preface (225–34). Reviewing the poems for the *Quarterly*, William Lyall contends that the self-centered poet fails to choose subjects of general interest (201–25).

Christian notes a mild resurgence toward the end of the second decade, especially with the publication of the River Duddon sonnets in 1820. The *Literary Gazette* sees Wordsworth escaping his early childishness and producing in these sonnets and in *Vaudracour and Julia* more important work (200–203). A review of *The River Duddon* in the *London Magazine; and Monthly Critical and Dramatic Review* calls attention once again to the Metaphysical poets, this time favorably, praising the poems because they bring together the meditative quality of those poets with the genuine simplicity and love of nature of the Elizabethans. It is the modesty of the poet's philosophy, rather than the idiosyncratic, that shines through his descriptions. Wordsworth's natural simplicity is at the heart of favorable reviews (618–27). The *Eclectic Review* finds him redeeming himself after the banalities of *Peter Bell* and *The Waggoner* (170–84). And the *British Review* lauds the Duddon sonnets for description informed by feeling, intensity, and originality (37–53).

At the same time more wide-ranging reviews tend to be favorable, noting his growing conservatism in politics, his greater orthodoxy in religious matters, but also in general less ideology and a greater directness of feeling and expression. John Scott in a "Living Authors" section of the *London Magazine* writes that Wordsworth's works express a real communion of moral and physical beauty, presenting not just literal truth but what that literal truth suggests. He may on occasion seemingly subvert his theory in poems such as *The Idiot Boy* and "The Sailor's Mother" by focusing too much on the accidental, but generally his own character marks his subjects (275–85). Thomas Noon Talfourd in an essay "On the Genius and Writings of Wordsworth" responds to critics who judge not by his poems, but by his theories. His is a genuine poetic genius, says the reviewer, probing the quiet passions and the interaction of mind and nature, and as evidence he cites Wordsworth's ruminations on "the grand abstractions of humanity" in the *Immortality Ode* (498–506, 648–55).

Wordsworth's more public posture can be seen in his *Ecclesiastical Sketches* (in 1837 reentitled *Ecclesiastical Sonnets*) and *Memorials of a*

Tour on the Continent, both published in 1822. He recalls in a long prefatory letter to the massive sonnet sequence a walk with his friend Sir George Beaumont through his Coleorton estate and a discussion of the possibility of building a church there. As their enthusiasm increased, the poet conceived of a poetic structure that captured the long tradition of Christianity with present gratitude and that looked to the future with hope. He was anxious about the prospects and problems of Catholic emancipation and eager to trace the development of the Church of England from its remote origins. Wordsworth had experience with matters of fact, and he maintained that there is something in history that "enslaves the fancy," but he nevertheless was eager to bring the force of his imagination to the institution of the great world beyond.

Reception of the *Ecclesiastical Sonnets* was mixed. The reviewer for the *General Weekly Register* sees Wordsworth as saying farewell to the religious power of nature and turning to "painted wood, gilt crosses, and priestcraft" (185). The reviewer of the *Sketches* for the *Literary Gazette* likes the "genuine song of the Duddon sonnets, but finds it quite astonishing to see a man of genius so far delude himself as to fancy he can render anything popular, no matter how intractable and how absurd the plan" (191–92). The same strongly negative feeling can be found about the *Memorials of a Tour on the Continent* as the critic finds it "painful to see a poet like Wordsworth impose so egregiously upon his better perceptions as to fancy that these teemings of egotistical complacency can possess any general interest" (210–12). Critics of both collections find in them the work of a more conservative and didactic poet. But there is also praise for both by the formidable Henry Crabb Robinson who writes of reading both collections with pleasure, especially "the glorious sonnets . . . which are lessons of wisdom and stimulants to inquiry" (282). Yet John Bowring in the *Monthly Repository* regards a later Wordsworth as forgetting the poor and pampering his own passions and prejudices (360–65). And Francis Jeffrey continues his critical war on the poet, citing in *Memorials of a Tour on the Continent* a weak sense of history and a distressing obscurity and preachiness (449–56).

Praise or blame, there is one critic who comes out unabashedly for the *Ecclesiastical Sketches* and the *Memorials* for their religious spirit and for their strong influence. John Wilson sees the volumes in the context of Wordsworth's whole career. Stressing the continuities in the work from the *Lyrical Ballads* forward, Wilson writes that Wordsworth is "indisputably the most ORIGINAL POET OF THE AGE" who "had a greater influence on the spirit of poetry in Britain, than was ever before exercised by any individual mind." Even "the enthusiast of nature" delighted by the poet's "images of beauty" must have felt as he finished the *Sketches* that "a profounder pathos and sublimer interest lie among the ruined walls of old religious houses and round the yet undecaying temples of the living God, than can ever be found in the solitude of the great hills; for the shadows that fall there, and the echoes that are heard, are all spiritual; the creature is brought nearer to the Creator, and the communion is felt to be more divine." Wordsworth's poetry "is to him religion; and we venture to say that it was felt to be by thousands" (175–91).

A May 18, 1822 review in the *Literary Museum* frames nicely the key issues in Wordsworth's evolving reputation. Taking the poet's self-centeredness as a starting point, the reviewer comments on a "power of spinning his web from himself, and affixing it to objects which have not usually been considered as admitted to the realms of poesy." Interestingly enough, he continues, we have "one main reason of the unpopularity which marked his rise, but which is now gradually disappearing, or which may be already said to be scattered before the increasing brilliancy of his fame" (52–53).

With the publication of *The Excursion, Duddon Sonnets, Ecclesiastical Sketches*, critics reviewing still later works began to take a longer view of a poet now well past middle-age and a career well past mid-point. Robert Stone Christian sees Wordsworth's reputation growing between 1824 and 1834, and, after the publication of *Yarrow Revisited and Other Poems* in 1835, reaching "a high point of fame which continued throughout the 1830s" (329). And the rise continued with the publication of *Poems, Chiefly of Early and Late Years* in 1842 with a notable number of highly positive reviews.

While the number of new poems declines, there are still fine individual poems — in the *Yarrow Revisited* volume, "Composed Upon an Evening of Extraordinary Splendour," the "Extempore Effusion," and others — and Wordsworth gains a notable amount of celebrity. The *Monthly Censor* for March 1823 speaks of Wordsworth as "indisputably the most original of all living and perhaps of all preceding poets" (324–25).

John Clare's "Essay on Popularity" in the *European Magazine* comments on Wordsworth's lack of popularity early in his career, but sees remarkable change. "The quiet progress of a name gaining ground by gentle degrees," he argues, "is the best living shadow of fame: fashionable popularity changes like the summer clouds, while the simplest trifle, and the meanest thing in nature is the same now and it shall continue to be till the world's end" (76–77). The reviewer for *The Specta-*

tor regards Wordsworth not as a popular poet, yet as one whose special gift is blending description and meditation in the *Yarrow* poems (493-94). And Henry Nelson Coleridge, reviewing the collection for the *Quarterly*, sees the poetry as added confirmation of an "established fame." Nobility of thought finds its proper expression as the shadows of a long life enrich the maturing of a poetic life (181–85).

Interesting in the *Yarrow Revisited* reception is the attempt to see continuities in the poet's life and career without any great sense, as is so often the case in the twentieth-century criticism, of early radical and later conservative periods. Henry Nelson Coleridge's already cited review in the July, 1835 *Quarterly* sees the Yarrow collection as "the work of the autumn day of a great poet's honoured life" with a "profound pensiveness, nevertheless, bursting occasionally into devotional rapture [as] the foundation of every one of them." Hartley Coleridge writes to his mother in a September, 1839 letter, "I hope Mr. Wordsworth feels some consolation in the complete victory of his poetic fame. He may at least feel assured, that no Great Poet ever lived to see his name of so full an age as Wordsworth has done. His last volume is exquisite" (176).

Wordsworth continued to bring out editions of his poetry almost to the end of his life, and he continued, now with increasing frequency, to be reviewed. We need to discuss the long delayed publication of *The Prelude* although doing so briefly brings this study back to early life and early career when Wordsworth was planning his *magnum opus* ,*The Recluse*. The facts of Wordsworth's plan need no elaborate rehearsal at this time. He may have developed this plan to take his place with great writers of epic poems (for him, with Milton in particular), to establish himself as more than a writer of short poems, or simply to enhance his reputation. That poem, although never published, was to have for "its principal subject the sensations and opinions of a poet living in retirement." Whatever the motivation — "the burden of the past" or "the anxiety of influence" — the plan was not realized. The middle section of the epic, *The Excursion*, was published in 1814. And, somewhat ironically, as a test of his qualifications he was prompted to write an introductory poem, a prelude, recording the origin and development of his poetic powers. That poem — *The Prelude* — according to the preface to *The Excursion*, was to be the "Ante-chapel" to "the body of a Gothic Church." Instead it became almost the church itself, his masterpiece.

The plan of *The Prelude*, however, became complicated almost immediately, as it evolved from the two-book version of 1799 to the fourteen books of 1805 — virtually the complete poem — and through

the long years of revision (some would say calculated procrastination)
to the final version which was unpublished at the time of his death in
1850 but published soon after that death by his wife in the same year.

Of theories concerning the delay — anxiety about revealing the dimensions of his involvement in the French Revolution; fear about any
mention of his love affair with Annette Vallon; his daughter Caroline; a
kind of perfectionism that simply wouldn't allow him to let go — there
are all too many, and it is not the purpose of this volume to deal with
them beyond this mention. We need to remember that the poem developed over a lifetime into a massive spiritual autobiography recounting his early life close to nature, the development of the poetic
imagination, the university days at Cambridge, European travels, enthusiasm for the French Revolution and later recantation, the maturing
and dedication of a poetic vocation. Indeed what was originally conceived as an introduction to the greater *Recluse* and its other related
poem *The Excursion*, has, somewhat from the beginning, but especially
in twentieth-century criticism, drawn critics and reading audiences in
general to it. *The Recluse* was, in fact, never completed, and *The Excursion* was seldom regarded as a major work.

It was his wife Mary Hutchinson who provided *The Prelude* with a
title and one of its sub-titles, "the poem to Coleridge," and Coleridge
himself called it a poem "on the growth of the poet's mind." Few were
aware of the poem at all during Wordsworth's long life. Only
Coleridge's memorable poem "To William Wordsworth," which he
wrote after hearing *The Prelude* read aloud, reveals some of the depth
of its probing the inner life of Wordsworth. *The Prelude* also received
very little significant extended notice in the years immediately following
its appearance. *The Examiner* review briefly speaks of the "vitality" in
the poem. A review in *Athenaeum* speaks of the poet's egotism and the
influence of Milton. *The Spectator* stresses the need for more biographical facts, more shortening. There are words of praise in *Critic: the London Literary Journal*, regarding it as Wordsworth's greatest work, a
work complete in itself. A review in *Tait's Edinburgh Magazine* complains about the wordiness of the piece and the triviality of its subjects,
yet finds it a poem to soothe the spirit. In September 1850 in an essay
entitled "The New Poem by Wordsworth," the *Dublin University
Magazine* reviewer has mixed reactions, complaining about the solemn
tone and prosy expression. And, strangely enough, he also complains
about its failure to reveal the development of the poet's mind and
about its pantheistic strain although he takes time to praise its instructive and elevated poetry. The *Eclectic Review* contrasts *The Prelude* with

Thomas Carlyle's *Sartor Resartus*. Wordsworth's only fault was in "loving nature too well. More metaphysical than biographical, he subordinates, as does Milton, the materials of art to art itself." A review in The *Prospective Review* comments that *The Prelude*, though often prosy, reveals an uncharacteristic "fulness of life," "vividness of thought," and "potency of passion."

Works Consulted

Bowring, John. Review of *Ecclesiastical Sketches* and *Memorials on a Tour on the Continent*. *Monthly Repository*. 17 (June 1822): 360–365.

Burney, Charles. Review of *Lyrical Ballads* (1798). *Monthly Review*, NS 29 (June 1799): 202–210.

Byron, George Gordon, Lord. Review of 1807 *Poems*. *Monthly Literary Recreations*. 3 (July 1807): 65–66.

Christian, Robert Stone. *Eclipse and Resurgence: A Study of William Wordsworth's English and American Literary Reputation, 1822–1851*. U of South Carolina Ph.D. Dissertation, 1978.

Clare, John. "Essay on Popularity." *European Magazine*. (November 1825): 76–77.

Coleridge, Hartley. *Letters of Hartley Coleridge*. Grace Evelyn Griggs and Earl Leslie Griggs, editors. London: Oxford UP, 1936.

Coleridge, Henry Nelson. Review of *Yarrow Revisited*. *Quarterly Review*. 54 (July 1835): 181–85.

Coleridge, Samuel Taylor. *The Collected Works of Samuel Taylor Coleridge, Biographia Literaria or Biographical Sketches of My Literary Life and Opinions*. 2 vols. James Engell and W. Jackson Bate, editors. London: Routledge and Kegan Paul; Bollingen Series 75, Princeton UP, 1983.

——. *Collected Letters of Samuel Taylor Coleridge*. 6 vols. Earl Leslie Griggs, editor. Oxford: Clarendon P, 1956.

——. *Poems on Various Subjects, 1796*. Oxford and New York: Woodstock Books, 1990.

Conder, Josiah. Review of *The White Doe of Rylstone*. *Eclectic Review*. NS. 5 (January 1816): 33–45 and NS. 6 (July 1816): 1–8.

Eaton, Horace Ainsworth. *Thomas DeQuincey: A Biography*. New York: Oxford UP, 1936.

"General View of Literature, 1808." *Edinburgh Annual Register*. 1–2 (1810): 417–430.

Hazlitt, William. *The Complete Works of William Hazlitt.* P. P. Howe, editor. 21 vols. London: Dent, 1930–34.

Holcroft, Thomas. Review of *An Evening Walk. Monthly Review.* NS 12 (October 1793): 216–18.

Jeffrey, Francis. Review of 1807 *Poems. Edinburgh Review.* 11 (October 1807): 214–231.

——. Review of *The Excursion. Edinburgh Review.* 24 (November 1814): 1–30.

——. Review of *The White Doe of Rylstone. Edinburgh Review.* 25 (October 1815): 355–63.

——. Review of *Memorials on a Tour of the Continent. Edinburgh Review.* 37 (November 1822): 449–56.

Johnston, Kenneth R. *The Hidden Wordsworth: Poet, Lover, Rebel, Spy.* New York, London: W. W. Norton & Co., 1998.

Jordan, John. *Why the Lyrical Ballads: The Background, Writing, and Character of Wordsworth's 1798 Lyrical Ballads.* Berkeley: U of California P, 1976.

Lamb, Charles and William Gifford. Review of *The Excursion. Quarterly Review.* 12 (October 1814): 100–111.

Lyall, William. Review of *Poems (1815)* and *The White Doe of Rylstone. Quarterly Review.* 14 (October 1815): 201–225.

Mahoney, John L. *Wordsworth: A Poetic Life.* New York: Fordham UP, 1997.

Montgomery, James. Review of 1807 *Poems. Eclectic Review.* (January 1808): 35–43.

——. Review of *The Excursion. Eclectic Review.* 21 (January 1815): 13–39.

Page, Judith. *Wordsworth and the Cultivation of Women.* Berkeley and Los Angeles: U of California P, 1994.

Raysor, Thomas M. "The Establishment of Wordsworth's Reputation." *Journal of English and Germanic Philology.* 54 (1965): 61–71.

Review of *An Evening Walk. Critical Review.* NS 8 (July 1793): 347–48.

Review of *An Evening Walk. Gentleman's Magazine.* 64 (March 1794): 252–53.

Review of *Descriptive Sketches. Critical Review.* NS 8 (July 1793): 472–74.

Review of *Descriptive Sketches. Analytical Review.* (March 1793): 294–99.

Review of *Ecclesiastical Sketches. Literary Gazette.* 271 (March 30, 1822): 191–92.

Review of *Ecclesiastical Sketches. General Weekly Register.* (May 5, 1822): 184–85.

Review of *Memorials of a Tour on the Continent. Literary Museum.* 4 (May 18, 1822): 52–53.

Review of *Memorials of a Tour on the Continent. Literary Gazette.* 272 (April 6, 1822): 210–12.

Review of *Lyrical Ballads. New London Review.* 1 (January 1799): 33–35.

Review of *Poems (1807). Critical Review.* 3rd Ser. 11 (August 1807): 399–403.

Review of *The White Doe of Rylstone. British Review.* 6 (November 1815): 370–77.

Review of *The White Doe of Rylstone. Gentleman's Magazine.* 85–2 (December 1815): 524–25.

Review of *The Excursion. New Monthly Magazine.* 11 (September 1814): 57.

Review of *The Excursion. British Critic.* 2nd Ser. 3 (May 1815): 449–467.

Review of *The Excursion. British Review.* 6 (August 1815): 50–64.

Review of *Poems in Two Volumes of 1807. Le Beau Monde.* 2 (October 1807): 138–42.

Review of the 1815 *Poems. Monthly Review.* NS. 78 (November 1815): 225–234.

Review of *The River Duddon. Literary Gazette.* 166 (March 25, 1820): 200–203.

Review of *The River Duddon. British Review.* 16 (September 1820): 37–53.

Review of *The River Duddon. London Magazine; and Monthly Critical and Dramatic Review.* 1 (June 1820): 618–27.

Review of *The River Duddon. Eclectic Review.* NS. 14 (August 1820): 170–84.

Review of *The Prelude. Examiner.* 2217 (July 27, 1850): 478–79.

Review of *The Prelude. Athenaeum.* 1188 (August 3, 1850): 805–807.

Review of *The Prelude. The Spectator.* 23 (August 3, 1850): 738–39.

Review of *The Prelude.* "The New Poem by Wordsworth." *Dublin University Magazine.* 36 (September 1850): 329–337.

Review of *The Prelude. Critic: the London Literary Journal.* NS. 9 (August 15, 1850): 402–404.

Review of *The Prelude. Tait's Edinburgh Magazine.* NS. 17 (September 1850): 521–27.

Review of *The Prelude. Eclectic Review.* 4th Ser. 28 (November 1850): 550–62.

Review of *Wordsworth: The Prelude. Prospective Review.* 7 (1851): 94–131.

Review of *Memorials of a Tour on the Continent* and *Ecclesiastical Sketches. Monthly Censor.* 2 (March 1823): 324–25.

Review of *Yarrow Revisited. The Spectator.* 8 (May 23, 1835): 493–94.

Reynolds, John Hamilton. "Sonnet to Wordsworth." *Champion.* 163 (February 18, 1816): 54.

Robinson, Henry Crabb. *Henry Crabb Robinson on Books and Their Writers.* Edith Morley, editor. London: J. M. Dent and Sons, Ltd. 1938.

Scott, John. "Living Authors." *London Magazine.* 1 (March 1820): 275–85.

Seward, Anna. *Letters of Anna Seward: Written Between the Years 1784 and 1807.* 6 vols. Printed for George Ramsay and Company, Edinburgh; and Longman, Hurst, Ries, Orme, and Brown, William Miller and John Murray, London, 1811. 6.258, 280.

Smith, Elsie. *An Estimate of W. W. by His Contemporaries, 1793–1832.* Oxford: Blackwell, 1932.

Southey, Robert. *The Life and Correspondence of the Late Robert Southey.* 6 vols. Charles Southey, editor. London: Longman Brown, 1850.

——. Review of *Lyrical Ballads* (1798). *Critical Review.* NS 24 (October 1798): 197–204.

Stoddart, John. Review of *Lyrical Ballads. British Critic.* 17 (February 1799): 125–26.

Talfourd, Thomas Noon. "On the Genius and Writings of Wordsworth." *New Monthly Magazine.* 14 (November 1820): 498–506; (December 1820): 648–655.

Wilson, John. "Essay on the Lake School of Poetry, No. II, On the Habits of Thought, inculcated by Wordsworth." *Blackwood's Edinburgh Magazine.* 4 (December 1818): 257–263.

——. Review of Ecclesiastical Sonnets and Memorials. *Blackwood's Edinburgh Magazine.* 12 (August 1822): 175–191.

Wordsworth, Christopher. *Memoirs of William Wordsworth.* 2 vols. London, 1851.

Wordsworth, William. *The Prose Works of William Wordsworth.* Ed. W. J. B. Owen and Jane Worthington Smyser. 3 vols. Oxford: Clarendon, 1974.

Wordsworth, William and Dorothy Wordsworth. *The Letters of William and Dorothy Wordsworth.* Ed. Ernest DeSelincourt. 7 vols. *The Middle Years,* Part I. *1806–1811.* Rev. Mary Moorman. Oxford: Clarendon, 1969-1993.

2: Eminent Victorians and Others

WE PAUSE AT THIS POINT and step back for a larger view of major nineteenth-century critics, of eminent Victorians such as Arnold, Ruskin, Mill, and others. Here Wordsworth seems to move into a new arena of criticism, as man of letters, public intellectual. Stephen Gill has recently dramatized the impact of Wordsworth on a large number of Victorian writers, indeed on the spirit of an age. He begins with a premise we have already underlined that "by the late 1830s . . . Wordsworth's fame was widespread and assured. Contrary to a belief, which the older Wordsworth and his disciples did little to dispel, his career did not follow a single trajectory from neglect to acclaim. *Lyrical Ballads* went through four editions between 1798 and 1805, establishing at least the beginnings of a reputation which *Poems, in Two Volumes* of 1807 ought to have consolidated. The unsparing attack on most of the 1807 poems, however, voiced most tellingly by the *Edinburgh Review*, but disseminated even down to the *ad hominem* tone, by most other reviews, silenced Wordsworth" (16).

Almost from the earliest Victorians there emerged a running debate between the pre-1810 Golden Decade fans of Wordsworth and those who find in the poet of *The Excursion* and the later works a philosopher whose poetry is a source of wisdom and instruction, a source of spiritual power. It is fascinating to hear some of the major players in the drama, highly regarded poets themselves in some cases, who find Wordsworth their guide and inspiration. Gill cites Matthew Arnold as "the one Victorian writer of whom it can be said without metaphor that he was nurtured in the Wordsworthian presence" (174). In late 1831, early 1832, his family had come to Rydal, taken a temporary residence at Allen Bank in Grasmere (the Wordsworths lived there for a time), and, thanks to the good offices of Wordsworth, finally settled in a house (Fox How) near Rydal Mount where the young Arnold became an ardent member of the literary circle around the poet.

Yet Arnold's distancing himself from the philosophic Wordsworth, from the poet whose ability is to make readers feel, becomes increasingly apparent. Gill contends that this distancing can be accounted for by Arnold's inability to "draw on the sense of connectedness which charges all of Wordsworth's poetry" (184). Arnold did, however, remain an admirer although a proponent of the "two Wordsworth" approach. "His poetry," Arnold writes, "is the reality, his philosophy — so far, at least, as it may put on the form and habit of 'a scientific system of thought,' and the more that it puts them on — is the illusion" (148–49). He clearly favors the shorter lyrical poems where Wordsworth's greatest achievement lies, "the extraordinary power with which, in case after case, he shows us this joy, and renders it so to make us share it." Poems such as *Michael* and "The Solitary Reaper" are superior to *The Excursion* and *The Prelude*, his longest poems. Even the *Immortality Ode* "has itself not the character of poetic truth of the best kind; it has no real solidity" (151).

Arnold's essay on Wordsworth first appeared in 1879 as "Preface" to his selection of *The Poems of Wordsworth* and was directed toward many readers who had turned away from the poet. Taking the long view, he envisions two audiences. It is probably true, he contends, that "Wordsworth has never either before or since, been so accepted and popular, so established in possession of the minds of all who profess to care for poetry, as he was between the years of 1830 and 1840, and at Cambridge." He did have admirers, to be sure, but "I myself heard him declare that, for he knew not how many years, his poetry had never brought him in enough to buy his shoestrings." The poetry-reading public was very slow to recognize him, and was very easily drawn away from him. The death of Scott and Coleridge helped to advance the poet's reputation, especially at Cambridge. "But even amongst the general public," says Arnold, "its sale grew large, the eminence of its author was widely recognized, and Rydal Mount became an object of pilgrimage" (122–24).

Another generation turned to Tennyson and not so much away from Wordsworth, and even in 1850, the year of Wordsworth's death, "this diminution of popularity has continued . . . . Even the abundance of Mr. Palgrave's fine and skillfully chosen specimens of Wordsworth, in the *Golden Treasury*, surprised many readers, and gave offense to not a few . . . . On the Continent he is almost unknown" (124–26). Arnold takes the long-range view even though the poet has been dead for some thirty years. He still firmly believes that "the poetical performance of Wordsworth is, after that of Shakespeare and Milton, of which all the world now recognizes the worth, undoubtedly the most considerable in our language from the Elizabethan age to the present time" (132).

Leslie Stephen, Victorian essayist *par excellence*, agreeing with Arnold about Wordsworth as a philosophic poet, nevertheless praises this dimension of his work. He finds not so much celebrity as genuine fame for a poet of youthful exuberance and then an older philosopher whose work has the richness and the staying power of great art. "We love him," writes Stephen, "the more as we grow older and become more deeply impressed with the sadness and seriousness of life," at the time "when we have finally quitted the regions of youthful enchantment. And I take the explanation to be that he is not only a melodious writer, or a powerful utterer of deep emotion, but a true philosopher" (3:136). Stephen agrees with Arnold that Wordsworth minimizes the dark side of life, and argues that the poet teaches readers to find strength in the midst of grief. For him the *Immortality Ode* establishes a connecting link between the ecstatic joys of childhood close to nature and the later wisdom of the poet-philosopher with its unifying of mind and heart.

John Stuart Mill, clearly an admirer, found Wordsworth's poetry therapeutic after coming down with a deep depression in his youth. Indeed Mill's account of his slow recovery in his *Autobiography* has become a major critical landmark. A youthful radical, as he describes himself in his chapter, "A Crisis in My Mental History: One Stage Onward," he emerged from his reading of Jeremy Bentham "with an object in life; to be a reformer of the world," only to awaken from what he calls the dream in 1826. "I was," he says, "in a dull state of nerves, such as everybody is occasionally liable to; unsusceptible to enjoyable or pleasurable excitement; one of those moods when what is pleasure at other times, becomes insipid or indifferent; the state, I should think, in which converts to Methodism usually are, when smitten by their first 'Conviction of sin'" (137). "I seemed to have nothing left to live for," quoting, as he writes, Coleridge's line from *Dejection: An Ode*, "A grief without a pang" (139).

Mill's state at this time, he records, "made the fact of my reading Wordsworth for the first time an important event in my life." And it was not *The Excursion* but the *Miscellaneous Poems* of 1815 with their "love of rural objects and natural scenery" that stirred something positive. It was not just the physical beauty of nature, "but states of feeling and of thought coloured by feeling, under the excitement of beauty. They seemed to be the very culture of the feelings, which I was in quest of. In them I seemed to draw from a source of inward joy, of sympathetic and imaginative pleasure, which could be shared by all human beings . . . . And I felt myself at once better and happier as I came under their influence" (151).

Wordsworth's poetry taught Mill that true happiness lay in "tranquil contemplation." The *Immortality Ode*, while not advancing his favorite philosophy, brought to "his usual sweetness of melody and rhythm" and "two passages of grand imagery" "special blessings." And in a sweeping general statement of his debt to Wordsworth's ode, and perhaps to his other poetry, Mill expresses his conviction that Wordsworth "too had had similar experiences to mine; that he had also felt the first freshness of youthful enjoyment of life was not lasting; but that he had sought for compensation, and found it in the way he was now teaching me to find it. The result was that I gradually, but completely, emerged from my habitual depression, and was never again subject to it" (153).

Still another eminent Victorian, Walter Pater, high priest of the nineteenth-century Aesthetes and Decadents, represents a strong critical emphasis on the subject in art, on what brings pleasure to the reader or spectator. Impatient with philosophizing and analysis, he writes in his celebrated "Preface" to his *Studies in the History of the Renaissance*: "What is important, then, is not that the critic should possess a correct abstract definition of poetry for the intellect, but a certain kind of temperament, the power of being deeply moved by the presence of beautiful objects" (282). Few artists in his judgment "work quite clearly, casting off all debris, and leaving us only what the heat of their imagination has wholly fused and transformed" (283).

Not an unqualified devotee of Wordsworth's poetry, he finds in it "much which might well be forgotten." Yet there is at the heart of it — in poems such as *Resolution and Independence* and the *Immortality Ode* — a certain magic, "sometimes as if at random, turning a fine crystal here and there, in a matter it does not wholly search through and transform . . . his unique incommunicable faculty, that strange mystical sense of a life in natural things, and of man's life as a part of nature, drawing strength and color and character from local influences, from the hills and streams, and from natural sights and sounds." Then, playing the role of pedagogue, he returns to this idea of the "active principle," urging critics of Wordsworth's poetry "to trace that active principle, to disengage it, to mark the degree in which it penetrates his verse" (283).

William Michael Rossetti in the prefatory notice to his edition of the *Poetical Works of William Wordsworth* (1870) cites John Ruskin as the poet's major disciple at the time. Ruskin, a major critic of the arts, especially painting, had made his mark in *Modern Painters, Stones of Venice, Sesame and Lilies, Unto This Last*, and other works. Finding longer works such as *The Prelude* unduly long, prosy, and difficult to read, and the *Immortality Ode* superficially philosophical, he favored the painterly poet (5.364). For him Wordsworth was like Turner in seeing what was "deep and essential in nature" (3.307); indeed he was a harbinger of the Pre-Raphaelites. Ruskin found absolute fidelity in Wordsworth's sketching of peasant life in a poem such as *Michael* (27.210). He saw "Lucy Gray" as best capturing the local English character that makes his work its "monument and epitaph." And he saw "a perfect description of 'womanly beauty' in 'Three years she grew in sun and shower' and 'She was a phantom of delight'" (18.124–25).

Stephen Gill describes Ruskin's generally favorable response to Wordsworth, despite his later reservations about *The Prelude,* and his sense that the older Wordsworth was out of touch with the great events of the world around him. Ruskin was a staunch devotee, writes Gill; for him "*The Excursion* had been, next to the Bible, the Book of Life, and there was no hyperbole in his declaration in 1880 that he had 'used Wordsworth as a daily text-book from youth to age, and [had] lived, moreover, in all essential points according to the tenor of his teachings'" (216).

Aubrey DeVere, friend of the poet and later to be an important member of the Wordsworth Association, is clearly an admirer of the poetry. In his *Recollections of Aubrey De Vere* he recalls his father describing Wordsworth as "the greatest modern poet" (60) and offering great praise for *Laodamia,* which the son subsequently reads and as a result switches his earlier admiration from Byron to Wordsworth. It is the love of and writing about nature that chiefly captures DeVere's attention. "For him," he says, "it was in her deeper meanings that the inspiring influences of nature chiefly resided. If one had demanded of him what were those deeper meanings, it would have been as if one had demanded of Beethoven what were the deeper meanings of the grandest symphonies, which are his obscurest. In both cases it is through the sense, not by the sense, that the meaning penetrates to the soul." As he and Wordsworth walked together, he recalls, "his chief theme, next to Nature, was poetry. He did not think very highly of our modern poetry except Coleridge, of whom he affirmed that no other poet had ever had so exquisite an ear, and that if he had gone on writing poetry for ten years more he must have been the greatest poet of the modern world" (122–24).

In DeVere's *Recollections* there is a revealing exchange of correspondence with Sara Coleridge about favorite Wordsworth poems. She contends that no one could be a "true Wordsworthian . . . who admired as much as I did some of his later 'poems' of 'accomplishment,' such as 'The Triad.' It implied a disparagement of his earlier poems, such as 'Resolution and Independence,' in which alone, she said, the

Wordsworthian inspiration uttered itself" (197). They agree on their admiration, but — the debate arises once again — differ in their attitudes toward his earlier and later work. Actually giving marks to the poems, Sara Coleridge favors "The Brothers" more than DeVere does. DeVere favors "The Happy Warrior" and *Laodamia*, "the most majestic poem in the language," and *The Old Cumberland Beggar* is regarded by Sara Coleridge as a "true Wordsworthian poem" (203). DeVere writes in conciliatory fashion that "the earlier poems, it will be said, are always strong. True, but they are greatly inferior in grace, sweetness, and refinement, both of thought and expression" (204). *Michael, Yarrow Revisited,* and the sonnets are favorites, and the *Immortality Ode* is "the highest cathedral of song . . . to which he always assigned the highest place in all his editions" (204–205).

No study of major Victorian response to Wordsworth's poetry should neglect at least brief mention and discussion of the poet's interesting connection to the Oxford Movement. Wordsworth's increasingly conservative politics is matched by a similar conservatism in religion as he became more firmly committed to the Church of England as a middle ground between the emotionalism of Methodism and the doctrinal dimension of Roman Catholicism. The young radical supporter of the French Revolution was not attracted to organized religion during his early years and during his studies at Cambridge. But marriage, children, and, the death of his brother John brought him closer, and he began regular attendance at Rydal Hall in 1813, and, as Stephen Gill contends in his life of the poet, he was firmly committed to the Church of England by 1822 (344).

Quite ironically his devotion to the Anglican Church brought Wordsworth into contact with younger members of the growing Oxford Movement — Hugh James Rose, John Keble, Roundell Palmer, Robert Aston Coffin, and especially Frederick W. Faber, a curate at the parish church of St. Mary the Virgin in Ambleside from 1837 to 1842 and a correspondent who in a letter of November 17, 1845 informs Wordsworth of his reception into the Roman Catholic Church. John Edward Bowden comments that among the friendships that Faber formed in Ambleside "was that of Mr. Wordsworth, whose poetry had been the object of his early admiration, and had contributed largely to the formation of his own pastoral spirit" (85). Faber had agreed to contribute to the *Lives of English Saints* launched by the now retired John Henry Newman, master spirit of the renewal within the Church of England that led to the entrance of many into the Roman Catholic Church. Newman had met Wordsworth in 1839 and singled out the

poet in an essay in the *British Critic* as "a writer of philosophical meditation whose works addressed themselves to . . . high principles and
feelings," an essay he later noted in his *Apologia Pro Vita Sua* (1864) as
an important document in his intellectual development (93–94). And,
Newman wrote to Edward Ballasis, Jr. in April 1872, "Wordsworth's
'Immortality Ode' is one of the most beautiful poems in our language.
It and Milton's *Lycidas* affect me more, I think, than anything in
Shakespeare, in Dryden, in Gray, or in Scott. It is partly the thought,
partly the harmony of verse, but Wordsworth is far the more touching
of the two" (*Letters* 26.56).

In 1842 Samuel Wilkinson of Leeds, the Anglican editor of *The
Christian Miscellany*, asked Wordsworth's permission to devote an entire issue to a series of passages from his poetry in *Contributions of William Wordsworth to a Revival of Catholic Truth* (1842). Newman,
according to Mary Moorman, had previously written that Wordsworth,
Coleridge, and Scott, though different poets and believers, "had . . .
borne witness in their writings to a progress in religious thinking, 'to
something deeper and truer than satisfied the last century'" (2.480–
81). Wordsworth, however, flattered as always by attention to his work,
feared to appear as an open Tractarian supporter.

John Taylor Coleridge notes that when John Keble's *Praelectiones*,
his *Lectures on Poetry 1832–1841*, were ready for publication, he dedicated the work to Wordsworth (250). Keble reverently addresses the
poet as "true philosopher and inspired poet who by the special gift and
calling of Almighty God whether he sang of man or of Nature failed
not to lift up men's hearts to holy things nor ever ceased to champion
the cause of the pure and simple and so in perilous times was raised up
to be a chief minister not only of sweetest poetry but also of high and
sacred truth" (1.10). He praises the *Immortality Ode* as the "finest
poem of the greatest poet within our own times," a poem "based on
this belief: namely, that our recollections of childhood are touched with
their peculiarly exquisite and far-reaching charm, simply because of its
feeling of a former existence and of a life closer to divine influence"
(2.453). Faber regards the poet as a "sage and high-souled bard" (99)
and "a reverent, cautious Christian" (161) whose *Excursion* resembles
Homer's *Odyssey* with a Christian underpinning (626–32), and sees, as
Stephen Gill puts it, Wordsworth's *Stanzas Suggested in a Steamboat off
St. Bees' Heads* as anticipating Catholic doctrine. He also notes that although Wordsworth had no great love for Roman Catholic doctrine,
he admired the Catholic past and tradition. He did succeed in securing
permission to append the poem to his saint's life (74).

Among major critics of Wordsworth later in the century is Algernon Charles Swinburne; especially important are his two long essays on "Wordsworth and Byron" in the April and May, 1884 issues of *The Nineteenth Century*. He is clearly a fan of Byron, and especially of Shelley, and he begins his critique by engaging Arnold with proper Victorian respect but with notable disagreement. Although Arnold "is clearly a critic to be reckoned with, yet I cannot feel that in his recent utterances or expositions regarding Wordsworth and Byron he has now and then spread a wider sail before a stronger wind of sheer paradox than ever has any critic of anything like equal or comparable reputations." Arnold "has at once a passion and genius for definitions, but while it is doubtless good to have such a genius, . . . it is surely dangerous to have such a passion" (583).

As the essay continues, Swinburne calls attention to the "ethical" side of Wordsworth, and warns that devotees like Arnold, the Dean of St. Paul's, and especially Sir Henry Taylor, if they have "a tendency to exalt," also have "a tendency to infatuate the judicial sense and spirit of his disciples," with Taylor praising Wordsworth's *Michael* over Aeschylus and Shakespeare (767).

Swinburne, although devoted to Shelley, has strong feelings for the more lyrical Wordsworth. He agrees with Arnold's "We must be on our guard against the Wordsworthian if we want to secure for Wordsworth his rank as a poet." Such disciples are mistaken in adopting the poet's own point of view as the only outlook on his genius and his work. In a stunning summation he argues: "Not that he did wrong to think himself a great teacher: he was a teacher no less beneficent than great: but he was wrong in thinking himself a poet because he was a teacher, whereas in fact he was a teacher because he was a poet" (772).

Swinburne admires *Michael* more than the Margaret section of *The Excursion*, and favors the "Ode to Duty" and "Song at the Feast of Brougham Castle" over the more critically acclaimed *Immortality Ode*. He admires "The Highland Girl," "Stepping Westward," *Resolution and Independence*, "We Are Seven," and "The Solitary Reaper" (the last line of which contains "the purest note of Wordsworth's genius"). *Tintern Abbey*, "with the exception of a few phrases and lines, can make perfect and unquestionable justice of its claim to be ranked with the most triumphant successes of English poetry" (782). And as for *The Affliction of Margaret*, "there is hardly in any literature a poem of more perfect power, more awful and triumphant beauty" (774).

For Swinburne Wordsworth is "the heroic poet of his age," and "there never was a poet whose power, whose success, whose unquestionable triumph was more independent of all his theories, more inexplicable by any of his rules" (774). Arnold's "Memorial Verses," Swinburne contends, capture his own sentiments.

In America there is limited but interesting response to Wordsworth's poetry. Professor Henry Reed of the University of Pennsylvania was the poet's first American editor, and he was an ardent supporter. After expressing major reservations about the early work, Ralph Waldo Emerson's opinions and judgments are quite positive. In 1840 he comments that "Wordsworth has done as much as any living man to restore sanity to cultivated society" (7.494). An 1856 journal entry remarks that the *Immortality Ode* is "the high-water mark which the intellect has reached in this age" (14.98–99). And in a retrospective mood in 1875, Emerson writes that "Wordsworth has secured his fame not only against his critics but against himself, a prey long time to the critics in his puerile poems, I may say infantile, and self-conceit which he could not exclude from his loftier strains. All this he outgrew at the last and . . . has established his claim to the highest thought in England in his time" (16.316).

Thoreau's reactions are limited but positive. "Dignifying the life of man, leading a simple, epic country life in these days of confusion and turmoil — that is what Wordsworth has done. Retaining the tastes and innocence of his youth. There is more wonderful talent, but nothing so cheering and world famous as this" (407).

A. C. Bradley's lectures on poetry, given in Edinburgh in the 1890s and at Oxford in April, 1903, are important in themselves, but even more so for the light they shed on Victorian and later criticism of Wordsworth, and especially on the popular approach that creates the image of two Wordsworths — one the lyrical and the other the more philosophical poet. In the Oxford lectures, published in 1909, Bradley surveys the major literary voices — Coleridge, Hazlitt, Arnold, Swinburne, Brooke, Myers, Pater, Lowell, Legouis, and others — concluding that with a century gone by, "there is now no other English poet, either of that period or any other, who has been the subject of criticism more just, more appreciative, we may even say more reverential" (99). Yet, favorable though that criticism may be, "a disproportionate emphasis is often laid on certain aspects of his mind and writings" (100). "Readers," he continues, "find his way of seeing the world, his poetic experience, what Arnold meant by his 'criticism of life,' to be something deep, and therefore something that will hold. It continues to bring them joy, peace, strength, exaltation . . . not like Shakespeare's myriad-mindedness; it is, for good or evil or both, peculiar" (101).

At the same time, he is unhappy with the "two Wordsworth" approach in both Arnold and Pater. He takes issue, for example, with Arnold's "partial-praise," his contention that Wordsworth was not an epic, tragic, or supernatural poet. True, says Bradley, "he would not choose *Endymion* or *Hyperion* for a subject, for he was determined to speak of what Englishmen may see every day; but what he wrote of Greek religion in *The Excursion* is full of imagination and brought inspiration to Keats, and the most famous expression in English of that longing for the perished glory of Greek myth which appears in much Romantic poetry came from Wordsworth's pen." And even though there are "dull pages" in *The Prelude* and *The Excursion*, both "contain much of Wordsworth's best and most characteristic poetry" (129).

While defending the long poems, Bradley doesn't play them off against the more lyrical Wordsworth. As Kenneth Johnston, author of the most recent study of the poet's life to the time of his writing *The Prelude*, puts it, "without *The Recluse* there would be no 'rustics' as they exist in Wordsworth's poetry," crediting Bradley's approach as a pioneering one (842–43). And, again advancing his idea of a Wordsworthian continuity, while the *Immortality Ode* is not one of Bradley's favorites, "it will never do to dismiss the final lines of the poem" as casually as Arnold does. "Without them Wordsworth is not Wordsworth" (134). At the same time *Resolution and Independence* is "the most Wordsworthian of Wordsworth's poems, and the best test of ability to understand him" (136).

Bradley is rhapsodical about "I wandered lonely as a cloud/That floats on high o'er vales and hills," which opening is "thrust into the reader's face." In "Alice Fell" he finds the directness and naturalness of the poet; "it was this poverty and this grief that Wordsworth described with his reiterated and hammering blows" (106). Eschewing again the idea of two Wordsworths, he argues that "the poet whose portrait we drew when we began might have been the author of the *White Doe*, and perhaps of *Brougham Castle*, and possibly of the *Happy Warrior*. He could no more have composed *Poems Dedicated to National Independence and Liberty* than the political sonnets of Milton. And yet Wordsworth wrote nothing more characteristic than these poems, which I am not going to praise, since Mr. Swinburne's praise of them is, to my mind, not less just than eloquent" (116–17). Bradley deftly makes his larger point that while on the whole "the later poems may be inferior and may reveal a decline, yet in these patriotic poems, in which he rejects his earlier overt Godwinism, the character of his ideal and of this national pride, with him, as with Milton, is connected with personal traits, — impatience of constraint, severity, a certain austere passion, and an inclination of imagination to the sublime" (119).

In the second of his lectures — "The Long Poem in Wordsworth's Age" — Bradley stresses the poet's work as part of an imaginative, poetic counterpart to the scientific (178), confirming Arnold's view, and "if we think of the periodical literature of the *Quarterly* and *Edinburgh* and *Blackwoods*— we shall be still more inclined to that view" (179). Rather than separating the long poem from the lyric, Bradley strives for some sort of reconciliation. The "eminence of Wordsworth's age in lyrical poetry, even if it is not also a pre-eminence, is a significant fact" (182). "Yet the longer poems have some of that lyrical spirit which accounts for their imperfection" (187). "A long poem . . . requires imaginative powers superfluous in a short one; and it will be easy to show that it admits of strictly poetic effects of the highest value which the mere brevity of a short one excludes. That the long poem is doomed is a possible, however groundless, belief; but it is futile to deny that, if it dies, something of inestimable worth will perish" (204).

Bradley stands as a major turn-of-the-century critic of Wordsworth, keenly aware of a tradition of criticism, yet bringing greater rigor and insight, and opening the way for a modern Wordsworthian aesthetic.

Speaking of Bradley and studying the slow process of critical revival after the Victorian response, it is important to note the appearance in 1935 of a helpful volume by Cornelius Howard Patton, *The Rediscovery of William Wordsworth*. In prefatory remarks Patton writes about the poet's steadily increasing influence, his becoming "*A Mighty Voice*" for the modern world and "how closely his teachings fit into our present post-war situation" (i).

Patton modestly describes his own approach as concerned with the "topical," with the ideas of the poet rather than with aesthetic matters (i). However one stands on the questions of a Golden Decade or a period of decline, "we shall still have a body of achievement of large dimensions and of supreme value in the realm of the spirit." He quotes with approval Bradley's statement that "There have been greater poets than Wordsworth, but none more original" (4).

Publishers, Patton continues, have been quick to pick up the growing interest in the poet and "have reached the conclusion that Wordsworth is appealing to a steadily widening circle of readers, and for a variety of reasons . . . since the opening of the World War [I] and the twenty-one years since that time have produced no less than ninety-five volumes relating to Wordsworth or his family, or having the message of this poet as a prevailing theme" (6).

After brief mention of some of this work — Ernest de Selincourt's editorial feats, Herbert Read's *Wordsworth*, Hugh Fausset's *The Lost Leader*, for examples — Patton provides some interesting anecdotes and asides. "Woodrow Wilson," he says, "was a life-long student of Wordsworth and . . . before his public career he rented a house at Ambleside, in the Lake District, so that he might be as close as possible to the scenes of *The Prelude* and of the nature-pieces which inspired so much of the Poet's work" (7). There is also his conjecture that "as a result of the War, American college men have come to appreciate Wordsworth as *par excellence* the Poet of Patriotism" and of how "from a revolutionist in France he came to be a patriot in England" (12–13).

After ranging in rather general fashion through the poetry, Patton concludes that "Wordsworth's sense of beauty and his sense of mission were one and the same thing. He was an artist in verse because he was an artist in truth . . . . It was from an experience of deep inner satisfaction that he devoted his life to the promulgation of a brighter and happier, because a spiritually conditioned world" (258).

The Wordsworth Society: Beginnings of a Tradition

Any study of Wordsworth and the critics and of the evolution of the poet's reputation must note the foundation of a Wordsworth Society in Grasmere on September 29, 1880. William Knight, a pioneering biographer, editor/anthologist of the poet, and the editor of the *English Lake District as Interpreted in the Poems of Wordsworth*, founded the Club, and his *Wordsworthiana: A Selection From Papers Read to the Wordsworth Society* is a treasury of information about the Society and its members as well as a collection of Presidential Addresses that offer a wide variety of contemporary critical opinion. Originally a private club whose members would travel yearly to the Lake District, the membership swelled to 344 in 1886, and the more formal organization developed.

At the original Grasmere meeting a Constitution was drafted, and from it we gather some of the purposes and hopes for the Society. Members were to be "in sympathy with the general teaching and spirit of Wordsworth, to support the study of the poems, especially those with local allusions," to collect letters and reminiscences, and, most interesting for the present writer, to "prepare a Record of Opinions, with reference to Wordsworth, from 1793 to the present time, and to inves-

tigate any points connected with the first appearance of his work."
Members included Robert Browning, James Russell Lowell, Leslie Stephen, Stopford Brooke, John Ruskin, Aubrey DeVere, Ellis Yarnall
(from Philadelphia), Roundell Palmer (Lord Selburne), and many others of note. The Society had only a seven year life, with meetings moving to London after the first two in Grasmere.

Reports of annual meetings were printed in newspapers of the day,
and the Secretary of the Society released the *Transactions* with reports
and published papers. *The Spectator* of October 6, 1880 reports on the
inaugural meeting — details, organization, and the understanding that
"membership of the Society was not to be regarded as implying literary
partisanship." As a matter of fact, some members felt that Wordsworth
lacked humor and passion, but on balance they praised "his meditative
depth . . . his power of teaching us, when the tumult of passion had
passed, by insight into the symbolism of Nature — an imaginative and
rational insight — which connects his poetry . . . at once with the genius of Plato, and with the latest and most elevated philosophy of
Europe" (Knight xiii–xviii).

The annual Presidential addresses cited by Knight are varied indeed.
Arnold's 1883 address is fulsome in its praise while having particular
reservations — "an exceedingly great poet," a rival of Shakespeare and
Milton, his "most distinctive virtue of all — his power of happiness and
hope," his "'deep power of joy'" (125–26). James Russell Lowell regrets that the poet "has too commonly been estimated rather as philosopher or teacher than as poet" (172). He has "that rare quality of
the minds that he has most attracted and influenced," but "he continues to be insular" and "makes no conquests beyond the boundaries of
his mother tongue" (173).

Lord Houghton (Richard Monckton Milnes), although not without
reservations, tries to be positive in his 1885 Address. He describes, as
does Arnold, the student enthusiasm for Wordsworth's poetry at Cambridge between 1830 and 1840, taking issue with what he regarded as
the unjust criticism of the language and the pastoral motifs. Houghton
nevertheless contrasts the "stirring" and "passionate" language of
Burns's poetry of common life with Wordsworth's, yet he must admit
that "there was something in the poems of Wordsworth and Shelley
that we knew to be our better and higher aspirations" (261). And he
cites Rawnsley's celebrated *Reminiscences* of the Westmoreland country
folk about the poet's eccentricity and want of humor. Then turning
positive, although still unwilling to rank him among the best, he says of
the poetry: "Its interest in so many forms of familiar life, its interest in

the common occupations of the world . . . its perfect enthusiasm for Nature, and from Nature to Nature's God — this gives to Wordsworth the assurance of a constant immortality, crowned, I think, by the production of some few poems which we may place at the very top of philosophic poetry" (266). Among those philosophic poems he regards the *Immortality Ode* as "the greatest embodiment of philosophic poetry . . . . It comprehends the life of man" (260).

Lord Selborne (Roundell Palmer), in his Presidential Address of July 7, 1886, recalled the beginning of years of worship "at the innermost shrine of Wordsworth," during his undergraduate days at Oxford. He prefers, Knight records, a more personal response than a technical analysis. His impressions are "real, and . . . have endured almost the whole of my life" (278). Wordsworth, he says, more than any other writer, is responsible for "anything I may recognize as good in the formation of my own mind and character." Not a great poet like Plato or Shakespeare, "nevertheless, I have learned more as an individual man than I ever learned from Plato or even Shakespeare." Wordsworth "speaks the truth, not as a man who comes down to ride the high horse of human ethics over his fellow-men, but simply as a part of human nature" (281).

Specifically, Selborne sees Wordsworth as a cultivator of human sympathy. His poetry resonates Christianity and the presence of God. *Tintern Abbey,* far from being pantheistic, "is a representation of that omnipresence," and the *Immortality Ode* reveals "a recognition of the divine origin of the human soul" (284). Wordsworth, says Selborne, never separates the spiritual and the physical. "The outward and the inward eye see together. He sees with them both deeply, and he teaches and helps others to do the same" (286).

For one reason or another the Society was dissolved in 1886, although the Master Spirit William Knight continued his dream with the publication of the *Transactions of the Wordsworth Society.* And work continued on the planned *Selections from William Wordsworth and Other Members of the Wordsworth Society* which was finally published in 1888. The great plan of Knight and Rawnsley was later carried out by Stopford Brooke with the purchase of Dove Cottage, opened to the public on July 27, 1891, and the inauguration of the National Trust for Places of Historic Interest or National Beauty on January 12, 1895.

Biographies and Memoirs

In recalling William Knight and his major role in founding the Words-worth Association, we also note the earliest beginnings of Wordsworth-ian memoirs and biographies. Shortly after the poet's death his nephew Christopher, clearly an admiring relative, published a two volume *Memoirs of William Wordsworth* which he describes as a "biographical commentary on the poet's works" (1.3). Remembering an 1847 visit to his uncle at Rydal Mount, he writes: "On that occasion as on many others, he expressed an opinion, that a poet's *Life* is written in his *Works*; and this is undoubtedly true, in a remarkable manner, in his own particular case" (1.1). Christopher Wordsworth, with this in mind, is firmly committed to the conviction that "His Works . . . are his Life," remaining both possessive and protective in his almost Biblical excla-mation, "Let them retain their supremacy in this respect; and let no other Life of Wordsworth be composed beside what has thus been written with his own hand" (1.2). Yet, despite this call, he calls the po-ems "no visionary dreams but practical realities," reminding readers that the poet "wrote as he lived, and he lived as he wrote," and that consequently "the circumstances of his life" require attention. He will, he says, "keep chronology central in his biography so that readers will gain a greater awareness of the poet's artistic development" (1.5).

Wordsworth, we are told, actually dictated autobiographical materi-als so that what the *Memoirs* amount to is family biography with rela-tively minor attention given to the poems as poems and with little of the kind of objectivity one expects in biography. There is, for example, no mention of the love affair between the poet and his French mistress, Annette Vallon, and of the birth of a child to them, and little informa-tion about Wordsworth's French interlude in general so that one is left without a vital dimension that might illuminate the life and work of a young artist.

A number of biographies and biographical studies followed, none es-pecially scholarly, but most contributing to the early images of Words-worth and the shaping of his poetic reputation. Among them are Edwin Paxton Hood's *William Wordsworth: A Biography*; encyclopedia essays like the one by Robert Carruthers in the *Encyclopedia Brittanica, or Dictionary of Arts, Sciences, and General Literature* for 1860; James Sutherland's *William Wordsworth: The Story of His Life with Critical Remarks on His Writings*; Elizabeth Wordsworth's *William Words-worth*, and others.

Yet it was William Knight who played a major role in bringing serious scholarship to bear on Wordsworth's life and work, and he did so in a variety of ways — from his *The English Lake District as Interpreted in the Poems of William Wordsworth*, to his "Preface" and "Notes" in *Selections from Wordsworth* edited by Knight and other members of the Wordsworth Society, to his full biography in three volumes with separate essays on "Wordsworth's View of Education and Its Methods" and "On the Portraits of Wordsworth."

Fortunately the crucial biographical work of Emile Legouis begins the process of revealing more fully Wordsworth's early days in France as he recounts a story told to him by Thomas Hutchinson about "a well-established tradition in the Coleridge family that William Wordsworth, during his stay in France, had by a young French lady a son, who afterwards visited him at Rydal Mount" (7), a matter missing from Legouis's *Early Life of Wordsworth* but later told to George Harper, an early and important biographer of Wordsworth. Harper then discovered in the British Museum a series of letters from Dorothy Wordsworth to Catharine Clarkson in which there is specific reference to a Madame Vallon and a daughter, Caroline, whom Dorothy describes as her niece. The first noting of this finding is in Harper's *William Wordsworth: His Life, Work, and Influence*, but more important is Harper's discovery during his World War I service that Annette was the sister-in-law of a Madame Vallon whose memoirs of the French Revolution appeared in 1913. When Harper returned to America after the War, he urged Legouis to tell the full story, which he did in a new edition of his *Early Life of Wordsworth*. Legouis's biography, his *Wordsworth and Annette Vallon*, and *Wordsworth in a New Light* combined to locate the poet's French episode in the larger context of the poet's life and to offer readers a more authoritative biography.

Other biographical studies — some recounting the whole life, others focusing on specific aspects of the life and work — include H. W. Garrod's *Wordsworth*, Herbert Read's *Wordsworth*, Edith Batho's *The Later Wordsworth*, and Willard Sperry's *Wordsworth's Anti-Climax*. Sperry's is especially interesting and important for its argument that Wordsworth's career is marked by sharp decline — from the youthful exuberance of his early poetry, to the steady erosion of his powers around 1806 and 1807, to his assuming of the mantle of didactic, philosophical, and ultimately uninspiring poet of the last forty years. Sperry takes his place with the school of "early" and "later" Wordsworth, praising the poetry of a "Golden Decade," bemoaning the dramatic falling-off, and even attempting his own analysis of the decline.

Wordsworth, he contends, "could not be relied upon, after about 1806, to write poetry which bore upon its face the credentials of its greatness, and, failing inspiration, he manufactured verses. In general, therefore, there is warrant for Professor Garrod's statement that the last forty years of Wordsworth's life are 'the most dismal anti-climax of which the history of literature holds record'" (29). Kinder but not less decisive, Sperry notes that "we see the end from the beginning and read the early work in the light of the later. Much as we might like to isolate the poems of the golden decade and rid ourselves of the embarrassment of the subsequent work, we cannot in good conscience do so. There must have been some initial defect which brought on untimely, and hastened unduly, the processes of Wordsworth's poetic decline. Hence we see the sources of the last sterility in the nature of the first fruitfulness" (30).

Catherine Macdonald Maclean in *Dorothy and William Wordsworth*, using Dorothy's journal technique, focuses on the close relationship of brother and sister, stressing the impact of Dorothy on William's life and work. Dorothy, says Maclean, did not have the "semi-mystical experiences" of the poet whose insights were "his own." Yet, as he wrote of Dorothy in "The Sparrow's Nest," "She gave me eyes, she gave me ears."

Maclean singles out three special gifts in Dorothy, each of which enriched the poet's work, "the gift of observation, the gift of receiving those impressions which became the substance of poetry, and the gift of getting in touch with all sorts of people and envisioning their lives . . . . The only proof of this that is needed is a comparison of Wordsworth's poems with Dorothy's journals" (38).

Harper, certainly a fan of Wordsworth, nevertheless sees decline also. Concentrating on the political and on the impact of the French Revolution on the poet, he argues that hopes give way to fears in both life and poetry and that "the best poems belong to the period before 1815." Harper, like the Victorians, attends to the later political and religious conservatism with *The Excursion* as his major exhibit. "The philosophical doctrine of the poem, is, first of all," he says, "a statement that the universe is ruled by a spiritual Person," "that human life on the whole is morally admirable and worthwhile," "that there may be enjoyed a communion with the divinity existing in all things fair" (24–25). And the later Wordsworth is fearful of political change, becoming "a spokesman for the reaction to the inevitable growth of social progress" (28).

Herbert Read plays the psychologist in telling the poet's story. For him, as for Christopher Wordsworth, although for different reasons,

Wordsworth's "poetry is his philosophy and neither can be distinguished from his private belief" (33). But, he continues, "Wordsworth was a poet, and a supreme poet, for a limited period of about ten years" (49). His is "that rare species of poetry in which thought is felt" (119). Read even proposes his own diagnosis of "the gradual decay of Wordsworth's poetic powers. Either there was no spontaneous overflow of powerful feelings of any kind — just mere prose rhetoric; or the feelings were crossed by the poet's own inhibitions, and thus reduced to confusion" (149).

Robert Gittings and Jo Manton offer an impressive study of Dorothy as both an individual and as a force in her brother's life. Possessed of a simple Christian faith and "with a warm and affectionate heart," and a lifelong love of reading, she ruled out marriage and devoted herself to her brother's work. Gittings and Manton cite the at times abnormal sisterly devotion and quote her remark in a 1793 letter to her friend Jane Pollard: "I am very sure that Love will never bind me closer to any human being than friendship binds me to William, my earliest and dearest male friend" (33).

Edith Batho in her *The Later Wordsworth* offers a strong portrait of the real opinions "in the last as in the first half of his life," and finds a mellowing rather than a hardening. Recognizing his Tory and Anglican loyalties, his opposition to Catholic Emancipation and to any grant of freedom to Non-Conformists, and to slavery in America, she sees a "continuum of orthodoxy throughout his life" (54–55). John Williams, stressing a dark side of the poet's life in his *William Wordsworth: A Literary Life*, finds in the poet's love of solitude "the face of a literary and political establishment of which he is emphatically not a part" (215).

Natalie Bober's *Wordsworth: The Wandering Poet* in 1975 and Hunter Davies's *Wordsworth: A Biography* in 1980 offer serviceable lives of the poet with Bober catching the zest for travel and the passion for nature in the poet and Davies offering interesting portraits of the Wordsworth family circle. I offer in *Wordsworth: A Poetic Life* what I consider to be a full-scale literary life, reversing the usual biographical method and telling the story of the life through a rigorous reading of poems from every phase of the poet's career in the context of the life he lived and the events that surrounded that life.

What might be called the great era of Wordsworth biography is launched with the publication in 1959 of the first volume of Mary Moorman's monumental life followed in 1965 by a second and final volume. A masterful biographer eager to capture the full richness of Wordsworth's long life, she moves adroitly from the poet's earliest days to his Cambridge years, the French adventure, the life of poetry at Grasmere, the presence of Dorothy, the marriage to Mary Hutchinson and the family that followed, his growing repute as the Squire of Rydal Mount, the celebrity of the later years, and a moving account of his final illness and death. Moorman skillfully interweaves life and work although she makes no great attempt at critical evaluation of the poetry.

It is Stephen Gill who, modestly recognizing the massive research efforts of Moorman, moves beyond her work and produces the now definitive *William Wordsworth: A Life* in 1989. Handsomely illustrated and a model of late twentieth-century scholarship, this long biography has the added advantage of lucid and graceful writing. While it is not a literary biography, it nevertheless weaves life and poetry exquisitely, connecting appropriate texts to specific episodes in the poet's life. Whether quoting from the *Lyrical Ballads*, the 1807 poems, *The Prelude*, *The Excursion*, the full body of the poet's work, Gill's sensitive reading enriches the story of a long life.

Yet the fascination with that life doesn't seem to end. Kenneth Johnston, known for his earlier work on *The Recluse*, brings his moderate New Historicist impulses to bear on what he considers to be a mysterious side of the poet in his 1998 *The Hidden Wordsworth: Poet, Lover, Revel, Spy*. In some eight hundred pages of the most dogged, yet riveting research on the pre-1805 Wordsworth, he cross-examines the poet on what he regards as the logic of his own self-creation as the hero of *The Prelude* and the poet of *The Recluse*. Against the image of a solemn pre-Annette Vallon celibate male, he juxtaposes vivid documentation of the thriving prostitution and the generally raucous social scene around the Cambridge campus in the 1790s, a scene and a trade the poet must certainly have known. And against the image of the dedicated poet, chastened by earlier political disillusionment and now committed only to his art, he juxtaposes a persuasive picture of that same poet concerned with commercial success and almost certainly involved in espionage activities during his trips to France. We will have occasion to consider Johnston's critical methodology later in the study.

Before leaving this brief account of biography as it provides a vehicle for the criticism of Wordsworth, it is important to take note of a still-to-be completed dazzling piece of scholarship: Mark Reed's *Wordsworth: The Chronology of the Early Years, 1770–1799* and *Wordsworth: The Chronology of the Middle Years, 1800–1815*. Reed's method is to provide, whenever possible, a day-by-day account of the poet's activities, travels, and, most crucial, writing with remarkable documentation from a mind-boggling array of sources. The two volumes are essential to the work of any Wordsworth student, and, with the completion of the final volume, one of the true miracles of Wordsworth, or, for that matter of almost any, scholarship will have been performed.

There have been two great twentieth-century editions of Wordsworth's poetry, each one proceeding from different editorial principles. First is *The Poetical Works of William Wordsworth with Textual and Critical Notes* edited by Ernest de Selincourt and Helen Darbishire, an edition that follows the six volume edition of 1849–1850, the last one overseen by Wordsworth himself.

There is also *The Prelude, or Growth of a Poet's Mind, Edited from the Manuscripts with Introduction, Textual and Critical Notes* edited by Ernest de Selincourt with a second edition revised by Helen Darbishire. This edition prints on the right hand page the 1850 text and on the left the text read to Coleridge in 1807. When Darbishire edited the second edition, she included the earliest manuscript of what was to become *The Prelude*. Edited by Jonathan Wordsworth, M. H. Abrams, and Stephen Gill, the Norton edition is an invaluable volume that includes the 1799 *Prelude* and on opposite pages, most helpful for studying changes and development, the 1805 and 1850 editions.

Nearing completion as I write is the notable, for some controversial, Cornell University Press edition of the poet's complete works under the general editorship of Stephen Maxfield Parrish. Unlike DeSelincourt's edition, Wordsworth's longer works are presented in their earliest completed form rather than the latest with all variant readings given.

The standard edition of Wordsworth's prose is the *Prose Works* edited by W. J. B. Owen and Jane Worthington Smyser, and the vital *Letters of William and Dorothy Wordsworth*.

Works Consulted

Arnold, Matthew. "Wordsworth." *Essays in Criticism*. 2nd Ser. London and New York: Macmillan, 1905.

Batho, Edith. *The Later Wordsworth*. Cambridge: Cambridge UP, 1933.

Bober, Natalie. *Wordsworth: The Wandering Poet*. New York: Thomas Nelson, Inc., 1975.

Bowden, John Edward. *Life and Letters of Frederick William Faber*. Baltimore: John Murphy & Co., 1869.

Bradley, A. C. *Oxford Lectures on Poetry*. London: Macmillan, 1909. [reprint 1950 by Macmillan].

Coleridge, John Taylor. *A Memoir of the Rev. John Keble*. Oxford: J. Parker, 1869.

Davies, Hunter. *Wordsworth: A Biography*. New York: Athenaeum, 1980.

DeVere, Aubrey. *Recollections of Aubrey DeVere*. New York: Edward Arnold, 1897.

Emerson, Ralph Waldo. *Journals and Miscellaneous Notebooks of Ralph Waldo Emerson*. 16 vols. Gillman, William H., editor. Cambridge, MA: Belknap P of Harvard UP, 1973.

Faber, Frederick William. *Sights and Thoughts in Foreign Churches and Among Foreign Peoples*. London: Rivington, 1842.

Garrod, Heathcote W. *Wordsworth*. Oxford: Clarendon, 1923.

Gill, Stephen. *Wordsworth: A Life*. Oxford: Clarendon, 1989.

——. *Wordsworth and the Victorians*. Oxford, Clarendon, 1998.

Gittings, Robert and Jo Manton. *Dorothy Wordsworth*. Oxford: Clarendon, 1985.

Harper, George Maclean. *William Wordsworth: His Life, Work, and Influence*. 2 vols. New York: Charles Scribner's Sons, 1916.

Hood, Edwin Paxton. *William Wordsworth: A Biography*. London, Edinburgh, Dublin: Cash, 1856.

Johnston, Kenneth R. *The Hidden Wordsworth: Poet, Lover, Rebel, Spy*. New York, London: W. W. Norton & Co., 1998.

——. *Wordsworth and "The Recluse."* New Haven and London: Yale UP, 1984.

Keble, John. *Keble's Lectures on Poetry, 1832–1841*. 2 vols. Edward Kershaw Francis, trans. Oxford: Clarendon, 1912.

Knight, William. *Wordsworthiana: A Selection From Papers Read to the Wordsworth Society.* London and New York: Macmillan and Co., 1889.

———. *The English Lake District as Interpreted in the Poems of William Wordsworth.* Edinburgh: D. Douglas, 1878; 3rd edition, 1890.

——— and Other Members of the Wordsworth Society, editors. *Selections from Wordsworth.* London: Moxon, 1888.

———. *The Life of William Wordsworth.* 3 vols. Edinburgh, 1889.

Legouis, Emile. *The Early Life of Wordsworth.* Trans. J. W. Matthews. London: J. W. Dent, 1921.

———. *Wordsworth and Annette Vallon.* New York: E. P. Dutton, 1922.

———. *Wordsworth in a New Light.* Cambridge, MA: Harvard UP, 1923.

Maclean, Catharine Macdonald. *Dorothy and William Wordsworth.* New York: Octagon Books, 1972.

Mahoney, John L. *William Wordsworth: A Poetic Life.* New York: Fordham UP, 1997.

Mill, John Stuart. *Autobiography and Literary Criticism of John Stuart Mill.* John M. Robson and Jack Stillinger, editors. Toronto: U of Toronto P, 1981.

Moorman, Mary. *William Wordsworth: A Biography.* I. *The Early Years: 1770–1803.* Oxford: Clarendon, 1957; II. *The Later Years: 1803–1850.* Oxford: Clarendon, 1965.

Newman, John Henry. *Apologia Pro Vita Sua.* 1864. Martin J. Svaglic, editor. Oxford: Clarendon P, 1967.

———. *Letters and Diaries of John Henry Newman.* Charles Dessain and Thomas Gornall, editors. 31 vols. Oxford: Clarendon P, 1974.

Pater, Walter. "Preface." *Studies in the History of the Renaissance in Aesthetes and Decadents of the 1890's: An Anthology of British Prose and Poetry.* Karl Beckson, editor. Chicago: Academy Chicago Publishers, 1981. 280–85.

Patton, Cornelius Howard. *The Rediscovery of William Wordsworth.* Boston, MA: The Stratford Company Publishers, 1935.

Read, Herbert. *Wordsworth.* London: J. Cape, 1930.

Reed, Mark. *Wordsworth: The Chronology of the Early Years, 1770–1799.* Cambridge, MA: Harvard UP, 1967.

———. *Wordsworth: The Chronology of the Middle Years, 1800–1815.* Cambridge: Harvard UP, 1975.

Rossetti, William Michael, editor. "Prefatory Notice." *The Poetical Works of William Wordsworth.* London: Moxon, 1870: xv–xxiv.

Ruskin, John. *The Works of John Ruskin*. 3 vols. E. T. Cook and Alexander Wenderburn, editors. London: George Allen; New York: Longmans, Green & Co., 1903–1912.

Sperry, Willard. *Wordsworth's Anti-Climax*. Cambridge, MA: Harvard UP, 1935.

Stephen, Leslie. "Wordsworth's Ethics." Vol. 3 in *Hours in a Library*. 4 vols. New York: G. P. Putnam, 1904.

Sutherland, James. *William Wordsworth: The Story of His Life with Critical Remarks on His Writings*. London: E Stock, 1887.

Swinburne, Algernon Charles. "Wordsworth and Byron." *The Nineteenth Century*. London: Twentieth Century Limited. (April 1884): 583–609; May (1884): 764–790.

Thoreau, Henry David. *The Journals of Henry D. Thoreau*. Torrey, Bradford and Francis H. Allen, editors. Boston: Houghton Mifflin Co., 1906, 1949.

Williams, John. *William Wordsworth: A Literary Life*. New York: St. Martin's P, 1996.

Wordsworth, Christopher. *Memoirs of William Wordsworth*. 2 vols. London, 1851.

Wordsworth, Elizabeth. *William Wordsworth*. London: Percival, 1891.

Wordsworth, William. *The Letters of William and Dorothy Wordsworth*. Ernest de Selincourt, editor. 8 vols. Oxford UP, 1969–93.

——. *The Poetical Works of William Wordsworth*. Ernest de Selincourt and Helen Darbishire, editors. 5 vols. Oxford: Clarendon P, 1940–49.

——. *The Prose Works of William Wordsworth*. Ed. W. J. B. Owen and Jane Worthington Smyser. 3 vols. Oxford: Clarendon P, 1974.

——. *The Prelude, 1799, 1805, 1850: Authoritative Texts; Context and Reception; Recent Critical Essays*. Jonathan Wordsworth, M. H. Abrams, and Stephen Gill, editors. London and New York: Norton, 1979.

3: Wordsworth and Twentieth-Century Criticism

Beginnings and Early Development

ALTHOUGH IT IS DIFFICULT TO CATEGORIZE PRECISELY Wordsworth's twentieth-century critics, it is nonetheless useful to examine what might be described as several phases of response to the poet and his work. One thing is clear, and that is the enormous bulk of material in books, scholarly journals, reviews, and the more popular publications dealing with Wordsworth from a variety of critical and theoretical angles. As already noted, biographical studies continue, studies that have become increasingly scholarly and, in some cases, highly specialized. Similarly, appreciation has slowly given way to more rigorous interpretation; as biography moves from the familial and laudatory, so does criticism move from unqualified praise or blame to more technical examination.

Much of this change can be attributed to shifting emphases in the curricula of British and American colleges and universities, in the introduction of more modern literature and eventually in the teaching of that literature in period fashion — Renaissance, Augustan, Romantic, and the like. With such teaching came anthologies and textbooks, Romantic poetry anthologies, for example, in which Wordsworth, given his nineteenth-century reputation, was a major presence. With greater emphasis on formal study and interpretation and on the training of professional scholars came a flood of publication, from essays and books on the poetry to examinations of Wordsworth's social, cultural, political, and religious interests and biases.

Along with the more straightforward telling of Wordsworth's life story in the early part of the century are a number of semi-biographical studies, in many cases revealing as much about the authors as the poet and offering relatively little technical analysis. Such a body of work includes Sir Walter Alexander Raleigh's *Wordsworth*; Frederick M. Robertson's *Lectures on the Influence of Poetry and Wordsworth*; Cornelius Howard Patton's *The Rediscovery of Wordsworth*; Mary Burton's *The*

One Wordsworth; George Wilber Meyer's *Wordsworth's Formative Years*; Katherine Mary Peek's *Wordsworth in England: Studies in the History of His Fame.*

An interesting and important development in the earlier century was a general critique of European Romanticism and a sharp rebuke of Wordsworth's faith in nature by the so-called New Humanists, critics such as Paul Elmore More and especially Irving Babbitt in his classic *Rousseau and Romanticism* and his essay on "The Primitivism of Wordsworth" in his book *On Being Creative*. Babbitt, very much in the tradition of Matthew Arnold, regards Rousseauism as "a throwing off of the yoke of both classical and Christian discipline in the name of temperament . . . in favor of original genius" (49). "No one," he contends in *Rousseau and Romanticism*, "would question that Wordsworth has passages of great ethical elevation. But in some of these passages he simply renews the error of the Stoics; he ascribes to the natural order virtues that the natural order does not give" (221).

Providing an effective counterbalance to the New Humanist position on Romantic/Wordsworthian naturalism are a number of studies that attempt a systematization and defense of Wordsworth's philosophy. Arthur Beatty's *William Wordsworth: His Doctrine and Art in Their Historical Relations* focuses on what he regards as the poet's debt to British Associationist psychology in his concern with the interaction of mind and nature. Abbie Findlay Potts, a hundred years after a war far greater than Wordsworth experienced, tries to understand the poet's quest for some larger meaning after a period of political and social turbulence. In her edition of *The Ecclesiastical Sonnets of William Wordsworth*, she finds a "poetic interpretation of the spiritual history of his country" (VII) and sees Wordsworth taking his place with Dante, Spenser, and Milton in accepting "the final challenge of his life and art" (4).

Important in countering the kind of emphasis on empirical psychology seen in Basil Willey's chapter "Wordsworth and the Locke Tradition" in his *Seventeenth Century Background* and leading the way to a view of the poet's anti-scientific naturalism are Alfred North Whitehead's chapters on "The Eighteenth Century" and "The Romantic Reaction" in his *Science and the Modern World* (his 1925 Lowell Lectures at Harvard). After describing "the influence upon the eighteenth century of the narrow and efficient scheme of scientific concepts which it had inherited from its predecessor" and the image of "man as helpless to cooperate with the irresistible mechanism of nature," he points to Romantic poetry, and particularly Wordsworth's, as counter forces. "Wordsworth," he argues, "was passionately absorbed in nature . . . .

His consistent theme is that the important facts of nature elude the scientific method . . . . His theme is nature *in solido*, that is to say, he dwells on the mysterious presence of surrounding things." His greatest poem is the first book of *The Prelude*, "pervaded by this sense of the haunting presences of nature" (79–80). Likewise Newton Stallknecht in *Strange Seas of Thought: Studies in William Wordsworth's Philosophy of Man and Nature* views Wordsworth not as a prisoner of Locke and Hartley, but as having a genuinely mystical vision. And T. S. Eliot in his Harvard Norton lecture of December 4, 1932 contends that there is in Wordsworth's "poetry and in his *Preface*, a profound spiritual revival, an inspiration communicated rather to Pusey and Newman, to Ruskin, and to the great humanitarians, than to the accredited poets of the next age" (73). His "revolutionary faith was more vital to him than it was to Coleridge. You cannot say that it inspired his revolution in poetry, but it cannot be disentangled from the motives of his poetry" (66).

Melvin Rader, stressing the influence of Coleridge, especially after the 1795 crises when Wordsworth's bewilderment was great and his Godwinian faith declining to the point that he was giving up moral questions in despair, maintains that the poet had a philosophy although not an elaborately technical one. That philosophy was transcendentalism, a faith that "the mightiest light is to be achieved by combining the empirical and transcendental factors into a most potent unity" (39). There are, argues Rader, two underlying assumptions in Wordsworth's theory of the external world: "that it is free and active, and that spiritual forces are at work. These unite in one idea, that outer things may be interpreted in idealistic terms" (51). In a later work, *Wordsworth: A Philosophical Approach*, Rader connects Wordsworth with a potpourri of philosophers — Plato, Spinoza, Rousseau, and Kant — to argue for a new transcendentalism of the poet, one that generates a new and higher unity.

Joseph Warren Beach in a chapter on Wordsworth in *The Concept of Nature in Nineteenth-Century English Poetry* and Raymond D. Havens in *The Mind of a Poet* are also part of a tradition that minimizes the impact of British empirical psychology and stresses a religion of nature rooted in feelings of the poet, advancing a conviction that the ultimate wisdom is achieved by bringing the inner life into a deeper union with the spiritual forces that pervade external nature. Beach is especially concerned with the impact of the Cambridge Platonists on Wordsworth.

D. G. James in his important book *Skepticism and Poetry: An Essay on the Poetic Imagination* links Wordsworth and Coleridge in their faith that "imagination is a primary factor in all knowledge whatsoever" (15–

16). Writing about *The Prelude* and its expression of personal crisis, he regards the poem as "amongst the greatest poetry. But, as time went on, he used the dogmas of Christianity which slowly were central to his imaginative life." And, continuing this emphasis on intersections of literature and religion, an emphasis that is increasingly notable in recent literary theory, James contends that the "urge to personal creation therefore weakened, and weakened not because he distrusted his own imagination, but because he saw in Christianity the consummation of his imaginative life" (209). In the case of Wordsworth, however, such a consummation "took its toll on the poetic life, for religion impaired the sense of his poetry" (258).

The New Criticism

Clearly one of the most influential, if at times negative, responses to Wordsworth, indeed to Romantic poetry generally, came from the so-called New Criticism, both the British and American varieties. Eschewing poetry as philosophy and large, often vague generalizations about the ideas of a poem, New Criticism became a movement away from appreciative response and toward rigorous, close reading attentive to the subtle presences of irony, paradox, and ambiguity. W. J. Bate saw it as essentially "a movement toward Arnoldian culture rooted in the premise of the centrality of literary studies," "especially in an age with strong religious conviction," "a movement toward a stricter and more involved formalism" (692).

T. E. Hulme's description of Romanticism as "spilt religion" and his objection to "even the best of the romantics" and "the sloppiness which doesn't consider that a poem is a poem unless it is moaning or whining about something or other" catch some of the flavor of the British faction. And T. S. Eliot and I. A. Richards, both of whom spent a good deal of time in the United States, energized what became a full blown American New Criticism in the late 1930s and the 1940s. For Eliot, Wordsworth and Coleridge "were the two most original minds of their generation" (61), and their criticism was the criticism of an age of change (73). Eliot's key concern in criticism was "to divert interest from the poet to the poetry." "There are many people," he writes, "who appreciate the expression of sincere emotion in verse, and there is a smaller number of people who can appreciate technical excellence. But very few know when there is an expression of *significant* emotion, emotion which has its life in the poem and not in the history of the poet. The emotion of art is impersonal." Eliot considers Wordsworth's "emotion recollected in tranquillity" an inexact formula. Far from "emotion" or "recollection," poetry "is a concentration, and a new thing resulting from the concentration, of a very great number of experiences which to the practical and active person would not seem to be experiences at all." Wordsworth's "Preface" to his *Lyrical Ballads*, Eliot argues, makes assertions about the nature of poetry which, if excessive, have a wider bearing than even Wordsworth may have realized. "There is in his poetry and in his *Preface*, a serious spiritual revival" (73). You will, he writes, "understand a great poem like 'Resolution and Independence' better if you understand the purposes and social passions which animated its author; and unless you understand these you will misread Wordsworth's literary criticism entirely" (64–65).

Eliot admired I. A. Richards greatly as the kind of scientific critic who combines both an intense knowledge of poetry and a capacity for objective psychological analysis. Even when he cannot accept his ethics or value system, he admires Richards's taste and the objectivity he brings to his criticism of poetry. For Richards, who represents still another pioneer admired by the American New Critics, the poem is the thing and the reader's experience of it, much more than its background or message, is central.

It is against this English and Anglo-American background that one can see more clearly both the influences and the special cultural concerns brought to the New Criticism by its American disciples. Names such as John Crowe Ransom, Cleanth Brooks, Robert Penn Warren, Allen Tate, and William K. Wimsatt come to mind as key players. Brooks may be the major spokesman, and his textbook *Understanding Poetry*, written with Robert Penn Warren, was a major influence on a generation of college and university students of poetry. The approach was always articulated directly: "By trying to understand the *nature* and *structure* of poetry, how that nature and structure are expressive, and how we respond to them, readers may accelerate and deepen the natural and more or less unconscious process by which they enlarge their experience of poetry." Criticism, the authors contend, "is ultimately of value *only insofar as it can return readers to the poem* itself" (16).

The Romantics, including Wordsworth, do not fare well. Much of their work, as Hazard Adams puts it, "insists on its portentous statements being taken out of context, as if the rest of the poem were merely a surrounding embellishment" (1971, 1032). In his now classic *The Well Wrought Urn*, Brooks begins his argument with the premise that "the language of poetry is the language of paradox . . . the language of sophistry, hard, bright, witty; it is hardly the language of the soul" (3). The case of Wordsworth is instructive, he contends, since his poetry "would not appear to promise many examples of the language of paradox. He usually prefers the direct attack. He insists on simplicity; he distrusts whatever seems sophistical." Yet, ironically, paradox explains the popularity of a sonnet like "Composed upon Westminster Bridge" which most students like, "but have the greatest difficulty in accounting for its goodness." For Brooks "the sonnet as a whole contains some very flat writing and some well-worn comparisons" when the reader probes closely (4–5).

As for the *Immortality Ode,* the poem's successes are countered by its "vagueness — which is not the rich multiplicity of the greatest poetry; and there are some loose ends; and there is at least one woeful anticlimax" (138). A key problem for the careful analyst is that "the solution to the problem of spiritual loss posed by the poem is asserted rather than dramatized" (137). For Brooks we can best understand the strengths and weaknesses of the great ode "if we see that what Wordsworth wanted to say demanded the use of paradox, that it could be said only powerfully through paradox, and if we remember in what suspicion Wordsworth held this kind of poetic strategy" (138). Unfortunately the "ambiguity" of the poem "breaks down into outright confusion" (115).

There is no underestimating the impact of the New Criticism on the reception of a great deal of Romantic poetry and theory, and that included Wordsworth's. As already suggested, the strong emphasis on a more scientific, textually-based approach to reading and judging poetry often found the strongly personal tone, the expansiveness of the language and imagery, and the overt struggle to communicate ideas and emotions undesirable and inappropriate. One of the most striking examples of the impact of the New Criticism and its emphasis on close reading is the celebrated Humanities 6 course at Harvard University in the 1950s and early 1960s, a course taught by a variety of people in a variety of fields, but all persuaded, as its master-spirits Reuben Brower and Richard Poirier put it, that "much of our effort in teaching and in communicating with one another has been directed at clarifying questions and testing answers" (viii). "Reading in Slow Motion" is Brower's manifesto essay, concerned not with putting down literary history and tradition, but with "slowing down the process of reading to observe what is happening, in order to attend very closely to the words, their uses and their meanings" (4), with teaching that brings out "the complete and agile response to words that is demanded by a good poem" (5).

Essays on Shakespeare, Milton, Pope, Frost, Stevens, and others reveal their authors' methodology at work, and Paul DeMan, later to become a guru of the phenomenon of Deconstruction, brings the method
to bear on Wordsworth in an essay on "Symbolic Landscape in Wordsworth and Yeats." Using Wordsworth's sonnet "Composed by the Side
of Grasmere Lake" and Yeats's "Coole Park and Ballylee, 1931," he argues for a different kind of romanticism in each poet by studying carefully the treatment of landscape in their respective poems. Yeats's
"symbolism," he contends, "has nothing in common with Wordsworth's second or symbolic kind of language . . . . Both, it is true, lead
from material to spiritual insights, but whereas Wordsworth's imagination remains patterned throughout on the physical process of sight,
Yeats's frame of reference, by the very nature of his statement, origi-
nates from experiences without earthly equivalence" (37).

Such an institutionalization of New Criticism in the new "close
reading" approach is an important phenomenon in literary study. *Tintern Abbey,* the *Immortality Ode,* the sonnets, sections of *The Prelude,*
and a good deal more of the poet's work has lent itself to the method,
in many cases quite tellingly.

Strong though the impact of the New Criticism and its variations
were, there remained the echoes of earlier semi-biographical and philosophical and religious approaches. Most important in what we might,
perhaps a bit too loosely, call post-World War II criticism of Wordsworth is a pronounced strain that combines close reading with a strong
emphasis on intellectual history. It is the era before the theoretical re-
volts of the late 1960s and the years following, and the names of M. H.
Abrams, Geoffrey Hartman, Harold Bloom, David Perkins are but a
few of those who provided a richer sense of the philosophical and religious roots of Romanticism. Yet even before the full flowering of this
phase in the evolution of Wordsworthian criticism, there were prominent critical voices calling attention to the centrality of Wordsworth not
only to British and European Romanticism, but to the arts, specifically
poetry, in the education and the life of men and women.

Centenary Celebrations and High
Romantic Criticism

1950 saw the hundredth anniversary of Wordsworth's death com-
memorated at ceremonies at Cornell and Princeton Universities and the
publication of the proceedings in a notable collection of essays, edited

by Gilbert Dunklin, on the poet's life and work. In an essay on "Words-worth Through Coleridge's Eyes," Earl Leslie Griggs regards Coleridge as a key to any full understanding of the poet, "for the inspiration he afforded Wordsworth in the development of his poetic genius, for be-ing his best defender during the long period of non-recognition and ridicule, for reading and evaluating his work with penetrating insight, for anticipating the twentieth century estimate of him, and for revealing some of the rich though hidden personality" (91). John Crowe Ran-som, mentioned earlier as one of the founding fathers of the New Criticism, presents in his essay "William Wordsworth: Notes Toward An Understanding of Poetry" the image of Wordsworth as one "who reversed the direction of English poetry in a bad time, and revitalized it" (91). He contends that "in choosing to deal directly with the natu-ral concretions, and with the feelings that engage them, Wordsworth was willing to throw away most of the tropology with which poetry was commonly identified," proposing "to stick to the *tenor* of his situation, and have little recourse to extraneous *vehicles* . . . . For some two years I have felt deeply grateful to Wordsworth for giving his authority to this special kind of language" (97). Recognizing what he regards as the religious, albeit non-sectarian, nature of *The Prelude*, Ransom wonders whether the poet "does not read back into the boy's mind some of the matured configurations of his own. And I think we prefer to take our poetry as an experience which is local, and plural, rather than cosmic and one. It will still give the quick joy, and the instant sense of com-munity with natural objects, and we can go a long way on that" (106). High tribute indeed, he also finds that "the important successors to Wordsworth in the poetry of nature have been Keats, and Hopkins, and our own Robert Frost" (106).

B. Ifor Evans, a fan of Harper's early biography, enters into the continuing discussion of the poet's theory and practice, arguing that Wordsworth is best when he turns away from systematic and writes a visionary poetry. His "true greatness," says Evans, "lies in a uniqueness of experience to be found in Tintern Abbey and parts of *The Prelude* and in some other places" (123). At times he reached "an order of mystical vision in poetry which is of a quality without parallel in our lit-erature" (127).

Lionel Trilling, still another contributor to *Centenary Studies*, brings the perspective of both critic and university don to his essay "Wordsworth and Iron Time." For him, he reminds his audience, "if Wordsworth were not kept in mind by the universities, he would scarcely be remembered at all." The ordinary reader most likely sees him as "the very type of poet whom life has passed by, presumably for the very good reason that he passed life by" (131). Ever the astute public intellectual and sharp observer of American culture, Trilling wonders why and speculates that possibly "for modern taste he is too Christian a poet" (132), taking issue with Hoxie Neale Fairchild's point in his *Religious Trends in English Poetry* that Wordsworth was never an authentic Christian poet (3.170). Agreeing that he "certainly did not in his great period accept as adequate what the Church taught about the nature of man," he did discover "much that a strong Christianity must take account of, and be easy with, and make use of" (135). Trilling probes more deeply into this problem of Wordsworth's difficulty in reaching a modern audience, advancing the idea of a certain "Judaic quality," of the Jewish Church Fathers of *Pirke Aboth*, and of an affinity between "the law as the Rabbis understood it and nature as Wordsworth understood that" (137–38).

In one respect, however, Wordsworth is a poet for contemporary culture, says Trilling. He "taught us to feel but to remember" (151). His may not be tragic art in the classical sense, but "it is precisely the true awareness of what Wordsworth called common life, and even of common life as it exists at a very low level of consciousness, pride, and assertiveness, that validates heroism and tragedy" (149). Trilling closes his rich argument sounding very much like the academic man issuing a clarion call. He recognizes the gap between the celebratory tone of the proceedings of which he is a part and the low standing of the poet with modern readers, but he urges his colleagues to maintain their spirit. In so doing, he appeals, "we do something to fulfill one of the essential functions of the university in our society" (151–52).

Willard Sperry, author of the earlier *Wordsworth's Anti-Climax* with its theory of the poet's decline, also contributed to the centenary celebration, focusing on the question of Wordsworth's religion. The poet was not a pantheist, he argues; he developed, especially in the skating and boat-stealing episodes in *The Prelude*, from a "sense of the world which was wholly alien to himself, if not potentially hostile, to a God-the-companion" sense after his eventual return to the Lake District, and it is in those detailed descriptions of the divine presence in nature that we come to the essence of his religion. It is, says Sperry, "a religion which gave to the poet the power to transmute his agonizing sorrows" (157–61).

Interestingly enough, the collection includes a "minority report," issued in the face of the celebratory spirit of the other participants. It is not the stern critique of an ideologue, but the warm, wise, and witty second thoughts of Douglas Bush, distinguished author of *Mythology and the Romantic Tradition* and a notable scholar and teacher of English Renaissance literature, in a way surprised that he had been invited to Princeton. With tongue in cheek he recalls days on his Vermont farm when he "could not reap the harvest of a quiet eye because my eyes were swollen with hay fever," "could not slake my thirst at every rill because our two springs had been condemned by the state laboratory," "could not appreciate the songs of cuckoos and sky larks" because "we had bees and hornets buzzing in the kitchen." He can only say, "Little I saw in nature that was mine" and resonate with Arnold's "admission that Wordsworth's eyes avert their ken from half of human fate" (3).

Bush's wit may not delight the ardent Wordsworthian, but it does give us something to think about and to question. Recognizing that historically Wordsworth "ranks among the first five or six English poets," "that his share in the *Lyrical Ballads* . . . inaugurated a poetical and spiritual revolution" that "set forth the romantic religion of nature that was to fill a growing spiritual vacuum," he still must pose a vital question: "Is he still, for us, a great poet?" (4).

Bush's answer to that question is a qualified negative. "In Wordsworth's gospel of nature and man," he notes, "the dualism of both classical and Christian ethics was pretty much dissolved." He can admire sections of *Tintern Abbey, The Prelude,* and the *Immortality Ode,* but miss the sense of original sin in the midst of Wordsworthian sentimentalism. "What Wordsworth mourned in *Tintern Abbey* and *Intimations of Immortality* was, to be sure, the sense of what he lived by, but that was the capacity for sensuous and emotional response to nature" (15–16). He admires and calls attention to the poems of questioning and of the quest for a stronger discipline: *Resolution and Independence,* "Ode to Duty," "Character of the Happy Warrior," and "Elegiac Stanzas" are among his examples. What he concludes is that the essential, truly memorable William Wordsworth can be found in a small anthology with a limited number of poems: "a few of the narrative and reflective poems, and of course *Tintern Abbey* and *Intimations of Immortality;* some short poems in which nature is subordinated to humanity and in which there is little or no philosophizing. Of these *The Solitary Reaper* may stand as a perfect example"; "the best of the Lucy poems"; and "a good many of the sonnets, those on Milton, on British ideals of the past and sins of the present, on Toussaint L'Ouverture, and kindred subjects, and some on various themes, from the sight of London at sunrise to mutability" (20–21). This would be a small anthology indeed. Bush contributes a special point of view to an important collection of Wordsworth criticism.

The post-Centenary celebrations and the volume we have just noted might in some ways be considered the beginning of a major outburst of critical attention to Wordsworth's poetry, an outburst that was to shape an image of the poet and his art for the better part of the next twenty-five years. Generalizations are dangerous, of course, but when we think of names such as Harold Bloom, M. H. Abrams, Geoffrey Hartman, Carl Woodring and Robert Langbaum, we think of critics, solidly grounded in the poetry and theory of the age, who nevertheless move beyond close reading as a dominant methodology, using philosophy, psychology, even religious thought to develop a High Romantic doctrine. In this sort of approach Wordsworth looms large even though Coleridge is, quite properly, cited as the guru of the period, the promulgator of fresh ideas of the poetic imagination, of nature as a source of inspiration and meaning, of poetry as something approaching prophetic utterance.

Wordsworth, however, who wrote poetry from his schooldays almost to the year of his death in 1850, seems like the spokesman for the movement, with his ringing description in his 1800 "Preface" to the *Lyrical Ballads* — of poetry as "the spontaneous overflow of powerful feeling," an "emotion recollected in tranquillity," as "the first and last of all knowledge"; of the poet as "a man speaking to men: a man, it is true, endowed with more lively sensibility, more enthusiasm and tenderness, who has a greater knowledge of human nature, and a more comprehensive soul, than are supposed to be common among mankind." It is this image of the poet and poetry that captures the attention of many critics of the time even though their individual approaches can be notably different.

M. H. Abrams in his now classic history of literary criticism and theory *The Mirror and the Lamp* sees Wordsworth's "Preface" as the harbinger of a movement of aesthetics from the classical mimetic to the Romantic expressive. As the first great Romantic poet, he contends, Wordsworth "may also be accounted the critic whose influential writings, by making the feelings of the poet the center of critical reference, mark a turning point in English literary theory" although he was more "thoroughly immersed in certain currents of eighteenth century thinking than any of his important contemporaries" (103–104). Furthermore, for Abrams Wordsworth unfolds a whole philosophy of poetic diction, declaring himself for nature over art (111).

Abrams makes another vital contribution to Wordsworth criticism with his oft-cited essay "Structure and Style in the Greater Romantic Lyric" in a splendid collection of essays, edited by Frederick Hilles and Harold Bloom, on the theme of a shifting sensibility in the latter half of the eighteenth century. Abrams notes that there had never been any adequate description of a distinctive kind of Romantic lyric, of what Coleridge called the "conversation poem" and Langbaum the "poem of experience." Wordsworth's key poems in this genre of lyric, meditative, ruminative writing are *Tintern Abbey,* the *Immortality Ode,* and, in a special way, his "Elegiac Stanzas Suggested by a Picture of Peele Castle in a Storm," and Abrams opens up a whole new way of thinking of poems like these. Such poems, he writes, have "lyric magnitude and a serious subject, feelingly meditated." They offer "a determinate speaker in a particularized, and usually a localized, outdoor setting, whom we overhear as he carries on, in a fluent vernacular which rises easily to a more formal speech, a sustained colloquy, sometimes with himself or with the outer scene, but more frequently with a silent human auditor, present or absent." The speaker moves from a description of the landscape, after noticing a change which evokes memory and feeling. And as the speaker meditates on the change, he "achieves an insight, faces up to a tragic loss, comes to a moral decision, or resolves an emotional problem" (527–528).

One of the earliest of such history of ideas approaches was E. D. Hirsch, Jr.'s influential *Wordsworth and Schelling: A Typological Study of Romanticism.* Following the familiar date of Romanticism's beginning in England in 1798 and citing Wordsworth as a key player, Hirsch sees Schelling's *Naturphilosophie,* and especially his *Ideen zu einer Philosophie der Natur,* as central to understanding the poet, although for Wordsworth, who was not a Germanist, the influence was indirect. Schelling is vital because "it is very difficult to deduce the contours of Wordsworth's outlook from his poetry alone" (6).

What Wordsworth and Schelling share, according to Hirsch, is "Enthusiasm," described as "a highly affirmative way of experiencing things" (15) with the subject feeling "a deep kinship with his object . . . a kind of love." The experience is fundamentally "religious"; the "beyond which it constantly senses is nothing other than God Himself" (26). For the enthusiast "everything is alive" and, citing the "sentiment of Being" passage from Book 2 of *The Prelude,* "There is no absolute separation between time and eternity" (62). In *Tintern Abbey* we see how a "new visit to the scene of an earlier experience becomes a renewal on a different level of the earlier affirmation" (76). And in a rigorous analysis of the *Immortality Ode,* Hirsch connects the theme of the poem with that of *The Prelude,* "the growth of the human heart" (173), "a song of thanks and praise to God" (174).

James Benziger in an influential book, *Images of Eternity: Studies in the Poetry of Religious Vision from Wordsworth to T. S. Eliot,* argues that Wordsworth recognized that the eighteenth century "had starved men's religious instincts . . . stunted the growth of men's imaginations" (12) and that he sought the restoration of that power in poetry. Anticipating the great premise of Abrams's *Natural Supernaturalism* (to be discussed later in this chapter), Benziger finds that "external nature was the first great religion in which deists and Romantics sought images to nourish religious instincts no longer sustained by Biblical narrative and religious tradition" (15). In *The Prelude* "beauty and love are seen as related by the imagination" which "is pronounced to be the indispensable moral agent in that growth of love which will alone enable us to play our full part in the great cosmic harmony" (43). And one sees Wordsworth's linking of beauty and the sublime in the *Immortality Ode* and the great Mount Snowdon scene in *The Prelude.*

Early on in his *The Excursion: A Study* Judson Lyon speaks to those many critics of *The Excursion* by calling attention to the poem as part of the poet's recovery from the failures of France, the death of his brother John, and the general rationalism of the age. "There is a faith at the end of the poem, but only after steps like appreciation of the mute agents which stir in nature and love for one's fellow-beings — and they seem to be important means in themselves, as well as means to the ultimate faith in God" (80).

Bloom is an ever-present and pioneering critic in this Romantic resurgence, highlighting from his earliest writing the visionary company and how "the central desire of Blake and Wordsworth, and of Keats and Shelley, was to find a final good in human existence itself" (xxv). Ranging through Wordsworth's poetry, he focuses on the so-called Golden Decade, arguing that "until *Peele Castle,* natural seeming and reality are one." The crisis of *Tintern Abbey* is that "perception and response are no longer simultaneous, and it is an act of meditation that must bring the two halves together" (135). The world of *The Prelude* is "exquisitely fitted to the individual mind of the young Wordsworth" (146). The *Immortality Ode* is also about separateness and consequent mortality, and about "the imaginative power that can bridge that separateness and so intimate immortality" (176)

Bloom, in *The Ringers in the Tower: Studies in the Romantic Tradition,* carves large and engaging images of his visionary tradition from

Blake to Wallace Stevens, to A. R. Ammons: "a renaissance of the Renaissance," "the Internalization of Quest Romance." Wordsworth has a large part in the drama of questing poets looking back with anxiety, and forward with excitement. As Milton, he says, "curbed his own Prometheanism, partly by showing its dangers through Satan's version of the heroic quest, so Wordsworth learned to restrain his, partly through making his own quest-romance in *The Prelude*, an account of learning both the enormous strength of nature and nature's wise and benevolent reining in of its own force" (20).

M. H. Abrams, already mentioned, is another continuingly valuable critic of Romanticism in general and of Wordsworth as the center of the inspired company. He is the editor of still another collection of distinguished essays, *English Romantic Poets: Modern Essays in Criticism*, this one with notables such as Trilling, T. S. Eliot, C. S. Lewis, W. J. Bate, Cleanth Brooks, and Geoffrey Hartman, and he wisely reprints his own memorable and insightful essay. Taking his cue from the lines in *The Prelude*, "Oh there is a blessing in this gentle breeze" and I "felt within/A corresponding mild creative breeze," he finds the "correspondent breeze" metaphor especially fertile in helping one to see "how often, in the major poems, the wind is not only a property of the landscape, but also a vehicle for radical change in the poet's mind" (40). In a comment that will bear full fruit in his magisterial study *Natural Supernaturalism* twenty years later, he finds the wind "both the stimulus and outer correspondent to a spring-like revival of the spirit after a wintry season, and also to a revival of poetic inspiration of the Prophets when touched by the Holy Spirit" (40). We will return to that classic work later in this chapter.

Earlier mention of Robert Langbaum brings to mind his seminal essay, "The Evolution of Soul in Wordsworth's Poetry." Sounding a bit like Arthur Beatty with his emphasis on the poet's debt to the Locke tradition, Langbaum quickly moves beyond Wordsworth's early Locke-Hartley empirical sympathies. He argues that "it is the main purport of Wordsworth's poetry to show the spiritual significance of this world, to show that we evolve a soul or identity through experience and that the very process of evolution is what we mean by soul." He further contends that Wordsworth in *The Prelude* was trying to deal with the questions raised by the Lockean idea of man as well as the Platonic belief in innate ideas, and to use both to get at "the mystery of life, vitality, organic connection" (25). Wordsworth's conclusion, like Coleridge's in his poetic theory, is "the idea of interchange between man and nature — the idea that the mind modifies sensation as much as sensation modifies the mind" (19–20). Langbaum, developing further the tradition of Wordsworth as the poet of High Romanticism, contends that the poet finds a language to match his prophetic hero. Focusing on the visionary Mount Snowdon passage at the end of *The Prelude*, he regards Wordsworth's "naturalistic revelation to be not only the equivalent of the Platonic idea, but this time the equivalent of Christian revelation" (36). It is this image of a secularized Christianity with poetry as its gospel and the poet as its priest that underlies much of the criticism of the period and finds its culmination and most potent articulation in Abrams's later study *Natural Supernaturalism.*

There is also among what we have been calling the school of celebratory critics of Wordsworth, and indeed of Romanticism in general, a darker side, one that in no way minimizes the richness of the poet's vision or the extraordinary beauty of the poetry. In its own way it enriches Wordsworth's achievement and belies Arnold's views of the poet as turning away from half of human experience or Bush's complaint that the poet lacks a sense of original sin. David Perkins and David Ferry, without any sense of siding with each other, nevertheless explore what they regard as the clichés about Wordsworth's unqualified love of nature, the limitless powers of the imagination, and the idea of a connection between a love of external nature and its translation into a philosophy of human nature.

Perkins focuses on the symbolism of Wordsworth, Shelley, and Keats in *The Quest for Permanence*. For him the poet is not a landscape-loving Rousseauist. Like his fellow poets, Wordsworth "tended to represent the poet in the image of the discoverer, a man isolated in some difficult exploration or quest." But for Perkins there is a gulf between man and nature in the poetry, the sense of man as "alien or intruder," citing "Nutting" and the boat-stealing scene in *The Prelude* as examples. "Where Wordsworth does describe change and process in the natural world, it is slowed down until it scarcely intrudes upon the sense of permanence" (33). "Only the 'living Presence' of nature can be regarded as permanent and undying" (35).

Perkins continued his critical reading of the poet in *Wordsworth and the Poetry of Sincerity*. The reviewer for *The Dalhousie Review*, R. W. Woof, had called *The Quest for Permanence* "a poised and adventurous study that made its strong mark" and with that mark "we know that the days of innocence about the Romantic poets were over" (93–95). The new book takes its cue from a dominant theme that developed in the eighteenth century, the theme of art as the direct expression of personal feeling. Perkins cites Wordsworth as a major beginning point and argues that with him "art tends less to distinguish between the outer world of events and the inner world of consciousness. Instead it renders their meeting point of interfusion" (16). It is important, says Perkins, sounding like an early New Historicist, to read the poet as his readers did. Such readers were invited to imagine that "they felt a sympathy and communion with the natural world, and, in such communion, a quasi-religious experience. For if the natural world was not itself divine, it was haunted by a divine presence" (24). Along with this ideal came a "continuing mistrust of language" and of traditional conventions and forms. Wordsworth's poetry, with its deep sensitivity to patterns of consciousness, struggles to describe them, ultimately falling back on metaphor, especially one that "compares the imagination exerting its power to a mist spreading within and without" (90). The late poetry, a subject treated by almost all the critics from a variety of angles, receives Perkins's attention also. That poetry, he says, reveals the "liabilities" of the ideal of sincerity. Wordsworth might have been confident that belief "ought not so much to be adopted as to rise organically out of past feelings and experience," but for Perkins this didn't happen in the later work. "One must," he explains, "account in other ways for the shackles of self-mutilating dogma Wordsworth had put on by 1815, and the main explanation is his desperate need for certitude" (241).

In *The Limits of Mortality: An Essay on Wordsworth's Major Poems*, David Ferry demonstrates remarkable close reading skills in moving beyond easy generalizations about Wordsworthian philosophy and proposing a critical strategy. "It is," he begins, "often as if the 'surface' meanings of the poems were a beautiful and intelligible message, apparent at once, and as if hidden in that message were clues to a 'deeper' meaning, still more beautiful though in some at odds with the message one had to read at first" (12).

Ferry is especially effective in dealing with particular poems as test cases. "Composed Upon Westminster Bridge," also discussed by J. Hillis Miller and noted later in this study, is a strong example, a striking example "of the sort of poem which has a satisfactory meaning 'with relation to a fixed time and place' and an equally wonderful, quite different meaning when understood 'under the aspect of eternity.'" Far from simply a beautiful capturing of a London sunrise as seen from a coach traveling over Westminster Bridge, the sonnet is a statement about "man's essential relations to his experience and to the real, the metaphysical nature which devaluates the temporal experience." The sonnet's crucial last line — "And all that mighty heart is lying still" — suggests that the city is not merely sleeping but dead, its heart stilled.

The poet looks at London and "sees it as a sort of corpse and admires it as such, welcomes a death which is the death of what the city has come to stand for in his symbolic world" (14).

In "Nutting," Ferry finds man an enemy of nature, indeed a destroyer, knowing that he alone must die. Nature is, however, only a symbol of eternity, coming "between man and the experience of eternity" (29). And in his probing comments on "To the Cuckoo" Ferry hears the speaker yearning for the time "when the bird was not a symbol at all, but the mystery itself, *literally*. It yearns for the time when the world expressed more truth than poetry is capable of" (29).

The *Immortality Ode* affords Ferry rich opportunities for amplification of his reading of Wordsworth. Citing the closing lines, he finds them "a statement of the acceptance of temporal nature as repository of symbols — as the only way left, for the man who has lost his mystical capabilities, to have an experience of the eternal" (47). And he exercises his typically civil revision of the sentimental optimism that characterizes some criticism of the poem, finding Wordsworth as "in a certain sense the most remote of our great poets from the ordinary reader," not a poet of the "sacramental" but the "mystical" imagination, a hater of "temporal nature" (51–53).

Ferry is equally penetrating in his comments on *The Prelude* (Book 2. 382 ff.) with its joyous faith in the "sentiment of being." He wonders whether it ignores the tensions "between the changeful and the unchanging that we have seen so powerfully expressed in other passages." Man, he believes, is always conditioned by time, but has "his saving link to the quietness and peace which lie outside time and yet inform it" (123). On Mount Snowdon, in the epiphanic closing of the poem, Wordsworth passes the "limits of mortality." He can only yearn for the transcendent, "remembering that he had once been with the things of nature and had required no symbols. Not clarity but mists attend his vision" (171).

Like so many of Wordsworth's critics, early and late, Ferry has a strong critical interest in the later poetry and the question of whether it signals decline, loss, or fuller development. He wonders whether the deep distress that the poet finds responsible for a humanizing of his spirit is "really a confession that the love of nature had not led to the love of man, and the declaration of a new interest which his imagination was not equipped to sustain?" (172–73). Ferry's summary comment is sharp but insightful: Wordsworth's genius was "his enmity to man which he mistook for love, and his mistake led him into confusions which he could not bear. But when he banished the confusions, he banished his distinctive greatness as well" (172–73).

As Bloom, Perkins, and Ferry pursue the philosophical Wordsworth, each with a differing point of view, but all with a strong sense of the poet not just as a landscape poet, a writer about rustic life, a further extension of the eighteenth-century ballad tradition, there are remarkable developments that reveal critics of Wordsworth focusing on particular poems, or particular strategies and techniques.

Abbie Findlay Potts in her useful *Wordsworth's Prelude: A Study of Its Literary Form* notes that when *The Prelude* finally appeared in 1850, after Wordsworth's death, it was *The Excursion*, "whether or not one read it," that "was acknowledged as his masterpiece." She reminds us tellingly, and the earlier reception of the poet already considered in this book bears out her reminder, that major critical publications of the time such as the *Edinburgh Review*, the *Quarterly Review*, and *Blackwoods* didn't even review it. Potts cites the later century praise of A. C. Bradley as vital to the canonization of *The Prelude*. And it remained for mid-century critics to provide a more systematic treatment, whether the psychoanalytic analysis of Richard Onorato or the structural approach of Herbert Lindenberger. Herbert Lindenberger, in an important early study of *The Prelude*, stresses the modernity of the poem in both content and form and yet attends to the poet's public voice. The poem, he says, "wavers quite explicitly between two areas of reference . . . the poem as personal history and as poetic utterance" (xiii), and he further observes that "what goes on in the poem is a constant flight from subjectivity of private experience to the assertion of publicly communicable and valid truths" (5).

Lindenberger sees the structure in interesting ways, the first half moving from the "awesome visionary experiences of early childhood" to the "tamer argument," as he puts it, of the human world of London. The second half "progressed from the terrors of the Revolution — with the corresponding turmoil that ensued within his mind — to the attainment of rural retirement" (38). Time — or "time consciousness" — is a major concern, and Lindenberger devotes two impressive chapters to the theme. As with another important critic of the same period, Christopher Salvesen, it is a felt or experienced time that determines the form of the poem. Taken as a whole, he says, the poem can be looked upon as a struggle between two worlds, inner and outer, for control of its hero. Taking his cue from David Ferry's influential thesis, Lindenberger feels that Wordsworth at times "seems to regard nature as an image of eternity" and at others "to insist on the inadequacy of nature except as a means beyond itself" (179).

Lindenberger sees the modernity of the poem in its attempt to "imitate the structure of experience," its "spots of time" anticipating Arnold's "Dover Beach" and Yeats's "Among School Children" (201–202). On the other hand, Ferry's influence is notable, as he cites his remark that Wordsworth's "genius was his enmity to man," in his treatment of the later poems, those of the "monumental" poet. Time may continue as a subject in the post-Golden Decade poetry, but except for very few examples, "we no longer find the intense exploration of private experience . . . . Time in the later Wordsworth is time with a capital T" (175).

Carl Woodring stands as another pioneering critic of the poet in the 1960s, and his work on the politics of Romanticism and of Wordsworth is a particular example. His simply but deceptively titled *Wordsworth* provides a valuable overview of the career and work with his fine critical eye providing a sharp look at a wide range of the poetry. For Woodring he was not only a "great" but a "revolutionary" poet of a movement "that elevated sincerity, or fidelity to personal feelings, above the objective truths of social organization" (20). He eschews previous negative criticism of the *Lyrical Ballads*, arguing that "no other poet of England, to anything like the same effect, had kept his eye on the object, his mind on the heart, or his ear to the vernacular." And he regards the frequently criticized language of the ballads as "not that of peasant or child, but of a poet disciplined to simplicity" (22).

Woodring sides with Lionel Trilling on the *Immortality Ode,* finding in it not a dirge for a dying life or career but rather "cries of despair that marked the spring of 1802" (72). And he regards the great Mount Snowdon scene of *The Prelude* as "the final transcendent experience of the poem" as the poet felt again "this sense of immateriality and again attributed it to the communing imagination" (112). He also rejects the easy assignment of the later poems to a period of decline, stating impressively that "day in and day out, he proclaims in hammered verse the thrill of the ordinary" (214).

At a time when adversarial political criticism of Wordsworth is widespread, Woodring's *Politics in English Romantic Poetry* (published in 1970) is still an invaluable treatment of the historical, cultural, and political setting with special focus on Wordsworth, Byron, and Shelley. Of Wordsworth he comments that "during his sixty years of contemplating the nature of the poetic office," he "spent very few moments questioning the degree of a poet's responsibility to society." That responsibility he nourished, "sometimes by intensifying it, sometimes by en-larging its objectives" (85). Woodring traces the path taken by the poet from early radicalism, especially his initial enthusiasm for the Revolu-tion in France, his revulsion at the violence and power-mongering, and his turn toward a more measured confidence in Tory politics and An-glican religion. "In representative poems of *Lyrical Ballads*, Word-sworth's figures, settings, and attitudes were each commonplaces of the day." Yet, says Woodring, he brought to these commonplaces "a novel aspect of the democratic idea" (94). In a rigorous reading of *The Prel-ude*, he deftly takes on the facile view that the second half of the poet's epic traces "the conversion of a republican into a Tory." And he argues persuasively for "the growth of a troubled liberal into a Wordsworthian romantic, who held slightly changed beliefs with deeper reason." The poem ends with the poet and Coleridge dubbed as "Prophets of Na-ture" committed "to communicate in the brief years left to them the truths needed for men's redemption from ignominy" (115).

Stephen Prickett in *Coleridge and Wordsworth: The Poetry of Growth* is one of several critics who chose to study the two Romantic compan-ions as they interact with each other and as each makes his own way. What they have in common is a view of imagination as a union of per-ceiver and perceived. As with so many of the twentieth-century critics already discussed, Wordsworth and Coleridge are seen by Prickett as part of a new vision, "a new model of the human mind as a thing whose characteristic activity was creation." Instead of "the older Lockean-Hartleyan view of the human being as the cumulative legacy of past events, the personality was felt to be a 'unity'" (44).

A new set of definitions emerges from Prickett's analysis: "Poetry, for them, was the imagination in words": it was that "sublime faculty by which a great mind becomes that which it meditates on" (94). The most representative of Wordsworth's and Coleridge's insights "is not the feeling of the Imagination at work in perception, but of its suspen-sion" (142). Their romanticism "is a continually modifying interaction between external and internal worlds." Yet they are not clones. Each is a very different person, thinker, poet. Prickett offers a remarkable and persuasive distinction: "In Wordsworth the poet of poetic creation seems almost always to well up from within, whereas in Coleridge it seems usually to come from establishing a rapport with the external world — through recognizing a kinship with other creatures, or from the rising wind in the aeolian harp" (156).

William Heath writes about Wordsworth-Coleridge associations, but from an engagingly different angle. In *Wordsworth and Coleridge:*

A Study of Their Literary Relations in 1801–1802, he focuses on a single year, indeed on only a part of that year, because "literary history records no other fruitful confrontation of will and talent so fully documented so exactly located in time and place." It is a story in which Dorothy also has a part, albeit one that has never fully been understood. Wordsworth may have had a long poetic life, may have in the 1797–1800 period been a busy writer, but all of this pales, according to Heath, when one does a "creativity chart." In less than twenty weeks, he contends, "between March 19th [1802] when Coleridge arrived at Town End in Grasmere, and July 29th when Wordsworth and his sister left Grasmere for Calais, Wordsworth had written at least twice as many poems as appeared in the whole *Lyrical Ballads* of 1798, including 'The Rainbow,' 'Resolution and Independence,' and half of 'Intimations of Immortality.'" And if, says Heath, you include the work done on *The Prelude* and *The Excursion* during this period, it is a period of sustained work never again equaled. Although hardly comparable, Coleridge's vision, revision, and completing in a sense of his *Dejection: An Ode* was also the work of this period, perhaps his "final successful effort in his career as a poet" (5).

It is a remarkable period, and Dorothy, the home at Grasmere, personal crises, physical and emotional, all play key parts. Heath contends that the weeks are "irresistibly fascinating to the literary critic because these personal crises are so obviously reflected in, if indeed conducted in, the words that survive in the letters, notebooks, journals and magnificent poems of the people involved." Paul Magnuson pursues the connection of the two poets in his *Coleridge and Wordsworth: A Lyrical Dialogue* some twenty years later, and we will have occasion to consider that work as part of another period of reception of Wordsworth's poetry.

The *Lyrical Ballads* and their several prefaces have been the object of critical attention from the beginning, and we have already noticed in this study the range of responses — from praise for the new directions that the poems represent to sharply negative responses to the limitations of such a system of subject matter and language. What we have missed, perhaps understandably because of the more general nature of nineteenth and a good deal of early twentieth-century criticism, is the kind of rigorous study these poems and the philosophy underlying them deserve.

As early as 1917, however, Marjorie L. Barstow was one of those who launched a tradition of more scholarly study of the roots of the new genre of early nineteenth-century poetry and a careful examination of a wide range of Wordsworth's poems. And Robert Mayo has been properly recognized for his argument that the *Lyrical Ballads* followed in most cases patterns found in the magazine poetry of the 1790s. No one, however, has written more forcefully about the ballads than Stephen Parrish — first in a series of periodical essays and then in his remarkable book, *The Art of the Lyrical Ballads*. Beginning with the premise that Wordsworth never really confirmed Coleridge's description of the "dual purpose" of the volume, with Coleridge focusing on the supernatural and Wordsworth on the natural, and that Coleridge himself in the *Biographia Literaria* called the Wordsworth poems experiments that "in a comparatively small number of poems he chose to try" a failure, Parrish proceeds with his path-breaking study.

The study begins with the image of Wordsworth as the major partner, the bolder and more interesting experimenter, the more formidable poet. He cites George Harper's early contention that Wordsworth, "through a stiffer and more practical nature, was the innovator, the iconoclast, the radical, both in theory and practice." On the one hand, Parrish accepts and critiques commonplaces about the *Lyrical Ballads*— their "conscious artistry"; Wordsworth's "tireless commitment to the poet's craft"; DeQuincey's description of them as "the greatest event in the unfolding of my own mind"; Hazlitt's response that the poems were "like the turning up of the fresh soil, or the first welcome breath of spring" (ix–x). On the other hand, he wants to offer a special kind of examination, "tracing the literary antecedents of Wordsworth's most experimental poems" (mainly to Burger in Germany and to Burns in Britain) and to show how the poet moved beyond these in "original directions" (x). Parrish writes of these new directions as heightened metrical patterns, a jocular, even at times mock-heroic technique, the effective use of drama and pastoral, and, most important, a stronger emphasis on feeling than story and a fascinating internalization of the action.

Parrish takes on the familiar and challenging task of defining the curious collocation of "lyrical" and "ballad" and ventures an engaging description: "A 'lyrical ballad,' we may venture, was distinctively lyrical in two respects: its passion ('Poetry is Passion') arose, as in any lyric, from the mind of the speaker; and this passion was communicated in heightened, hence more lyrical ballad meter" (114). Recognizing the "major influence of Burns," he sees Wordsworth combining the two traditions of eighteenth-century poetry that he inherited and wanted to invigorate — "the pastoral with its truth to nature, and the ballad, with its authentic voice of passion and its truth to the elementary feelings of the human heart" (186). Parrish's treatment of a wide range of ballads is detailed and insightful, most notably his conclusion about *Michael*, a ballad that is converted into a blank-verse narrative and serves as a signal of "Wordsworth's movement in 1800 away from his early experimental voices into the main region of his song" (187).

John Jordan in *Why the Lyrical Ballads: The Background, Writing, and Character of Wordsworth's 1798 Lyrical Ballads* some years later continues the tradition of scholarly excellence set in Parrish's work. Its title suggests its remarkable comprehensiveness as Jordan, like Parrish in his skepticism about Coleridge's account of the origins of the volume, speaks of Wordsworth's simple dedication to writing a certain kind of poetry and of Coleridge's somewhat later push for a joint publishing venture (20–23). Jordan then takes us through the evolution of the volumes, dividing the poems into three groups, the most memorable the last group, "probably the *piece de resistance* of the *Lyrical Ballads* as Wordsworth conceived it, the core of the 'experiment,' for which the Advertisement and later the Preface were written" (35). "More likely Wordsworth acquiesced for financial reasons to Coleridge's suggestion that they query Cottle as to what he *could* give for the two volumes" (24).

Jordan's book has been enormously helpful to the present writer in his review of early critical response to the *Lyrical Ballads*. Challenging what was for a long while a popular myth about negative criticism, he demonstrates, from a thorough review of journal and magazine response, that the poems turned out to be "something of a popular success." The collection went on to see a total of four British and one American edition in seven years, and undoubtedly would have been brought out again if it had not been merged into Wordsworth's works in 1815" (111–112).

But Jordan goes beyond historical backgrounds and critical reception, advancing sound and thoughtful approaches of his own to explain the aesthetic success of the poems. Taking the "I have felt" section of *Tintern Abbey*, unquestionably the greatest of the ballads, as a cue, he feels that Wordsworth "tries to recreate that feeling for the reader by describing it thematically and circumstantially." More important than event or setting is "the feeling observer, who — despite the 'I' — is not simply William Wordsworth, but rather observing humanity, 'the mind of man'" (5–6). Wordsworth, says Jordan, denies the "trivially simple," but values the "essentially simple." His favorite critical terms were "elemental" and "external." In a word, the simple was "the quintessence of art" (99).

Paul Sheats in *The Making of Wordsworth's Poetry, 1785–1798* carefully follows Wordsworth's career from his earliest schoolday poems to the publication of *Lyrical Ballads*, emphasizing how the poet elaborated but also disciplined the central premises of English Romanticism as he examines the shifting relations in Wordsworth's work between external nature, the human mind, and poetic style. Sheats aims to offer a fresh context for the reading and interpretation of the mature poetry.

Admitting the difficulty of the task he undertakes, he recalls how Wordsworth himself "mocked the presumption of those who reduce the mysterious to single and extrinsic causes," mimicking them in *The Prelude* (2.213–15) as those "who point, as with a wand" and say "This portion of the river of my mind/Came from you fountain" (x). Sheats will follow the poet's own recommendation for studying his artistic development, reading the poems, not the biographies. He sees, as others in our study have, in the 1792–1797 period "the central moral and philosophical dilemma bequeathed to the modern poet by the rise of empirical science and rationalism" and makes the case for Wordsworth forging "a poetic language adequate to his perception" (xi).

To develop his argument he begins at the beginning. He would find the origins of the Wordsworthian paradoxes in some of the more accessible early poems despite the "aesthetic condescension" of Arnold in the nineteenth and H. W. Garrod in the twentieth century. In those earliest Hawkshead poems, so seldom discussed at the time, he sees Wordsworth's lifelong concern with "the relation with mind and object" (20). Preparing to leave the security and pleasure of the Lakes to enter Cambridge, Sheats writes, Wordsworth "presents himself as a man who has already survived the ambush of hope, and dedicated himself, by implication, to a poetry of reason and truth" (40).

Sheats reads the early poems with a fine eye, refusing to group them simplistically, but observing the uniqueness of each in a process of artistic development. *An Evening Walk*, for example, unlike the schoolday poetry exercises, values "the common range of visual things," yet "he presents the object without reference to the heart" (57), and "we sense a silently moving eye" (58). *Descriptive Sketches*, on the other hand, reveals a "revolutionary style, which suggests that Wordsworth's vision of landscape was profoundly changed by the events of 1791 and 1792" (61). Still trusting the poems as he unfolds his idea of development or making of poetic style, he finds the poet emerging from political and emotional distress in *The Borderers* as Wordsworth "turns once again to the sole remaining support available to the mind, nature in its role as epistemological and emotional object" (133). At Racedown and then at Alfoxden — with Coleridge and Dorothy — his art becomes the vehicle for pursuing the ideal of a revitalized human nature with the "I" returning to a new and lofty conception of poetry.

Tintern Abbey, for most readers the greatest of the *Lyrical Ballads,* is a poem of transition in Sheats's argument, its form representing "a unique blending of mimetic and expressionistic modes, as Wordsworth in effect imitates the activity of his own mind and moves toward the openly personal voice of the years to come" (244). It is a "first" in the developing career of the poet, "a presentational structure of immense complexity and eloquence . . . allowed to imitate the full range of his own consciousness" (230). Yet there is a "passionate protest against subjectivism," the vice of which Wordsworth and other Romantic poets have been accused. Sheats's closing tribute to Wordsworth is powerful indeed, that "he disciplined both the romantic and neoclassic practice on behalf of a Christian humanism that is rooted in the Renaissance" (249).

Two volumes of the period we are examining are worth noting here. The first, already mentioned in connection with Herbert Lindenberger's work on *The Prelude,* is Christopher Salvesen's *The Landscape of Memory: A Study of Wordsworth's Poetry,* which ranges widely in dealing with one of the most frequently used words in Wordsworth's poetry. Connecting memory with the poet's love of and devotion to the natural world, Salvesen makes the point that Wordsworth was becoming increasingly conscious that "his true understanding of nature was by way of remembered impressions" (74). Wordsworth himself had come to fear the tyranny of the eye and to feel the need of taming an "over-dominant sense of sight." The result was the "wise passiveness" he celebrates so often in the poetry, a state of the spirit effected by memory, "of allowing past experience to form itself and reappear — from the seeing of nature to the experiencing of time" (127). Time became a felt thing — Wordsworth's "felt in the blood and felt along the heart" in *Tintern Abbey* comes to mind — and the workings of memory "restorative." Salvesen's book treats a familiar subject with an engaging freshness.

The second book, James Scoggins' *Imagination and Fancy: Complementary Modes in the Poetry of Wordsworth,* juxtaposes the poet's poetry and critical writing to examine in depth fundamental differences between his 1815 classification of certain poems as those of "fancy" and others of "imagination." After exploring some of the roots of Wordsworth's poetic theory, he proceeds with his association of each with certain qualities and powers. The poems of fancy, generally written in the present tense and concerned with a general situation, lack wonder. The poems of imagination, evoking the past and focusing on particular settings, reveal a dominant speaker and are obviously autobiographical while those of the fancy rely on more sharply defined memories of childhood. Scoggins in effect offers us two Wordsworths, one the poet of fancy and beauty, the other the poet of imagination and the sublime.

If there is something like a Wordsworth critical tradition, even a tradition of High Romantic theory, it can certainly be seen as centering around the work of Geoffrey Hartman, Harold Bloom, and M. H. Abrams. This certainly must be the tradition that came to be known as the Romantic ideology which prompted a significant response in the new literary theory of the period from the mid-1970s to the present. Although hardly a school with master and disciples, there are certain key motifs, cultural critiques, mythologies and myth-makers that persisted in critical writing for a long time. While chronology is not a major key to understanding this phenomenon, one is naturally drawn to M. H. Abrams in beginning this section on Wordsworth and his critics.

We've already had occasion to discuss the very early work of Abrams in *The Mirror and the Lamp: Romantic Theory and the Critical Tradition* with its underlining of the expressive dimension of Romantic poetics and its movement away from a more classical mimesis toward a Wordsworthian emphasis on poetry as spontaneous self-expression. The Wordsworthian aesthetic, as found in the various versions of the poet's "Preface" to the *Lyrical Ballads* and in the poetry itself, is a central point of reference as Abrams unfolds a theory of Romantic, indeed of modern poetry. We've also seen how his now classic essay on "Structure and Style in the Greater Romantic Lyric" provided not only keen insights into the subject of a new kind of poetry but also into a new way of writing that poetry.

It's fair to say that Abrams continued, as theorist and critic, to maintain a strong interest in the Romantic movement, especially in ways of understanding it more fully. His second major book, *Natural Supernaturalism: Tradition and Revolution in Romantic Literature*, opens with a description of "a remarkable period of creativity, the three decades following the outbreak of the French Revolution" and with an explanation that his title "indicates that my recurrent, but far from exclusive concern will be the secularization of inherited theological ideas and ways of thinking" (12). Alerting his reader to how commonplace his concern might appear, he sets forth his sense of how that secularization evolved. Far from abandoning the tradition of Western thought since the Renaissance, secular thinkers, he argues, "have no more been able to work free of the centuries-old Judeo-Christian culture than

Christians were able to work free of their inheritance of classical and pagan thought" (13). Theirs is a *natural supernaturalism*.

Abrams's book is, to say the least, expansively ambitious, finding, for example, the roots of Wordsworth's *Prelude* and of his program for poetry itself in the circuitous journey motif of a great Christian autobiography such as Augustine's *Confessions*. Pilgrims and prodigals, says Abrams, move from alienation to integration with Holderlin's *Hyperion*, Goethe's *Faust*, and the romances of Novalis serving as examples. Abrams pursues the journey motif from Blake to D. H. Lawrence, pausing to consider Marx, Nietzsche, T. S. Eliot, and others. He also devotes chapters to major Romantic themes of apocalypse and poetic vision.

Wordsworth is clearly a key player in the unfolding drama, for Abrams "the great and exemplary poet of the age" with the "Prospectus" to his planned masterwork *The Excursion* "the manifesto of a central Romantic enterprise." No "wrath of Achilles," or "arms and the man" or "man's first disobedience" will be the theme of his song. Instead it will be a poetic epic "On Man, on Nature, and on Human Life" as he muses in solitude, he the poet-prophet of a new era, praying for a "fit audience . . . though few!" and rendering tribute to his great predecessor Milton. The "Prospectus" introduces a whole new epic subject matter, argues Abrams; "the heights and depths of the mind of man are to replace heaven and hell, and the powers of mind are to replace the divine protagonist" of Milton. For Wordsworth the power of the human mind is itself adequate, "by consummating a holy marriage with the external universe, to create out of the world of all of us, in a quotidian and recurrent miracle, a new world which is the equivalent of paradise" (25–26).

Abrams's reading of *The Prelude* is admirably rigorous and engaging as he takes the reader from the paradise of Wordsworth's childhood to the disenchantment with city-life and Cambridge education, to personal and political disillusionment in France, and finally to a mature joy in his return to a life with family, friends, and the nurturing beauty of nature. For Abrams the poem uses two great innovations in prose fiction which developed only a short while before Wordsworth began his epic: "the Bildungsroman (Wordsworth called *The Prelude* a poem on 'the growth of my own mind') and the Kunstlerroman (Wordsworth also spoke of it as 'a poem on my own poetical education')" (74).

Abrams's citation of the great lines toward the end of *The Prelude* capture his sense of Wordsworth's faith in the redemptive power of the human imagination, a power for him stronger than any creed:

> Imagination having been our theme,
> So also hath that intellectual love,
> For they are each in each, and cannot stand
> Dividually. — Here must then be, O Man!
> Strength to thyself; no Helper hast thou here
>
> (13.185–9)

Geoffrey Hartman is another powerfully influential force in this era of Wordsworthian criticism, and there are ways in which he anticipates Abrams's *Natural Supernaturalism* and Bloom's *Anxiety of Influence*. "Two powers," he argues, "fought for his soul — Nature and Milton" (xiv). But Nature became a more forceful "counter-myth to Milton," leading Wordsworth "beyond nature to the borders of vision." And "he never wavered in future years from the project of marrying mind to nature" (xv). Writing about the earlier poetry, specifically the *Lyrical Ballads*, he feels that the poet "does not deny the supernatural but says nature is already so much. Why multiply entities, or suppose special intervention, when nature is supernatural in its powers to renovate man?" (154).

What Hartman brings to the criticism of Wordsworth's poetry is the sense that the poet is coming to recognize the autonomy of imagination. No longer an ancillary faculty, a force to adorn ideas, imagination is instead a creative, mediating power that makes meaning. His survey of the evolution of that power in the poetry is thorough and persuasive, advancing the image of the poet beginning a career "with less between himself and his imagination than perhaps any poet before him" (104–5).

His early *Descriptive Sketches*, for example, offers a transcendence that "is still mainly visual" (111) although there is a prefiguring of his "inner preparedness for a break with nature." As a matter of fact, the major poems of the 1793–1798 years continue to be "haunted by a concern for a specific place." Yet, and here again there seems to be an anticipation of Abrams, "from the point of view of the history of Christianity *Lyrical Ballads* represents the furthest possible extension of the concept of the Light of Nature, and that his readers did sense." "For those who followed Wordsworth this was religion in a new dress, the dress of feeling. Religion was once more opened to all, as in the primitive Christianity of St. Paul" (153).

Hartman speaks of a developing Wordsworth giving a particular kind of careful attention to nature, not so much numbering the "streaks of the tulip," but continually detailing "the state of his mind."

The *1807 Poems*, including "I wandered lonely as a cloud" and "The Solitary Reaper," reveal his feelings not so much of "elation" or "salvation," but rather of "renovation (regeneration)" and "a heightened intimacy with seventeenth-century traditions" (5). And the Lucy poems are lyrics of passage with Lucy hovering between spirit and human.

Then there are the great questionings surrounding both Wordsworth's professional life and his personal: Must all be lost when the "marvellous boy" of the *Intimations Ode* and *The Prelude* achieves the "philosophic mind"? Must the power of poetry at its most inspired give way to periods of decline? Wordsworth will say "No" to such questions, however, finding in change growth, "and the passage from one mode of being to another should resemble the storm at the beginning of 'Resolution and Independence' which passes into the calm, sunny energies of a new day" (203). Already one hears the great stirrings of *The Prelude*.

We should note at this point James Heffernan's *Wordsworth's Theory of Poetry: The Transforming Imagination*. While recognizing the work of René Wellek, Raymond Havens, Geoffrey Hartman, and of James Scoggins, Heffernan still feels the need for a fuller and more thorough study of the poet's aesthetic theory and particularly of his theory of imagination. His book will, he says, deal with that need, viewing Wordsworth's concept of imagination "as the key to his poetry and to the evolution of his critical perspective, which at first focuses narrowly on feeling as the source of poetry, and then expands to see imagination — a much greater power — as the 'soul of poetry'" (1).

At the time of his writing, Heffernan regards recent criticism as stressing Wordsworth's "mystical, introspective tendencies" (17). Hartman describes imagination as "consciousness of self raised to an apocalyptic pitch" while David Ferry separates the "sacramental" Wordsworth, the one who regards nature as a symbol of eternity, from the "mystical" poet who saw nature as "nothing more than a hindrance to his communion with eternity" (3). In chapters on "The Eye and the Heart," "Spontaneous Feeling," "Creative Sensibility," "Transformation," "The Unity of Mutual Modification," "The Making of Emblems," and "Revelation," he blends both Wordsworth's aesthetic theory and poetic practice, contending that "no theorist of poetry before Wordsworth was more intimately, intensely, and consistently concerned with the world of sight and sound," with what the poet described as "exact and accurate detail (PW.4.430)." In this connection Heffernan, whose later work has devoted much attention to poetry-painting connections and to the large field of ekphrastic poetry, calls attention to Wordsworth's strong interest in painting. He cites Martha Shackford's demonstration that the poet was "at least *familiar* with approximately one hundred painters, and of these a dozen produced pictures which inspired him to write poems" (73), and notes Wordsworth's strong interest in William Gilpin's and Uvedale Price's work on the phenomenon of the picturesque (16–17).

Discussing the strengths and dangers of Wordsworthian spontaneity, Heffernan, conscious of a theory of poetry that would seem to exaggerate "the role of the natural, undirected response" (49), underlines how nature is "mentor, guide, and stimulus" (64) and how imagination at its best is a "transforming power" (150) that "must imitate the power of nature" (192). And he is eloquent in describing Wordsworth's sense of poetry as prophecy, his conviction that "part of his mission as a poet was to communicate a sense of moral values" and his central belief that imagination is "an instrument of divine revelation" (231).

The conclusion of his impressive book continues this spirit of informed and scholarly eloquence as he attempts to capture briefly the center of the poet's theory: "Seizing the infinite through the finite, the eternal through the temporal, and the invisible through the visible, the exercise of imagination for Wordsworth is an act of faith, a mode of apprehension, that yielded the 'sensuous incarnation' of 'ethereal and transcendent' truths. In the final reckoning, Wordsworth conceived of imagination as the power by which the poet bears witness to the inexhaustible mystery of the word made flesh" (271).

The Wordsworth Exhibition and "The Wordsworth Circle"

No study of the reception of Wordsworth's poetry in the late twentieth century should avoid adequate mention of the major exhibition organized by Rutgers, the State University of New Jersey, and the Wordsworth Trust, Dove Cottage, Grasmere. Entitled *William Wordsworth and the Age of English Romanticism* and planned by Michael Jaye, Robert Woof, and Jonathan Wordsworth, it had three major exhibition sites: the New York Public Library, the Indiana University Art Museum, and the Chicago Historical Society during 1987 and 1988. Consisting of manuscripts and paintings of the period, the catalogue is now available as a handsome volume with Jonathan Wordsworth's splendid overview of the period and chapters on "The Age of Revolution," "The

Spirit of the Age," "The Child is Father of the Man," "The Discovery of Nature," "Unity Entire," "Memory, Imagination, and the Sublime," a descriptive catalogue of paintings, and a 1770–1850 chronology by Duncan Wu.

One of the most important sections for this study is the foreword by M. H. Abrams. Written at a time when High Romantic Criticism is being called into question, including criticism of Wordsworth, it seems to offer a reaffirmation of a more traditional view. Recognizing that "'The Age of Romanticism' is a title imposed by later historians on the four decades after 1790," it nevertheless affirms that "a number of writers who lived during that turbulent time had recognized that in both its literature and thought it constituted an era that was distinctive, vital, and innovative, and had identified its distinguishing features by the term 'the spirit of the age'" (vii). And Wordsworth, Abrams continues, was recognized "by his major contemporaries . . . whatever objections they might have to some of his opinions and achievements" as "the greatest and most representative poet of his time" (viii). And they would have understood the Revolution as the focus of the exhibition, Wordsworth's "master theme," "an event that he, uniquely among contemporary poets, had known at first hand" (vii).

Abrams notes that "almost all of Wordsworth's greatest poems were written little more than a decade following the spiritual crisis and recovery he recorded in *The Prelude*, in the attempt to reconstitute for himself and for his readers, hope, courage, and a revised basis for civilized values in an age of profound cultural demoralization" (viii). He says, in considering the *Lyrical Ballads*, that the poet's revolution against the *ancien regime* in poetry "was more than merely egalitarian, it inverted the established social hierarchy by choosing not only the lowly — a shepherd, a cottage-wife — but also the ignominious, the scorned, and the social outcasts as the protagonists in serious, and sometimes tragic poems" (ix). And the *Ballads*, especially *Tintern Abbey*, launched the "major theme of his next and greatest decade — the theme of the individual mind, and what it is to grow older and to pass, by way of a personal crisis, from the stage of what William Blake called 'innocence' to that of 'experience'" (ix).

Abrams closes his foreword with the strong contention that this theme of loss and pain "managed in terms of an interaction between the individual mind and the environing world, is the subject and tactic not only of 'Tintern Abbey,' and of such later lyric poems as the 'Intimations Ode' and *Elegiac Stanzas*," but also appears in the massive expanse of his autobiographical *Prelude*.

The year 1970 also saw the founding of what is now the key journal of Wordsworth studies, *The Wordsworth Circle*. Founded by Professors Marilyn Gaull and Charles Mauskopf of the English Department at Temple University, and still edited by Professor Gaull, the first issue of the journal has an enthusiastic opening. "First conceived," write the editors, "during some moments of heady conversations in the riotous spring of 1968" when a good many scholars and students realized that there was "no publication devoted specifically to the first generation Romantic writers, we proposed a quarterly newsletter which would focus that interest." With unbounded confidence they planned an international bibliography of books, articles, reviews, reevaluations of the field, a plan too ambitious to implement.

The editors received strongly positive response from notable scholars such as Richard Haven, Geoffrey Hartman, David Perkins, and M. H. Abrams. David Whitten, then editor of the *Keats-Shelley Journal*, felt strongly about the need for a journal devoted to first generation Romantic writers. Chester Shaver, still another distinguished Wordsworthian, made a key point with his words about the need "to revive a sense of community among teachers and scholars of English Romanticism." And Earl Wasserman favored a merger of the new journal and the *Keats-Shelley Journal*.

After many conversations and much correspondence, W. P. Albrecht, a notable Hazlitt scholar, announced the plan for the new journal *The Wordsworth Circle* at the New York annual meeting of the Modern Language Association of America in 1968. With a modest format and contents that took the form of a forum on topics like Wordsworth's reputation in Japan by Paul Betz, Karl Kroeber's Concordance to the 1805 *Prelude*, and Richard Wordsworth's efforts to purchase Rydal Mount, the editors decided on a greater emphasis on fresh scholarship on the Circle with occasional single author issues, and news about meetings and seminars.

The rest is history, and especially for Wordsworthians interested in some of the best criticism of the poet and his work, with the following just a few of many examples: in the 1970s Bishop Hunt's "Wordsworth and Charlotte Smith" (1.3) and Marilyn Gaull's "From Wordworth to Darwin" (10.1); in the 1980s Kenneth Johnston's "The Politics of Tintern Abbey" (14.1) and Richard Gravil's "Coleridge's Wordsworth" (15.2); and in the 1990s Scott Harshbarger's "Transatlantic Transcendentalism: The Wordsworth-Peabody-Hawthorne Connection" (21.3) and Nicola Trott's "Wordsworth's Tranquilizers" (24.1); Aileen Ward's

"Romantic Castles and Real Prisons: Wordsworth, Blake and Revolution"; and Peter Manning's "Lyrical Ballads 1798 and 1998."

Works Consulted

Abrams, M. H. *Natural Supernaturalism: Tradition and Revolution in Romantic Literature.* New York: W. W. Norton and Co., Inc., 1971.

——. *The Mirror and the Lamp: Romantic Poetry and the Critical Tradition.* London, Oxford, New York: Oxford UP, 1953.

——. "Structure and Style in the Greater Romantic Lyric." *From Sensibility to Romanticism: Essays Presented to Frederick A. Pottle.* Frederick W. Hilles and Harold Bloom, editors. New York: Oxford UP, 1975. 527–560.

Abrams, M. H., editor. *English Romantic Poets: Modern Essays in Criticism.* 2nd edition. London, Oxford and New York: Oxford UP, 1975.

Adams, Hazard. *Critical Theory Since Plato.* New York: Harcourt Brace Jovanovich, Inc., 1971.

Babbitt, Irving. *Rousseau and Romanticism.* New York: Houghton Mifflin, 1919.

——. "The Primitivism of Wordsworth." *On Being Creative.* New York: Houghton Mifflin, 1932.

Barstow, Marjorie L. *Wordsworth's Theory of Poetic Diction: A Study of the Historical and Personal Background of the "Lyrical Ballads."* New Haven: Yale UP, 1917.

Bate, W. J., editor. *Criticism: The Major Texts.* Enlarged Edition. New York: Harcourt Brace Jovanovich, Inc., 1970.

Batho, Edith. *The Later Wordsworth.* Cambridge UP, 1933.

Beach, Joseph Warren. *The Concept of Nature in Nineteenth-Century English Poetry.* New York: Pageant Book Co., 1956.

Beatty, Arthur. *William Wordsworth: His Doctrine and Art in Their Historical Relations.* Madison: U of Wisconsin P, 1960.

Benziger, James. *Images of Eternity: Studies in the Poetry of Religious Vision from Wordsworth to T. S. Eliot.* Carbondale and Edwardsville: Southern Illinois UP, 1962.

Bloom, Harold. *The Ringers in the Tower: Studies in the Romantic Tradition.* Chicago and London: U of Chicago P, 1971.

——. *The Visionary Company: A Reading of Romantic Poetry.* Revised and Enlarged Edition. Ithaca and London: Cornell UP, 1971.

Brooks, Cleanth. *The Well Wrought Urn: Studies in the Structure of Poetry.* New York: Reynal and Hitchcock, 1947.

Brooks, Cleanth and Robert Penn Warren. *Understanding Poetry.* 4th edition. New York: Holt, Rinehart, and Winston, 1976.

Brower, Reuben A. and Richard Poirier, editors. *In Defense of Reading: A Reader's Approach to Literary Criticism.* New York: E. P. Dutton & Co., Inc., 1962.

Burton, Mary. *The One Wordsworth.* Chapel Hill, NC: U of North Carolina P, 1942.

De Man, Paul. "Symbolic Landscape in Wordsworth and Yeats." in *The Rhetoric of Romanticism.* New York: Columbia UP, 1984. 125–143.

De Vere, Aubrey. *Recollections of Aubrey De Vere.* New York: Edward Arnold, 1897.

Dunklin, Gilbert T., editor. *Wordsworth: Centenary Studies Presented at Cornell and Princeton Universities.* Princeton: Princeton UP, 1951.

Eliot, T. S. *The Use of Poetry and the Use of Criticism: Studies in Relation of Criticism to Poetry in England.* Cambridge, MA: Harvard UP, 1961.

Fairchild, Hoxie Neale. *Religious Trends in English Poetry.* 3 vols. New York: Columbia UP, 1937–1968.

Ferry, David. *The Limits of Mortality: An Essay on Wordsworth's Major Poems.* Middletown, CT: Wesleyan UP, 1959.

Harper, George Maclean. *William Wordsworth: His Life, Work, and Influence.* 2 vols. New York: Charles Scribner's Sons, 1916.

Hartman, Geoffrey. *Wordsworth's Poetry, 1787–1814.* Cambridge, MA and London: Harvard UP, 1964.

Havens, Raymond D. *The Mind of a Poet.* Baltimore: Johns Hopkins UP, 1941.

Heath, William. *Wordsworth and Coleridge: A Study of Their Literary Relations in 1801–1802.* Oxford: Clarendon, 1970.

Heffernan, James A. *Wordsworth's Theory of Poetry: The Transforming Imagination.* Ithaca and London: Cornell UP, 1969.

Hirsch, E. D. *Wordsworth and Schelling: A Typological Study of Romanticism.* New Haven: Yale UP, 1960.

Hulme, T. E. *Speculations: Essays on Humanism and the Philosophy of Art.* Herbert Read, editor. New York: Harcourt, Brace, and Co., 1924.

James, D. G. *Skepticism and Poetry: An Essay on the Poetic Imagination.* London: George Allen and Unwin Ltd., 1937.

Johnston, Kenneth R. *Wordsworth and "The Recluse."* New Haven and London: Yale UP, 1984.

Jordan, John. *Why the Lyrical Ballads: The Background, Writing, and Character of Wordsworth's 1798 Lyrical Ballads.* Berkeley: U of California P, 1976.

Langbaum, Robert. "The Evolution of Soul in Wordsworth's Poetry." *PMLA.* 82.2 (1967): 265–272. Rpt. in *The Modern Spirit: Essays on the Continuity of Nineteenth and Twentiety Century Literature.* New York: W. W. Norton, 1970.

Legouis, Emile. *The Early Life of William Wordsworth, 1770–1798: A Study of The Prelude.* Trans. J. W. Matthews, with a Prefatory Note by Leslie Stephen. London: J. M. Dent and Company, 1897.

——. *Wordsworth in a New Light.* Cambridge, MA: Harvard UP, 1921.

——. *Wordsworth and Annette Vallon.* New York: E. P. Dutton, 1922.

Lindenberger, Herbert. *On Wordsworth's "Prelude."* Princeton: Princeton UP, 1963.

Lyon, Judson. *The Excursion: A Study.* New Haven: Yale UP, 1950 [reprint 1970 Archon Books].

Magnuson, Paul. *Coleridge and Wordsworth: A Lyrical Dialogue.* Princeton: Princeton UP, 1988.

Mayo, Robert. "The Contemporaneity of the Lyrical Ballads." *PMLA* 69 (June 1954): 486–522.

Meyer, George Wilber. *Wordsworth's Formative Years.* Ann Arbor: U of Michigan P, 1943.

Onorato, Richard. The Character of the Poet: Wordsworth in *The Prelude.* Princeton: Princeton UP, 1971.

Parrish, Stephen. *The Art of the Lyrical Ballads.* Cambridge: Harvard UP, 1971.

Patton, Cornelius Howard. *The Rediscovery of William Wordsworth.* Boston, MA: The Stratford Company Publishers, 1935.

Peek, Katherine Mary. *Wordsworth in England: Studies in the History of His Fame.* Bryn Mawr, PA, 1943.

Perkins, David. *The Quest for Permanence: The Symbolism of Wordsworth, Shelley, Keats.* Cambridge: Harvard UP, 1959.

——. *Wordsworth and the Poetry of Sincerity.* Cambridge: Harvard UP, 1964.

Potts, Abbie Findlay. *Wordsworth's Prelude: A Study of Its Literary Form.* Ithaca: Cornell UP, 1953.

——. *The Ecclesiastical Sonnets of William Wordsworth.* New Haven: Yale UP, 1922.

Prickett, Stephen. *Coleridge and Wordsworth: The Poetry of Growth.* Cambridge: Cambridge UP, 1970.

Rader, Melvin. *Presiding Ideas in Wordsworth's Poetry.* U of Washington Publications in Language and Literature. 8.2. Seattle: U of Washington P, 1931. Rpt. New York: Gordian Press, 1968.

———. *Wordsworth: A Philosophical Approach.* Oxford: Clarendon P, 1967.

Raleigh, Sir Walter Alexander. *Wordsworth.* London: E. Arnold, 1903.

Richards, I. A. *Practical Criticism: A Study of Literary Judgment.* New York: Harcourt, Brace, and Co., 1929.

Robertson, Frederick M. *Lectures on the Influence of Poetry and Wordsworth.* London: H. R. Allenson, 1906.

Salvesen, Christopher. *The Landscape of Memory: A Study of Wordsworth's Poetry.* Lincoln: U of Nebraska P, 1965.

Scoggins, James. *Imagination and Fancy: Complementary Modes in the Poetry of Wordsworth.* Lincoln: U of Nebraska P, 1966.

Shackford, Martha. *Wordsworth's Interest in Painters and Pictures.* Wellesley, MA: The Wellesley Press, 1945.

Sheats, Paul. *The Making of Wordsworth's Poetry, 1785–1798.* Cambridge, MA: Harvard UP, 1972.

Sperry, Willard. *Wordsworth's Anti-Climax.* Cambridge, MA: Harvard UP, 1935.

Stallknecht, Newton. *Strange Seas of Thought: Wordsworth's Philosophy of Man and Nature.* Durham: Duke UP, 1945.

Whitehead, Alfred North. *Science and the Modern World.* New York: New American Library, 1964.

Willey, Basil. *The Seventeenth Century Background: Studies in the Thought of the Age in Relation to Poetry and Religion.* London: Chatto and Windus, 1934.

Woodring, Carl. *Politics in English Romantic Poetry.* Cambridge, MA: Harvard UP, 1970.

———. *Wordsworth.* Boston: Houghton Mifflin, 1965.

Woof, R. F. Review of David Perkins, *The Quest for Permanence: The Symbolism of Wordsworth, Shelley, Keats.* Cambridge, MA: Harvard UP, 1939. In *Dalhousie Review.* 41.1 (Spring 1961): 93–95.

Wordsworth, Jonathan, Michael C. Jaye, Robert Woof, with the assistance of Peter Funnell. Foreword by M. H. Abrams. *William Wordsworth and the Age of English Romanticism.* New Brunswick and London: Rutgers UP and Grasmere, England: Wordsworth Trust, Dove Cottage, 1987.

4: Wordsworth and the New Theory

IT IS DIFFICULT TO DATE WITH ABSOLUTE ACCURACY, but the emergence of post-structuralism, or of what has come to be known as
"literary theory," or quite simply "theory," is certainly a phenomenon
of the last thirty years. Hazard Adams marks 1965 as "the midpoint of
a decade of profound change and disquiet, particularly in its latter half,
that did not leave the world of criticism and theory untouched." And
although the roots of the new theory, in its many forms and variations,
are ultimately European, it developed with great speed and force in its
American incarnation where, as Adams puts it, structuralist criticism
waned and was transformed into "poststructuralism or deconstruction"
(1986, 1). We linger briefly to discuss some of the dominant manifestations not as we might in an extended treatment of contemporary approaches to criticism, but rather as we might connect these manifestations to notable differences in the ways Wordsworth's poetry has
been received. Alan Grob, in calling attention to one notable example
which we shall consider as we proceed, argues that "of all the convul-
sive changes that have worked their way through the field of Romantic — and especially Wordsworthian — studies during the post-
modernity of the past thirty years, none seems more truly ominous than
many critics' wholesale adoption in the past decade of those adversarial
positions that now seem to shape and govern almost all undertakings of
any real influence in the field" (187).

Grob is, of course, referring chiefly to his and some others' *bête
noire*, New Historicism, and we will have occasion to consider later that
specific phenomenon, especially as it triggered a notable debate in
Wordsworthian studies. But we should perhaps begin with some general observations about specific poststructuralist theoretical postures,
especially as they have a bearing on Romantic, and in particular Wordsworthian criticism.

Jacques Derrida is clearly a pioneering force in the critique of
structuralism, and his highly regarded 1966 lecture on "Structure,
Sign, and Play in the Discourse of the Human Sciences" represents one
of his major statements. With theorists such as Levi-Strauss and Northrop Frye as major targets, he contends that elaborate structures like
Western metaphysics and patterns of mythology ultimately deconstruct.

His critique of Ferdinand Saussure's linguistics finds the notion of signifier and signified outmoded. Language has come to speak man, and the whole idea of the human, the essential, is called into question. Michel Foucault, another formidable figure, brings the political to bear on the linguistic, also questioning the idea of man, of human, indeed of the author, and finding in institutions like prisons, hospitals, and asylums instruments of capitalist domination. With Derrida even the last vestiges of structuralism are lost with language itself deconstructing and leaving an "endless play of meaning," *différance*.

Paul De Man and J. Hillis Miller, both at Yale at the time, became major spokesmen for the deconstructive impulse, especially as it relates to literature. Miller, both theorist and critic, responds to M. H. Abrams's assault on deconstruction in a celebrated essay, "The Critic as Host." Rallying at the end of his argument, he values deconstruction for its "attempts to resist the totalizing and totalitarian tendencies" of criticism as he has seen it practiced. Its resistance comes "in the name of an uneasy joy of interpretation, beyond nihilism, always in movement, a going beyond which remains in place, as the parasite is outside the door but also always ready within, uncanniest of guests" (Adams, 1986, 468).

Over the last thirty years feminist theory has made its mark in the life and literature of our culture. "Since the late 1960s," writes Elaine Showalter, "when feminist criticism developed as part of the international women's movement, the assumptions of literary study have been profoundly altered." While no one voice or party-line dominates, names such as Kate Millet, Patricia Spacks, Sandra Gilbert and Susan Gubar, and Showalter herself have made special contributions. They do share, however, a continuing concern with "the literary representation of sexual difference, with the ways that literary genres have been shaped by masculine or feminine values, or with the exclusion of the female voice." In a word, "feminist criticism has established gender as a fundamental category" (3).

Showalter's anthology, with a variety of essays by notable scholars in the field, ranges widely over major theoretical issues while Gilbert and Gubar focus more sharply on the Wordsworthian century in their *The Madwoman in the Attic: The Woman Writer and the Nineteenth Century Literary Imagination*. Both have energized a generation of Romantic feminist critics, and, for our study, of critics of Wordsworth. We single out for attention but a few of the strong voices attending to the poetry and theory of the poet.

Anne Mellor is clearly a critic to be reckoned with in a study like this one, and her two volumes — *Romanticism and Gender* and *Romanticism and Feminism* — while dealing with a literary era, have a good deal to say about Wordsworth. Mellor makes a clear distinction between the masculine and feminine imagination in her approaches. The masculine mind is a dominating force, and its Romantic manifestation, she says, "has traditionally been identified with the assertion of a self that is unified, unique, enduring, capable of initiating activity, and above all aware of itself as a self" (*Gender,* 20). Such a mind, however, triggers a female silencing in one form or another. Like some other feminist readers of Wordsworth, Mellor often introduces Dorothy for purposes of comparison, arguing that "Dorothy's sense of self is fluid, relational, exhibiting the permeable ego boundaries" (*Gender,* 156).

Mellor imagines how Hartman's reading of Wordsworth might be cast with a change of gender. "Wordsworth," she writes, "finally replaces (feminine) nature with the production of the (masculine) imagination" (*Gender,* 20). In *The Ruined Cottage* Margaret's slow physical and mental decline after the loss of her husband and its representation in the deterioration of her house and garden become "a source of 'comfort' and 'happiness' for both the Old Man who tells her tale of unrelieved suffering and the Pedlar who hears it" (*Gender,* 19). Lucy and other female figures in the earlier poems "do not exist as independent self-conscious human beings with minds as capable as the poet's." They are "rarely allowed to speak for themselves" (*Gender,* 106).

The Prelude, according to Mellor, is clearly a poem of "a masculine self" (*Gender,* 147), and "the construction of such self-consciousness was the project of one of the most influential literary autobiographies ever written" (*Gender,* 145). Dorothy's "floating island" images a different self, however, "a self *that does not name itself as a self:* the metaphor of the floating island as a life or self is one that has to be intertextually transferred from her brother's poem" (*Gender,* 156).

In a sharp feminist critique of what had for many years come to be regarded as a Romantic canon, Mellor concludes that "these six male poets have been heralded because they endorsed a concept of the self as a power that gains control over and gives significance to nature, a nature troped in their writings as female" (*Feminism,* 8).

Judith Page's *Wordsworth and the Cultivation of Women* attempts a representative look at the poetry, both early and later. She clarifies at once the key word in her title, explaining that it works two ways — "to refer to a certain quality associated with women and the feminine and to suggest a process by which Wordsworth was formed, fostered, and nurtured by women and his ideas of the feminine." At the same time she sees him cultivating women, seeking "their company and friendship" even though he identified himself as a poet by distinguishing himself from women (10). Yet Page would strike a conciliatory tone, wanting to critique underlying assumptions about women in his life and work while offering a way to admire Wordsworth and his poetry.

Aware of fellow feminist readers and their critique of his egotistical sublimity, she finds a positive, "a paradoxical yearning for relationship, a tension that in the later poetry resolves itself in images of beauty and domesticity constructed from a masculine point of view" (6). Page sees the conflict in the early poetry, in the two-part *Prelude* of 1799, for example. Here Wordsworth, she contends, organizes his early experience around the Burkean categories of the sublime and the beautiful, taking a cue from Burke's connecting these categories to gender. The poet, says Page, "dramatizes an inner conflict between sublime impulses associated with masculinity and solitude, and the attractions of the beautiful, associated with feminine nurturing and community" (6).

Page calls attention to what she sees as Wordsworth dissociating himself from women writers and, in effect, feminine weaknesses in the 1800 "Preface" to *Lyrical Ballads* while at the same time defending "writing about figures on the margins of society" (7). At the same time, however, he "depends on a supportive private audience (composed largely of women), as both his letters and his great poem 'Tintern Abbey' make clear" (7). In short he is cultivating women while ignoring the possibility that women writers are part of the audience that cultivated him.

In an early chapter Page moves to a discussion of Wordsworth's French connection and with ways in which the Revolution impacted the poetry, with his need to control his own sexual and political excesses as the body politic in France did. Yet, says Page, as he comes to terms with his own moral lapses, he "spiritualizes or silences women so that he does not have to come to terms with them as sexual Other" (7).

In succeeding chapters Page moves to the later poetry — *The White Doe* and *Laodamia* in particular, *The Excursion* to some extent — still attending to conflicts of order and revolution, passion and control. Interestingly, she concludes that both poems "end in silence and death, one woman sainted for her passivity and the other condemned for passion" (8).

Page makes Wordsworth's daughter Dora a key to understanding the late Wordsworth. The poet, she says, is making a transition from "rebellious son to Victorian father" (8). That later poetry "is marked by a need to control and circumscribe women and the feminine often represented by a daughter" (8).

If New Historicism has one leadership voice, especially in the field of Romantic/Wordsworthian studies, it is certainly that of Jerome McGann. His *The Romantic Ideology* captures the essential spirit of the movement, and his creedal statements are sharp and provocative. Unlike the old literary history which sought to interpret texts in terms of "past historical texts" and how they shape them — a futile activity, says McGann — the New Historicism takes a different approach. Instead of allowing poets like Wordsworth and Coleridge to set the ground rules by which future critics approach their work — McGann's idea of a Romantic "ideology" — he advocates rigorous historicizing. Such a process focuses on and makes explicit "first, the dialectical relation of the analyzed texts to present interests and concerns; and second, the immediate and projected ideological involvements of the criticism, critical theory, and reading we practice, study, and promote." New Historicism at its best would "cease reproducing texts and begin *re*producing them" (159–160).

Clifford Siskin, another Historicist theorist and practitioner, brings his own particular slant to the methodology. Arguing that the Romantic view of the self is of "a mind that grows" and that "writing became an index to that growth" through the creative imagination, he is skeptical about this imagination. It is, he says, "not a timeless producer but a culture-specific product." And he finds that knowledge is "not discovered in the course of mankind's inevitable progress" — but "made at a particular point in time" (5).

We proceed to some representative samples of specific poststructuralist critical approaches to Wordsworth. J. Hillis Miller, perhaps the major American representative of deconstructionist reading, offers in his *The Linguistic Moment: From Wordsworth to Stevens* what he describes as a book of "slow reading" and proposes "a search to locate a ground beyond language for the linguistic patterns present in my poems" (xvii). His Wordsworth poem is the famous sonnet "Composed Upon Westminster Bridge," and he attends to it as an example of the important role played by the poet in "the deconstruction of metaphysics" and also of "ways in which the problem of form enters into his work as one of its essential themes" (63). The poem's meaning is for Miller ultimately indeterminate, "partly from a pattern of metaphors that lies like an invisible garment of light over the realistic texture of the poem" (68). While not attacking the more mimetic reading of a critic such as Earl Wasserman, he nevertheless feels that the subjective response of a poet can be just as mimetic. Negatives and imagery within the text of "Westminster Bridge" move aside the mimetic to create a new place for the "sovereignty of the mind over things" (72). The memorable closing lines of the poem, argues Miller, set up a striking contrast — between the second last line which suggests that the city/lady is asleep and the final line which suggests that "the city is like a corpse" (73). The poet is "both there and not there, as if he were his own ghost," and his poem expresses "an oscillation between con- sciousness and nature, life and death, presence and absence, motion and stillness." As in the great Lucy poem "A slumber did my spirit steal," the poet is "a survivor of a death that is by implication his own death" (74).

Paul Fry's take on "Westminster Bridge" is different. Responding not only to Miller, but also to other notables, including Geoffrey Hartman, Carl Woodring, and Alan Liu, he agrees with the power of "historical reality" in the text, but chooses to concentrate on the poem as poem, subtly critiquing that reality. The continuing debate about the exact date of the poem "is a mockery of living by the calendar." A truly poetic awareness, he contends, reveals that "the very uniqueness of this experience, its suspension of movement in stillness, shows how rare it is that the veil, the garment of history is drawn aside" (162).

One way of getting at the varied and complex New Historicist criti- cal response to Wordsworth is to focus on what might be called one episode that catches the many nuances — pro and con — of a criticism that connects literature and history in very special ways. The episode revolves around the Wordsworth of *Tintern Abbey* with Marjorie Levin- son at center stage, a smart, venturesome New Historicist and author of *Wordsworth's Great Period Poems* and a number of critical essays. Be- ginning with the premise that much current American writing on Wordsworth has developed uncritically from the Hartman/Bloom High Romantic discourse, she argues that all the talk about vision and transcendence "is a bit of a white elephant." We need, she writes, to suspend our ecstatic praise "until such time as we can trace its source and explain its character. The romanticized landscape of Wordsworth's poem avoids the vagrants and the poor as well as the coal and timber barges on the river." She continues with the observation that far from the transcendence of "the thing he loved," the poem betrays his flight from "something that he dreads" (37). Similarly in "Peele Castle" the power whose loss Wordsworth mourns is "the power of the Real — the experientially extrinsic stable datum — to impress itself as such on the mind of the poet, a mind which, by its ceaseless digestion of the uni-

verse of things, has finally incapacitated itself." The poem is his chance
to escape. Without ever being mentioned, the French Revolution is the
power overshadowing the poem (102). For Levinson, "Peele Castle"
"resumes but reverses the '93 to '94 despair-to-hope, shock-to-calm,
sublime-to-beautiful dynamic" (120).

Thomas McFarland, a major Romantic scholar known especially for
his work on the Princeton University Bollingen edition of Coleridge
and for a seminal work *Romanticism and the Forms of Ruin*, responds
directly to Levinson's chapter on *Tintern Abbey* in his *William Wordsworth: Intensity and Achievement* and provides a clear critical alternative to reading the poem, and perhaps to reading Wordsworth more
generally. His opening chapter, "The Clamour of Absence: Reading
and Misreading in Wordsworthian Criticism" sets the tone. Pulling no
punches from the beginning, he picks up on Levinson's enthusiastic account of a student's puzzlement at the title of the poem, noting that
from the beginning her argument is "built upon sentimentality . . . by
which student ignorance is transmuted into a higher wisdom" (2).

McFarland then focuses on Levinson's fascination with "absences"
in the poem, especially with the absence of any details about the industrial smoke from the river and about the poor people in the area. Levinson's charge concerned the poet's escapism, his "acts of exclusion,"
including exclusion of the abbey itself. McFarland, however, advances a
strong case for misreading. Wordsworth, he recalls, had written that he
began the poem after leaving Tintern, actually the evening "after a
ramble of four or five days with my sister" and that the poem is a classic
example of his definition of poetry as "emotion recollected in tranquillity." He further reminds the reader of John Keble's tribute to Wordsworth as the poet of the poor, adding that poems such as *Resolution
and Independence* and *The Ruined Cottage* could well have been written by Marx or Engels. Recalling the full title of the poem, he argues
that it evokes "a process that depended upon an emotional experience
above, not below, Tintern Abbey" (9).

McFarland also attends to a familiar New Historicist/Feminist
reading of the Dorothy passage at the end of the poem. Reading it as
"a textual device," Dorothy, Levinson says, "is felt to exist on the margins of the poet's enclosure and to have access both to the haven and
to the unimaginable relations outside it" (56). John Barrell was to critique the Dorothy lines even more sharply, regarding the poet's attitude as patronizing in the extreme. Dorothy's wild ecstasies will simply
mature into a sober pleasure, like fruit or cheese. It's all just a "matter
of growing up." The simple fact is that women in eighteenth-century

England from the Republic of Letters, lacking as they did "the ability to reduce the data of experience to abstract categories," had the capacity to "think in terms only of the particular and the concrete" (160–61).

McFarland also responds to the Levinson charge that *Michael,* "Peele Castle," and the *Immortality Ode* avoid or evade important socio-political themes. He would, he writes, treat poetry as poetry while Levinson and the kind of criticism she practices have "little real connection with the forms of culture. A poem is a concretion, the idea of a poem — obviously an abstraction" (56). In her preoccupation with "absence," he continues, Levinson misses the "intensity" of Wordsworth's poetry — the "vulnerability of the human heart" in "Ruth"; in *Home at Grasmere* its power of "generating maximum intensity without the related rush from absence to presence" (79).

If there is a New Historicism monument to this date, it surely must be Alan Liu's *Wordsworth: The Sense of History,* a continuing and relentless survey of Wordsworth's evasions of the realities of history by taking the route of sublimation. Beginning with the story of James Bruce's *Travels to Discover the Source of the Nile,* a book Wordsworth knew, he finds the parallels between Bruce's disappointment that he had not, as he thought, found the fountains of the Nile, and Wordsworth's similar disappointment that he had, without realizing it, crossed the Alps *via* the Simplon Pass (9). While history serves as ornament in poems such as Denham's *Cooper's Hill* and Pope's *Windsor Forest,* in Wordsworth "the arrow of signification from historical ornament toward the background is curiously blunted: historical markers point nowhere and decorate nature to no purpose" (11). The "I" dominates the circumstances in which it is present.

Liu's range of reference is extraordinary as he traces the poet's aesthetic evasions and his "crowning denial of history: autobiography" (31). A major example is, of course, *The Prelude* and the aforementioned Simplon Pass setting. Liu boldly and confidently contends that Napoleon lurks tellingly in the episode. "Recall," he says, "the diversionary force that Napoleon sent to demonstrate in the Simplon Pass. If my presentation has even the barest plausibility, it will appear that Wordsworthian nature is such an imaginary antagonist against which the self battles in feint, in a play to divert attention from the real battle between history and self" (31).

But Liu doesn't stop with *The Prelude.* He finds denial in the early tours — in *An Evening Walk* and *Descriptive Sketches* — as they "trace the development of a terrorized consciousness of time at once miming and denying the violence of the Revolution" (58). The poetry of the

Great Decade is characterized by a "rustic transcendence of history" to a place "for the mind to explore its empire" (214). And Liu doesn't neglect the later poetry, a subject of continuing interest to so many critics in this study. It is, he says, a poetry of "recollection," and suggests that where "the poetry of denial once formed itself in lyric," this later poetry "formed itself at a higher level of organization that gathered lyrics into sequences-within-sequences." The "I" gave in to the "we." And in the unkindest cut of all, "Like Eliot proclaiming himself classicist, royalist, and Anglo-Catholic, we may say, Wordsworth at last confessed himself conventional" (490).

James Chandler's New Historicist reading of the poet seems more moderate than Liu's and Levinson's although history still looms large in his appraisal. He begins with a recognition of the philosophy and the power of the poetry, and, like his colleagues, he locates it in a large part in Wordsworth's intellectual involvement in the philosophy of the French Revolution. Looking back at what we have been calling the High Romantic criticism of Abrams, Bloom, and Hartman, he finds them missing or misplotting the poet's position on "the crucial intellectual axes represented by Burke and Rousseau" (xxi). Although, he contends, the early Wordsworthian faith in nature was Rousseauistic, he is chiefly indebted to Burke who was the source of a "second nature" as appeal, of what DeQuincey regarded as the "literature of power."

For Chandler, Burke was an important force in the formation of an English radical ideology in the 1790s, and there is a notable turning toward Burke in Wordsworth. Even in the poetry of "humble and rustic life" one can find in the poet's conception of culture evidences of the Burkean philosophy. When the speaker of *The Old Cumberland Beggar* decides that "we all of us have one human heart," he is advocating "the same democracy of the emotions" (90), the sense that while "material equality is inevitable but inconsequential, moral equality . . . is crucial and, with virtue, attainable" (91).

Burke is for Chandler "the presiding genius" behind *The Prelude*, and the "Ode to Duty," far from simply a poem of decline that turns away from the freedom of *Tintern Abbey* and *The Prelude*, is a sharper articulation of the ideals of those major poems and a rededication of the poet to "a life of disciplined mental conduct" (249). And the more strongly societal concerns of *The Ruined Cottage* and the later poetry nevertheless govern "the most exclusively personal or psychological moments of his poetry" (265). These are moments when "the light of sense goes out" and the invisible world is revealed, Burke's and Wordsworth's "second nature" (56).

Chandler summarizes his argument nicely, saying that Wordsworth's "conception of the psychological life" is close to Burke's "high traditionalism . . . . That Wordsworth could not destroy his second nature, not even in the name of nature itself, is 'proved' in *The Prelude* by the eventual emergence of the 'spots of time'" (198).

David Simpson is still another important New Historicist critic of Wordsworth as seen in his *Wordsworth and the Figurings of the Real* and *Wordsworth's Historical Imagination: The Poetry of Displacement*. His position on the poet/author is clear from the beginning; in his or her work there is "no such thing as a private or individual imagination capable of complete and entire self-determination" (*Displacement* 1). External circumstances shape and sustain the imagination, and, if we study Wordsworth's poems well, we should be persuaded of this determination.

Simpson's book is dedicated to dramatizing how Wordsworth, in spite of his eagerness to address many contemporary political questions and issues which are "imaged in the language of work and property," nevertheless reveal "forms of displacement" (2–3). In explaining his sharply negative criticism of signs of urbanization, Simpson argues that "implicit or explicit reference to an ideal of agrarian civic virtue is the major organizational energy that runs through a great deal of Wordsworth's prose and poetry" (56). The plan to reform poetic language may have been regarded as a failure since the larger force of history prevailed.

Turning to the poetry Simpson again finds displacement in *The Prelude* and *Home at Grasmere* as Wordsworth offers "his most detailed representations of himself as, respectively, a mobile subject and a person in habitual contact with others in a dear perpetual place" (108). Poems such as "Gipsies," *Michael,* and "Simon Lee" reveal complicated interactions between the mind and reality outside. "As they address the objective features of the rural life, so they also dramatize the unstable position of the poet reporting upon them" (159).

Simpson finds in *The Excursion* the strongest manifestation of the didactic Wordsworth and also "his most searching and anxious inquiries into the relations between poetry, property and labor, and into the potential of the agrarian life to respond to or modify the challenge of urbanization" (186). In compromising, he found some satisfaction but no real answers.

Clifford Siskin's *The Historicity of Romantic Discourse* includes Wordsworth among several poets discussed. The poet of the Great Decade, Siskin argues, is, quite ironically, "the most blatant victim of that very myth of creativity *he* helped to articulate," a poet who developed from lyrical intensity and imaginative insight into the philosopher of the later years. Siskin offers as his contribution to Wordsworth criticism not a "history of genre" but a "generic history" that would explain how, in a remarkable shift, "man reconstituted himself as the modern psychologized subject" with a mind "capable of limitless growth that takes itself to be the primary object of its own inquiries" (11).

Taking issue with Abrams's essay on the "Greater Romantic Lyric" and citing *Tintern Abbey* as a major example, Siskin regards the poem as a "dead end" for the poet. And, he continues, what happens to the ode in *Tintern Abbey*, especially in the Dorothy passage, or in the drowned man episode in *The Prelude*, and, perhaps, to poetry in general through "extratextual activity," is not transcendence at all but "transformation." With a stronger methodology and careful textual study, a reader will see "these generic differences of the past" and note "the politics of the resulting work of Literature . . . a labor that naturally demands more labor, as the text that is the object of that labor, and as the subject that is the very product of the text it labors to produce" (124).

Tellingly, Siskin introduces one of our already discussed critics, James Heffernan, and cites his suggestion that the poet who produced the 1815 system of poetic categories was not "the Wordsworth we all know and love," but rather a poet who was pretty much finished by 1814. Heffernan, argues Siskin, cannot reconcile the youthful poet of *Tintern Abbey*, "a poem that proceeds through the positing of overlapping alternations," with the deviser of a system that "classifies a poet *either* generically *or* thematically *or* psychologically" (114).

We introduced the name of Alan Grob earlier as the author of a long essay directed against what he described as adversarial criticism generally and especially as it is directed against Wordsworth, and we return to that essay as we close this section. Grob's essay is what amounts to an important although a sharply negative critique of the whole New Historicist project as well as some of its manifestations in allied new theoretical movements. Returning to his strong sense that the project is a major player in a larger "hermeneutic of disparagement," he calls up Marjorie Levinson's suggestion that Feminism and New Historicism, originally disparate movements, had coalesced notably in their postures and approaches. And, he argues, what has developed in Romantic studies over the last twenty to thirty years is "an interpretive community adversarially self-defined whose quarrel, astonishingly enough for those of us who came before, is not *over* but *with* the subject of its criticism." It is, he continues, nothing less than a paradigm shift from "an older historical criticism . . . and a deconstructive postmodernism that New Historicism and feminism would still in essential respects claim as their theoretical forerunner" (188).

Returning to Levinson and her designated "destructive materialism" and recognition of Derrida and consequent preoccupation with the "absent or displaced," Grob addresses her already discussed essay on *Tintern Abbey*, noting her argument that the absence of the abbey in the poem "is made the primary pointer to meaning." For him the New Historicism "would go back to the past so that it might help take us to the future" (180), and it would offer us a Wordsworth as "the product of a certain historical causation, to be understood in terms of his class and gender as these were directed and determined by the socially constructing forces of his place and time" (191).

Turning to Alan Liu, Grob argues that his astonishing collection of historical materials to make his case for Wordsworthian evasion actually flattens and oversimplifies and offers "a rigid social and economic determinism that overrides all other explanatory possibilities" (191). The 1790s with intellectual options ranging from republican to monarchist, from Tom Paine to Edmund Burke for young idealistic intellectuals simply cannot be neatly summed up nor can a poet like Wordsworth be made to embody a particular option.

The adversarial position as it relates to gender in engaging *Tintern Abbey* and the Wordsworth-Dorothy connection is also considered by Grob. Levinson had relatively little to say about this issue, but an essay by John Barrell, according to Grob, finds male domination carried to the point of insult in the oft-cited words of Wordsworth to Dorothy at the end of the poem. Grob quotes Barrell's major point that in eighteenth-century Britain "women were excluded from what was called the 'republic of letters,'" a bastion reserved for those capable of abstraction from which women like Dorothy who could think only in terms of the particular and concrete "were excluded" (194). David Simpson is also cited in connection with Barrell's thesis, finding it necessary for a full understanding of a relationship between gender and class at the time Wordsworth was writing *Tintern Abbey* with its "poetic construction of a preliterate female" and its "marginalization of the exemplary female, who may be a worshipful or proleptic companion but who can never be a reader" (195).

Judith Page is also summoned to Grob's witness stand where, although less strident, she too finds a masculine bias in Wordsworth's representation of Dorothy, seeing "in 'her wild eyes' *himself*" and "imposing a 'masculine narrative' where a feminine narrative is required."

Grob's response is that Page's feminist reading simply ignores the middle-class plot of the time in which the unmarried sister or daughter lived in the household of a father or brother and contributed to the economy of the household and the raising of the children.

Grob's essay, although revealing his own literary historical and formalistic biases, nevertheless succeeds in framing nicely the contemporary theoretical debate about literary theory, especially in the context of British Romantic poetry and of Wordsworth as one of its major representatives.

Interest in Wordsworth continues unabated as a new century begins, and consequently there must be a sense of incompleteness about a study like this one. Yet we close with two important recent studies, one of them a massive revisionary work, the other a superior, more limited and measured study of one aspect of the poet's career, both by distinguished Romantic/Wordsworthian scholars. In a way they reveal a good many of the critical theoretical approaches we have been following throughout this survey of Wordsworth's critics.

If there is a genuine *tour de force* in Wordsworth revisionist criticism, it must be Kenneth Johnston's already mentioned massive semi-biographical study of the poet and his work through the *1807 Poems*. Johnston, a highly regarded Wordsworthian known especially for his work on *The Recluse*, sets out to give us a "true story" of the life, one not rooted in sentimentality or in a Romantic ideology, but in an amazing, some might say sensational, process of historicizing that has taken him to virtually every place the poet ever visited, to every record of comings and goings, to every set of social and political circumstances in which the poet could possible have found himself. The result, as Hermione Lee in a *New York Times Book Review* puts it, is that "the poet may have lived a far more adventurous life than we think" (14). Johnston has been to the Simplon Pass in the Alps to determine how Wordsworth might have lost his way on August 17, 1790, has crossed military territory on Salisbury Plain to check the poetic account, and has followed the poet's exact route to Tintern Abbey to understand more fully the geography of the area. He has also countered easy generalizations about a lonely, reclusive Laker with evidence of a Wordsworth enmeshed in hard realities — his family's battle with Sir James Lowther, the Earl of Lonsdale, for some sort of settlement for his father's many services rendered; his life among peddlers, miners, loggers, discharged Army veterans; his unhappiness with the Cambridge "getting on in the world" educational philosophy; his love affair with Annette Vallon and the child he fathered with her; his movement toward and then away from 1790s political radicalism. Johnston's total image, rooted in the most thoroughgoing research, is of a vibrant, politically engaged young man during these years.

The most notable revelation concerns what Johnston regards as Wordsworth's post-Revolutionary conservatism, a period when he might well have functioned as a spy for the Foreign Office while he was in Germany. He would also have us revise glib accounts of Wordsworth's sexual history, especially the idea that he remained celibate after Annette and before he married Mary Hutchinson. After careful research into the widespread prevalence of prostitution around Cambridge during Wordsworth's college years, he wonders how any healthy, passionate young man could have ignored the many occasions for encounters. He also attends to the poet's 1793 trip to France in search of Annette, and calls up the F. W. Bateson speculation about a sexual relationship with Dorothy.

Johnston is ready to account for both successes and failures, and, even when his scholarly adventures seem to some reviewers to reach unjustified conclusions, one cannot help being impressed by his impeccable research, his deep knowledge of the poetry, and the complete command of the materials he has amassed over many years.

Also recently published is a study of the early poetry, David Bromwich's *Disowned by Memory: Wordsworth's Poetry of the 1790s*. Less informed by the historicizing impulse of so much contemporary Romantic criticism and theorizing but not without a rich awareness of the contexts of the poetry, Bromwich sees Wordsworth after the Revolution not locked into a "single prescriptive doctrine" except perhaps "a sense of radical humanity," and turning to poetry as a vocation in order to remind himself that he "was still a human being" (1). *The Old Cumberland Beggar* is an example of "what it means to be alienated from one's purposes, or dispossessed of one's full human faculties." And *The Borderers* reflects the poet's "hopes and fears reacting upon the impersonal principles of the French Revolution" (44).

Bromwich's treatment of *Tintern Abbey* appears less tied to a narrow historicist paradigm, and he cites Levinson's political reading that the poet evaded what he knew about the setting, particularly "the causes of the vagrancy then common in the region" (75). He agrees with some aspects of this claim, but he cannot accept the "moralism" of this interpretation (91). He regards the poem as "about the peace and rest that one can know only by a sublimation of remembered terror" (73) and the poet as nevertheless concerned about the displacement of laborers in a utilitarian value system.

Wordsworth, he contends, "was always interested in people who continue to be themselves, who insist on themselves, weirdly or helplessly, whatever the cost to utility or convention" (172). Even when ballads like *The Idiot Boy* and *The Thorn* are targets for satire, Bromwitch nevertheless likes the risk-taking, its sincerity and involvement, "a baffling alienation of pathos and geniality" (94). *The Ruined Cottage* and *Michael* invent a "new sympathy — a new relation among the phenomena of pleasure" (184). Wordsworth's great appeal is "from the power of reflection to the dignity of mere existence" (178).

Works Consulted

Adams, Hazard, and Leroy Searle, editors. *Critical Theory Since 1965*. Tallahassee: Florida State UP, 1986.

Barrell, John. "The Uses of Dorothy: 'The Language of the Sense' in *Tintern Abbey*." *Poetry, Language, and Politics*. London: St. Martin's Press, 1988. 137–167.

Bromwitch, David. *Disowned by Memory: Wordsworth's Poetry of the 1790s*. Chicago and London: U of Chicago P, 1998.

Chandler, James. *Wordsworth's Second Nature: A Study of the Poetry and Politics*. Chicago: U of Chicago P, 1984.

Derrida, Jacques. "Structure, Sign and Play in the Discourse of the Human Sciences." In *Writing and Difference*. Tr. with Introduction and Additional Notes by Alan Bass. Chicago: U of Chicago P, 1978.

Fry, Paul. "The Diligence of Desire: Critics On and Around Westminster Bridge." *The Wordsworth Circle*. 23.3 (Summer 1992): 162–64.

Gilbert, Sandra, and Susan Gubar. *The Madwoman in the Attic: The Woman Writer and the Nineteenth Century Literary Imagination*. New Haven: Yale UP, 1979.

Grob, Alan. "William and Dorothy: A Case Study in the Hermeneutics of Disparagement." *Journal of English Literary History*. 65(1998): 187–221.

Johnston, Kenneth R. *The Hidden Wordsworth: Poet, Lover, Rebel, Spy*. New York, London: Norton, 1998.

Lee, Hermione. Review of Kenneth Johnston, *The Hidden Wordsworth: Poet, Lover, Rebel, Spy*. New York: Norton, 1998. *New York Times Book Review*. 2 (May 1999): 14–15.

Levinson, Marjorie. *Wordsworth's Great Period Poems*. Cambridge: Cambridge UP, 1986.

————. "The New Historicism: Back to the Future." In *Rethinking Historicism: Critical Reading in Romantic History*. Marjorie Levinson, editor. Oxford: Basil Blackwell, 1989. 18–63.

Liu, Alan. *Wordsworth: The Sense of History*. Stanford: Stanford UP, 1989.

McFarland, Thomas. *Romanticism and the Forms of Ruin: Wordsworth,*

————. *Coleridge and Modalities of Fragmentation*. Princeton: Princeton UP, 1981.

————. *William Wordsworth: Intensity and Achievement*. Oxford: Clarendon Press, 1992.

McGann, Jerome. *The Romantic Ideology: A Critical Investigation*. Chicago and London: U of Chicago P, 1983.

Mellor, Anne. *Romanticism and Feminism*. Bloomington and Indianapolis: Indiana UP, 1988.

————. *Romanticism and Gender*. New York and London: Routledge, 1993.

Miller, J. Hillis. *The Linguistic Moment: From Wordsworth to Stevens*. Princeton: Princeton UP, 1985.

Page, Judith. *Wordsworth and the Cultivation of Women*. Berkeley and Los Angeles: U of California P, 1994.

Showalter, Elaine, editor. *The New Feminist Criticism: Essays on Women, Literature, and Theory*. New York: Pantheon, 1985.

Simpson, David. *Wordsworth and the Figurings of the Real*. Atlantic Highlands, NJ: Humanities Press, 1982.

————. *Wordsworth's Historical Imagination: The Poetry of Displacement*. New York: Methuen, 1987.

Siskin, Clifford. *The Historicity of Romantic Discourse*. New York: Oxford UP, 1988.

5: An Abundance of Riches: Varieties of Later Twentieth-Century Criticism

WE TURN IN THE LAST SECTION OF OUR STUDY to a range of critical approaches to Wordsworth's poetry. This is not to lessen the impact of theory — whether historicist, feminist, or other — but rather to point up the persistence of a more traditional approach as well as the development of new discourses.

Politics

The last twenty years, for example, have seen a continuing emphasis on politics as a backdrop for studying the poetry. Michael Friedman's *The Making of a Tory Humanist: William Wordsworth and the Idea of Community* is a remarkably comprehensive study of the poet's politics, in the tradition of Carl Woodring's work on politics and Romantic poetry, yet exploring in more depth Woodring's contention that none of the philosophical defenses of liberalism available to the English poets from 1789–1832 "could be harmonized with the convictions that motivated their poetic practice" (103). Wordsworth's genius, Friedman argues at the outset, began to flourish at a time of social and economic turbulence, "when patriarchal political economy was disintegrating and England was being propelled into developed industrial capitalism." With a melodramatic ring, he continues, "England was being destroyed even as he wrote his major works" (1).

The Wordsworth of the Golden Decade lacked a firm sense of self and consequently was uncertain of how that self might connect with the great world beyond. Friedman proposes to trace the evolution of an "ardent revolutionary" as the forces and energies of the French Revolution were set in motion. Combining psychological, economic, and political tools in his analysis, he describes the poet's "fears of maternal loss and paternal retribution," and his fear of a threatening poverty as bringing about a "contracted self" (25).

Friedman's strong contention is that such a Wordsworth fell in love with "the internationalist enthusiasm of the Girondins," with the dream of "a universal community of brotherhood and liberty, a universal world of natural affection" (86). He, of course, turned sharply against the violence and power politics of the Revolution, but, according to Friedman, never lost his passion for community, finding a form of it in "the social community of the dalesmen in the Lake counties of England" (119), even though "corrosive forces of historical change" would take their toll (205). Such forces would lead to the sharp decline in Wordsworth's poetic power after 1807. Friedman concludes by returning to his title. Although never "a mean-spirited Tory who had contempt for the poor," Wordsworth "was certainly by 1808 and . . . had been since 1800, a Tory humanist" (234).

James A. Heffernan's *Representing the French Revolution: Literature, Historiography, and Art* is a notable collection of essays that attends in an essay of his own to the presence of the Revolution in *The Prelude*. While he argues for Burke's influence on the way Wordsworth saw the events in France, it cannot explain the poet's evocation of "the myth of paradise to describe the way the world appeared to him and his fellow enthusiasts at the outbreak" (50). Wordsworth saw the revolution as violent, as an unleashing of power that could effect radical change and bring a new freedom and justice. And he distinguishes the brutality and violence from the power and energy that preceded it. In an engaging comment Heffernan contends that "by imbedding the history of the French Revolution within a history of his own life, he sought to show why the power released by the Revolution had to pass from the world of politics . . . to the world of poetry, where he could demonstrate his spiritually redemptive force" (58).

Gordon K. Thomas, on the other hand, finds Thomas Paine a force to reckon with in any full understanding of Wordsworthian politics and *The Prelude*. Although never mentioned by name, he says, Paine was a kind of role model for Wordsworth of defiance and "undaunted confidence" (4) and "a representative of all the nameless victims of Terror and repression" (9). Thomas sees Wordsworth recognizing a glorious opportunity gone wrong and expressing "his own personal frustration at the prospect of failure and irredeemable loss" (4).

John Rieder studies Wordsworth's emphasis on poetry's unique power to build community and to effect political change. That power, he writes, "must be grounded in, and mediated in pleasure." Poetry "constructs a fantasy of community and draws its readers into it"; in its own special way it ministers to "widespread anxieties about social cohesion in late-eighteenth-century British writing." As he studies the Salisbury Plain poems, *The Borderers*, and *The Ruined Cottage*, he moves away from the overtly political. It is the pleasure of the literary experience rather than his own idealized rural communities that become important. Rieder's final chapter focuses on the poet's turn inward, especially in *Tintern Abbey*. "Wordsworth's counter-revolutionary turn is to assert that poetry itself can lodge a quasi-familial intimacy in the interstices of a class-driven commercial society" (228).

John Williams follows a middle ground in discussing Wordsworth's politics. Moving from *An Evening Walk* and *Descriptive Sketches* to the 1805 *Prelude*, he aims to study the extent to which the political situation in late eighteenth-century England exerted an influence on Wordsworth's poetry. Williams is eager to avoid a general politicizing of the poetry and to speculate on "the extent to which his political views were the product of a tradition of British political dissidence that pre-dates the impact of French revolutionary political philosophy and action on the British political scene" (vii).

Williams begins by rehearsing eighteenth-century pastoral motifs and how they were adapted from classical models in the poetry of the age "to reflect and reinforce a variety of ideological assumptions that underpinned political evolution in England in the course of the century" (1). *An Evening Walk* follows a traditional pastoral mode that was to evolve as Wordsworth's career developed. *Descriptive Sketches* challenges the poetical conventions, however, but "with the instinct of one who sought the restoration of an ideal commonwealth of virtue, rather than to usher in a radically conceived new order" (35). The *Sketches* and the poet's celebrated "Letter to the Bishop of Llandoff" recognize the connection between violence and political change, Williams contends, but he also sees an evolution in Wordsworth's thinking almost from the beginning. In the Salisbury Plain poetry the poet addresses "issues that had become real to him as a consequence of the French Revolution through setting the action of the poem in the period of the American War of Independence" (71). He wanted to express his sense of political disillusionment without following the extremist gospel.

As his study continues, the focus is on the Dorset and Somerset poetry — the *Lyrical Ballads* in particular — in which Wordsworth develops "new strategies to engage with fundamentally the same issues — public and private — which had dominated his thoughts since his second visit to France in 1792" (84). And the politics of the two-part *Prelude* of the late 1790s "remains best understood when placed alongside the radical Whig, Commonwealthman traditions of eighteenth-century political philosophy" (121). Williams continues to seek the middle ground as he sees the Wordsworth of the late 1790s writing a poem of personal crisis, "a crisis to which the Revolution had given dramatic political substance" (139). To the end Williams recognizes the influence of the French Revolution while insisting on the radical political tradition that is so much a part of eighteenth-century England. Wordsworth, he argues, is better understood when both forces are understood.

The Golden Decade and Wordsworth's Decline

The matter of Wordsworth's Golden Decade and the related problem of his decline continues to be a subject for a fair amount of critical attention and speculation. John Jones in *The Egotistical Sublime: A History of Wordsworth's Imagination* juxtaposes Wordsworth and Coleridge for his own purposes. Both poets, he argues, "continue to illuminate each other, by way of contrast, throughout their lives" (vii). But Wordsworth was "no philosopher" (viii). Indeed it is difficult to see how he can be called Romantic, "for he begins with a vision of Sympathy that belongs, in so far as genius can belong anywhere, to the eighteenth century, and he ends with the Religion of gratitude, tractarian and Catholic in its associations" (vii).

Wordsworth's best poetry, Jones argues, "deals with lonely places and solitary people," citing Coleridge's emphasis on the "self-centeredness" of his masculine mind and Hazlitt's and Keats's focus on his egotism (29–31). A member of the Golden Decade school, he sees Wordsworth in this period "involved in a huge, sustained argument from solitude to relationship," a relationship between the self and nature (33–34). In the Lucy poems one finds "a preoccupation with perfect solitude discovered in perfect relationship with environment" (73). But this poetry of relationship gives way to one of indecision, "of glances behind and before — the poetry, preeminently of *The Excursion* and *The White Doe*, long works of middle age" (53). And while the 1798–1799 *Prelude* "is in the high tradition of solitude and relationship," the later 1804–1805 poem is different. A "vital concentration has been lost" in a "dispersal of effort" (125–26).

Jones sees still a final phase of decline in Wordsworth's poetry, a phase he calls that of the "baptized imagination," that leaves the real world to roam in transcendental realms. What happened in the later versions of *The Prelude* is that "Wordsworth practised a kind of theological surgery on the body of his poem, grafting on to it pious digressions, and cutting away parts so distempered as to offend sound doctrine" (157).

Thomas Rountree, still another proponent of a Golden Decade William Wordsworth, singles out a dominant theme of "benevolent necessity" that appears in full flower in the years following 1797. He defines the theme as "an optimistic concept of the world as directed inevitably toward perfectibility by a cosmic force that pays special attention to the educative effect of nature in the mental and moral progress of man" (13). Rooted in his reading in Godwin and Hartley and his interest in Newtonian science, the poet's optimism and necessitarianism develop from the starkness of early negativism to later more Christian shadings. In the best poetry of the Great Decade — the "present" that pervades *Tintern Abbey* or the image of Mount Snowdon in *The Prelude* — "benevolent necessity is shown working primarily through nature" (92).

One related continuing theme in Wordsworth criticism is that of a Wordsworthian period of decline or anti-climax. And even though it might seem less a matter of concern in periods of critical sophistication and complexity, there is a fair amount of evidence to the contrary. A. S. Byatt, perhaps better known for her academic novel *Possession*, addresses it straightforwardly in *Wordsworth and Coleridge in Their Time*. Singling out the *Ecclesiastical Sonnets*, many of the monastery poems in *Memorials of a Tour in Italy, 1837*, and *The White Doe of Rylstone* as examples of the later poetry, she writes, "one is struck by a kind of ferocious monastic piety" that subverts them. Instead of the familiar Wordsworthian image of "the solitary man alone with Nature," we have "the voluntary confined ascetic in the chosen cell." The great irony is that "the self Wordsworth is contemplating and praising is increasingly not the creative mind but the created reputation, not energy but responsibility and moral truth" (47).

And Richard McGhee in a frequently cited article finds nearly all critics agreeing that "there was a falling off in his achievement around 1814" (641). "The difference," he continues, "is one of substance rather than exclusively one of degree." The same Wordsworth whose "earlier poetry embodied an existential discovery of meaning and beauty in the natural creation" sought in the later work to escape "the bounds of natural existence and penetrate to a perception of the essential values which transcend and give ultimate meaning to earthly beauty" (641). The poet's new concerns developed out a paradigm shift from the "things of this world" to the "things of the next world as they are communicated through the experience of apocalypse, of prophetic revelation, of uncovering the appearances of things in order to view the infinite and eternal realities beneath" (644).

Using the *Vernal Ode* as a test case and the image of the appearance on a bright April day of "The form and rich habiliments of One/Whose countenance bore resemblance to the sun,/When it reveals, in evening majesty,/Features half lost amid their own pure light" as specific example, McGhee sees "no attempt here to identify the Angel with the sun itself as there might have been in a poem of Wordsworth's earlier career." He concludes with the observation that the simile in a way typifies something about a Wordsworth in "declining age" as it "suggests that nature shares with infinity certain characteristics which can be revealed to mortal man only at times of twilight" (647–648).

D. D. Devlin is one of several critics who have called attention to the importance of Wordsworth's "Essays upon Epitaphs" in understanding and coming to terms with his poetry and poetic theory. In *Wordsworth and the Poetry of Epitaphs*, Devlin describes the epitaph as bringing together "the several publics which a poet might have or wish to have" (110), and in the process making "a heroic attempt at inclusiveness . . . at that 'reconciliation of opposites' which was in so many ways his greatest achievement" (6).

Audience is a key consideration for the poet, and he finds himself at a "meeting-point of Renaissance and Romantic views of poetry and their different implications for the kind of audience the poet will have or will wish to have" (5). This search for an audience pervades prefaces, critical essays, and letters as he struggles for a genuine relationship with readers. The "Essays upon Epitaphs," writes Devlin, reveals Wordsworth's doubts about the adequacy of language, especially language as ornament or decoration. Elsewhere in the "Essays," he continues, "Wordsworth insists that words are not a clothing of thought but an incarnation of it" (77), and it's in his special poetic attention to the thing, to the reality that leads to a point where that thing or reality "becomes the word itself that the morality (sincerity) and poetry of the poem as epitaph are to be found" (83).

In the "Essays," Devlin argues, Wordsworth eschews Johnsonian notions of the grandeur of generality and of not numbering the streaks of the tulip. The epitaph restricts; "it speaks of a particular person who is now dead and lamented, and it must therefore achieve a reconciliation of general truth with a particular case" (99).

In a concluding chapter on "The Poem as Epitaph," Devlin advances his key point that it is in Wordsworth's epitaphs that "through the transforming, modifying power of imagination or love, we can see Wordsworth most clearly and typically poised between a realist reading of the world and a purely subjective one" (112). Epitaphs are the truest poetry, and for a time, perhaps a Golden Decade and a bit longer, they flourished. *The White Doe of Rylstone* is perhaps the last success, for the poetry following "was no longer a reconcilement of opposites but a denial of opposites" (124).

Peter J. Manning in a useful collection of critical essays, *Reading Romantics: Texts and Contexts*, enters the discussion of the poet's later poetry. His own essay, "Wordsworth at St. Bees: Scandals, Sisterhood, and Wordsworth's Later Poetry," begins by acknowledging a general lack of concern with the subject and a strong image of the post-Golden Decade poet in decline, conservative in his politics and in his art. Yet he will not join the company of naysayers who enjoy only the strongly personal, lyrical work of the early years. Once understood "within their historical situation," he contends, "their contexts widen and their procedures gain meaning," and he proceeds with an analysis of Wordsworth's "St. Bees" poem. The poem, he continues, "by revealing the unexpected conjunction of Anglican idealism and Tory scandal" reveals the power and range of implication in the later work (273).

Manning also points to the popular success of *Yarrow Revisited and Other Poems* as another example of the special quality of an artist's late career work and another reason to argue "that a poet's final period should not be held in thrall to his earlier one, just because the earlier is more appealing." And returning to the theme of the "St. Bees" poem, he concludes that "where once he had sought in his personal past for renewal, now he returned to an earlier period of history" (294–295).

Ecology and the Poetry of Nature

While the poet's close, even intimate connection with the forces of nature has been a major concern of critics of the Romantics, and of Wordsworth in particular, from the beginning, it is only in recent years that a more rigorous body of ecological/nature writing discourse has developed. Some of this discourse has been seen as a response to New Historicist and other post-structuralist readings, but the bulk of it represents a genuine attempt to attend to a distinctively Romantic, indeed Wordsworthian, poetic response to nature. James McKusick in a short essay in *The Wordsworth Circle* maintains that "much of Romantic writing emerges from a desperate sense of alienation from the natural world and expresses an anxious endeavor to establish a vital, sustainable relationship between mankind and the fragile planet on which he dwells" (123).

As early as 1977 Laurence Goldstein felt that "Wordsworth's poetry made something happen; it awakened the moral conscience of posterity to the value of places which bear a habitual resemblance to Eden, our profound dream of harmony and joy." And this harmony and joy owes much to the Wordsworthian magic places. "Magical presences haunt the sites of Hawkshead, or Esthwaite Water, or the daffodils of Gowbarrow Park because Wordsworth felt and articulated their character" (103). Karl Kroeber, a continuingly perceptive and versatile critic of Wordsworth and the Romantics over the years, has consistently attended to poetry/landscape, poet/painter connections in his work. Early on in an influential essay on the poet's *Home at Grasmere* and its natural settings, he uses the phrase "ecological holiness" to describe their special qualities.

Alan Bewell in *Wordsworth and the Enlightenment: Nature, Man, and Society in the Experimental Poetry* moves from sections on "The Origin of Language," "The Origin of Poetry, Myth and Religion," and "Death" to an intriguing section on "The History of the Earth" with a specific section on "A Power Like One of Nature's: The Geological History of Revolution." Needless to say, as he attempts to come to terms with Wordsworth's master plan for *The Recluse*, the *Lyrical Ballads* and *The Excursion*, his approach is mainly philosophical and specifically anthropological in his study of the poet's response to Enlightenment attitudes toward nature and society. But there are fertile suggestions in the latter part of the book that have the ring of ecological rhetoric. As Wordsworth throughout his life and career tried "to explain how he had passed from a volcanic revolutionary to a revolutionary poet," he "continually drew on geology and environmental theory" (189). Bewell also notes that the lack of such a discourse actually "has led to a fundamental misreading of Wordsworth's poetry, which treats nature as if it were a stable, a historical phenomenon, opposed to mine." The poet's nature "is not simply an object or thought. . . . It is as much a historical phenomenon as the mind" (239).

Karl Kroeber, although still puzzled by the mysteries of Wordsworth's poetry, is unhappy with the anti-aesthetic approach of New Historicist criticism, an approach that "precludes recovering from within Romantic poems imaginative revelations that might revitalize the practice of criticism itself." Among those revelations are the "palpably unseen and unheard-presences, including finally self-presences"

(4). Kroeber agrees with the argument of Toby Bemis in *Romanticism on the Road* that *The Prelude* reveals its "essential originality by attempting to identify his life story with the masterplot of his generation." His epic poem moves away from earlier representations of homelessness and now savors a kind of "a-social subjectivity" (5), one that is "environmentally participative." The Wordsworthian vagrancy is one of mind evoking not so much "presences" but "absences" because "they offer only potentialities of community beyond any merely human community, a *conceivable* fittingness of humankind to the livingness of the natural earth" (6).

Wordsworth, continues Kroeber, resisted traditional social structures and sought a home in nature although, like us, he wondered about such a home in the face of technological advances. In the *Immortality Ode*, however, there is a falling away from any further probing of ecological concerns. He knew geology reasonably well, but instead of a help, this proved an excuse for his "literary preference for shepherds over farmers, ignoring practices of working land, sustaining it, keeping it healthy so that we can be healthy" (7). The consolation of the *Ode* is hardly one to delight an environmentalist as he envisions an imperial palace to replace the freshness of mother earth, for Kroeber the place where all of us can be "self-conscious participants in the everchanging connectedness of a material environment that is, finally, the nurturing source of all the imagined communities of humankind" (9).

It is Jonathan Bate, however, who has written something approaching a definitive treatment of a Romantic/Wordsworthian ecology in *Romantic Ecology: Wordsworth and the Environmental Tradition*, a book he describes as "a preliminary sketch toward a literary ecocriticism" (10), a book "dedicated to the proposition that the way in which Wordsworth sought to enable his readers better to enjoy or endure life was by teaching them to look at and dwell in the natural world" (4). Eschewing the historicizers and politicizers of the poetry, he trusts "the intuition that locates Wordsworth firmly in nature and I reject the counter-intuitive readings" (10), and he believes that poetry is not only a "means of verbal expression, it is also a means of emotional communication between man and the natural world" (17). Hence, he continues, "we must abandon the model of Wordsworth the young radical with his 'outraged' social and political instincts. An ideology rooted in a harmonious relationship with nature goes beyond . . . the political model we have become used to thinking with" (19–20).

Grasmere is Wordsworth's "visionary republic" (21) in *The Prelude*, a "working paradise" (22) where his shepherds are "free," "work for themselves," and "represent the spirit of unalienated labor." Using Burke's categories in his treatise on the sublime and the beautiful, Bate distinguishes the traditional pastoral as beautiful from the Wordsworthian as sublime. Wordsworth's pastoral is not simply another manifestation of a literary tradition, but a poetry about life as lived by real people (25–28). *The Ruined Cottage,* he contends, "proposes that the survival of humanity comes with nature's mastery over the edifices of civilization" (34).

In following chapters Bate addresses "The Ecology of Nature," "The Moral of Landscape," and, most interestingly, "The Naming of Places." He is careful in describing ecology as "a holistic science concerned in the largest sense with the relationship between living things and their environment" (36), adding that Romantic ecology is "an attempt to enable mankind the better to live in the material world by entering into harmony with the environment" (40). And, as far as Wordsworth is concerned, we must move beyond *Tintern Abbey* and *The Prelude* and find his ecological philosophy most fully articulated in his *Guide to the Lakes.*

As the poet of nature, Wordsworth offers landscapes that "reflect his own spiritual state" (76). Drawing parallels between Wordsworth and John Ruskin, Bate finds both looking through the phenomena of nature. Both at "certain moments of intense feeling" reveal the "optical" becoming the "visionary" (89). "The point of Wordsworth's project was to teach the intellect of man to wed itself to 'the green earth' which is its 'living home,' and the point of Ruskin's was to expose the limitations of nineteenth-century political economy by moving from the material to the spiritual" (83).

In his concluding chapter Bate would return Wordsworth's "Poems on the Naming of Places" to their rightful positions of importance in his repertoire, exemplifying as they do "an ecological tradition of English place-poetry" (90–91). At the same time he singles out the poet's classic "Essays upon Epitaphs" as exploring "the nature of the human's after-life" and establishing how vitally the poet connects poetry and place (86).

Bate's book, a creature of the 1990s, carries out in notable ways his early statement of purpose, which is to see Wordsworth as "going before us in some of the steps we are now taking in our thinking about the environment" (5).

Aesthetics

John H. Talbot's *The Nature of Aesthetic Experience in Wordsworth* offers a sweepingly general treatment of the poet's theorizing on the topic. Beginning with the premise that the poetry embodies that theorizing, he proceeds to define the term "aesthetic experience," to trace its eighteenth-century backgrounds, and to show it at work in selected poems. He describes aesthetic experience as "heightened awareness," a state in which "our consciousness is . . . expanded, and our sensitivity to the aesthetic features of the object" is "made more acute than in ordinary perception" (3).

With A. C. Bradley, René Wellek, and E. D. Hirsch among his scholarly guides on the topic, Talbot proceeds in several chapters to examine the extraordinary vitality of eighteenth-century theory — in phenomena like empirical psychology, association of ideas, disinterestedness, sympathy, and in key figures such as Joseph Addison, Francis Hutcheson, Henry Home, Lord Kames, and Archibald Alison. Wordsworth's debt to his predecessors is considerable, he contends, and examines *Tintern Abbey,* the *Immortality Ode* and *The Prelude* as well as the critical prose as evidence.

Talbot's primary evidence for the impact of associationism on the poet is the 1800 "Preface" to *Lyrical Ballads.* The remarkable achievement in Wordsworth is his movement beyond the mechanistic dimensions of association to advance the idea of "the creative aspect of the associative imagination in shaping feeling to thought" (181). "Through sympathetic association," he continues, "poet, and through poet, his audience, also gains access to a more complete, more intimate aesthetic experience of the object of poetic contemplation" (192).

Imagination and feeling are underlined as key dimensions of experience. Distinguished from fancy, Wordsworth's poetic imagination in *The Prelude* "is more akin to Coleridge's conception" (205). And "it is feeling which draws us to the 'source of things,' which gives meaning and life to our perceptions of the beauty which is everywhere around us" (233). Talbot, citing W. J. B. Owen, finds the notion of power another strong dimension of the poet's concept of aesthetic experience. And it is the notion of power that becomes "both the cause and effect, and above all, the highest manifestation, of poetic genius" (248–49).

Talbot closes his study with a section on his high regard for *Tintern Abbey* with its "consolidation of feeling and the poetic imagination in their highest manifestations: as component parts of an experience which aesthetically transcends human awareness" (264). It is this notion that remains for Wordsworth "the triumph of the human heart and the spirit of man" (270).

Theresa Kelley sees a revolutionary quality in Wordsworth's aesthetics. Taking issue with modern theorists who emphasize "the transcendent vision of the sublime speaker or hero," she cites the poet's Arab Don Quixote as revealing the dark side of transcendence, someone "who wants to be alone" and manifests "a rebellious disregard for the rest of society" (1). Kelley underlines Wordsworth's suspicion of sublime transcendence as perhaps a form of egotism.

This suspicion prompted the development of a dual aesthetics ultimately rooted in Edmund Burke's distinction between the sublime and the beautiful. Wordsworth, argues Kelley, saw not so much opposition as "aesthetic conflict" with beauty and sublimity as steps in a process. The beautiful offers "a sense of known limits in art as well as society" and connects with "the poetic project . . . announced in the 1800 *Lyrical Ballads*— to create a poetic speech adequate for a community of speakers and listeners." The sublime, on the other hand, is "revolutionary" and can be felt in the post-1800 poems as "a resonant image of poetic figures that speak for, or of, what resists representation (political as well as linguistic)" (3). In the 1805 *Prelude*, says Kelley, "a revisionary aesthetics recuperates what the earlier 'Lines Composed a few miles above Tintern Abbey, July 13, 1798' barely acknowledges" (61–62).

W. J. B. Owen, co-editor with Jane Worthington Smyser of the definitive edition of Wordsworth's prose, has also written *Wordsworth as Critic* in which he attempts to show the growth of the poet's thinking about his own theory of art. His study utilizes the several prefaces and essay associated with the *Lyrical Ballads* as well as the important "Essays upon Epitaphs" and key ideas on the mind of the poet in *The Prelude* and the letters. "Wordsworth's new ideas," he claims, "are commonplaces of certain eighteenth and nineteenth-century poetics which are based, in particular, on primitivistic theories of language and literature" (65).

Important is Owen's tracing of a theory of meter and especially his treatment of the Wordsworthian expressivism rooted in his notion of poetry as the "spontaneous overflow of powerful feeling." Here he notably distinguishes theory and practice, the theory "being widely but not generally applicable." Some poems, for example, "are written under the stimulus of immediate feeling and draw on no particular recollected emotion." Others, his own included, need the stimulus of an emotion immediately felt before composition can begin. Whatever general force the theory may lack, it remains "a valuable record of a psychological process" (50).

Owen offers a full view of the 1802 additions on the poet in the *Preface*. And he praises the *Essays upon Epitaphs* for its firm reiteration of certain poetic principles "which can be extracted from the tangled arguments of the *Preface*" — on poetic language, on the discipline of art, on the essential humanity of the poet (115).

Owen is also interested in a Burke-Wordsworth connection in the realm of landscape aesthetics in his essay "Wordsworth's Aesthetics of Landscape." Examining the prose documents, he finds Wordsworth essentially talking about Burke's sublime and beautiful. But he also finds a pre-1790 aesthetic of landscape, especially in *The Vale of Esthwaite*. It's more Gothic, drawing on "episodes of *terror*, not of the sublime which is an aesthetic based on the concept of *terror removed*" (70–79). He concludes that around 1790 — a point between *The Vale* and the publication of *An Evening Walk* and *Descriptive Sketches* — Wordsworth "learned about the sublime and adopted it as a way of looking at the environment, and its language as a way of talking about the effect of the environment on the mind of the observer." So greatly impressed was the poet by the majestic power of the Alps that he turned from "the crude Gothic aesthetics of terror . . . to the Burkean sublime" (80–82).

James Averill's *Wordsworth and the Poetry of Human Suffering* represents an important critical attempt to deal with the Wordsworthian spectator and with his or her response to suffering. This spectator — clearly the "authorial self of the narrative poems of Wordsworth's early career — is certainly a throwback to the self-conscious figures of the late eighteenth-century Poetry of Sensibility" (9). Wordsworth, however, Averill contends, adds a deeper dimension with his "intermediary presence between reader and story" and his concern with "the interplay of mind and suffering" (9). In a way the earliest verse suggests the first signs of the dramatic monologue, the poetry of experience so aptly defined and described earlier in this study by M. H. Abrams and Robert Langbaum. In moving from the schoolboy exercises to *The Vale of Esthwaite* and *An Evening Walk*, sympathy in the observer is not merely pity, but "the feelings of the 'accordant heart' beating in harmony with nature" (48). Going to the "Preface" to *Lyrical Ballads*, and specifically to the section on the character of the poet, Averill focuses on the "psychological" depth, the "interest in tragic response," and the "self-conscious art" that are the marks of not just another sentimental poet but of "an original Genius of a high order" (54).

Robert Griffin in *Wordsworth's Pope: A Study in Literary Historiography* offers a remarkably different discussion of the Romantic ideology, how it came to be constructed, and how it continues to shape our thinking today. The source, he argues, is in the Romantic view of Pope, "the one that confirms by contrast" (2) and that offers "a narrative of periodization that posits an epochal break at some indeterminate point in the eighteenth century" (4). Wordsworth is the villain of the piece in that Romantic literary history has unquestioningly offered a negative view of Pope and a canonization of Wordsworth.

Griffin proposes to write a "defamiliarizing history," one that is "counter-intuitive," playing down the intimidating image of Pope and inviting stronger consideration of Wartons, Edward Young, and William Cowper. He regards Pope as playing the part of Ancient and Modern, and claims that "Wordsworth's greatness . . . is not to be found in his rejection of Pope's 'classicism,' so much as in his successful use of it" (90).

Griffin further questions the parallel development of criticism's relation to Romantic literary history, and uses M. H. Abrams' *The Mirror and the Lamp* as his test case. His argument is rooted in devising a method of viewing literary history "horizontally . . . without the vertical metaphysical dimension of a teleological master narrative" (132). In a word, he speculates that "Romanticism's 'Pope' . . . refers to something within Romanticism itself" (134).

Susan Edwards Meisenhelder in *Wordsworth's Informed Reader: Structures of Experience* offers an interesting reader-response approach to the poetry. She tries, she says, to avoid a single-minded theory for approaching all texts, and chooses instead Wordsworth's own aesthetic as her vehicle. That aesthetic "invites . . . a study of the means by which he shapes his reader's response," and she cites the poet's own words as evidence: "The true province of the philosopher is . . . to look into his own mind and determine the law by which he is affected (PW.2.357)." In Meisenhelder's view, Wordsworth, by probing his own psyche, "discovers strategies for educating his audience" (1).

Elizabeth Fay is interested in the performative nature of Wordsworth's aesthetic, "the imaginative impetus" that compels the creation of such poems, with chapters on "The Wordsworthian Performative," "The Chartered Valley," "Authoring Selves, Traversing Ground," "Mountains and Abysses," and "The Politics of Negotiating Charts." Offering a map of the poet's imaginary terrain, she focuses on the pastoral mode where one finds what she describes as a "transgressive space" in which time stands still in a sublime moment in the drama of a female figure in the landscape. Fay offers her particular performative approach by imagining "how Dorothy wrote herself into being and into the aesthetic map" (12). With a strong emphasis on gender, Fay stresses the Dorothy factor in key poems by her brother, a variation on the Romantic sublime now seen "in terms of the woman's subjective trial and alternative routes of poetic discovery" (12).

John Beer's *Wordsworth and the Human Heart* also deals with the Wordsworth Circle, but with interesting and engaging variations. Wordsworth's sense of humanity, Beer contends, is a thing unto itself, but "it owed a good deal to his relationship with Coleridge and with his sister." Dorothy's gift for wonderfully direct and vivid expression as evidenced in her journals often seemed stronger than her brother's, but to understand this phenomenon fully, it must be "set in the context of speculation about the links between human consciousness and the human heart which were at the same time reaching Wordsworth from Coleridge" (xiii).

Many forces were operating on the younger Wordsworth — the "simple manliness" of Burns and the border ballads; the Cowper tradition and its concern "to reconcile the old intellectual order with the cultivation of sensibility" (7); Godwin's *Political Justice* with "the openness of the reasoning and the welcome invocation of sincerity" (25). Yet he turned from his own philosophical ruminations, especially those about the one life in all things, "to the more ready bond between himself and his sister" (78). In Dorothy he could see "kindred perceptions and might hope to see his solitary quest bear fruit in solid benefit" (78). *Tintern Abbey* becomes the map of his whole process of development, and the celebrated and puzzling closing lines express "his hope that she too would be drawn into a sense of the 'one life,' so finding a mainstay for her emotions in future years" (78).

Examining the Bateson speculation about an abnormally close relationship between brother and sister, Beer finds no evidence of the sexual and much "intensity of the heart" (161). Indeed by making "Mary central to his future household," Beer argues, "Wordsworth no doubt hoped that the affection between himself and Dorothy might find a continuing life within a larger mediating community of relationships where the quiet work of the mature human heart, anchored in a deeply physical human love, could contain, and find a place for, more intense and extreme attachments" (164).

Don Bialostosky in *Wordsworth, Dialogics, and the Practice of Criticism* makes friends with the general approach of Mikhail Bakhtin, the Russian theoretician, in his reading of Wordsworth. With a strong emphasis on the aesthetic, he proceeds autobiographically as he recalls an undergraduate teacher who directed him to the *Prelude* at a time of vocational crisis and how this led to a dissertation on the "Preface" to the *Lyrical Ballads.*

Wordsworth, Bialostosky contends, is both Founding Father and promulgator of a new "constitution for literature" (1). "The principal expositors of nearly every theoretical program for criticism during the past two decades (and some decades earlier) have found it necessary to take up Wordsworth's poetry along with his and Coleridge's poetic theories" (xiii–xiv). Wordsworth, however, is the central character in the drama of the book with his new image of the poet, his emphasis on a poetry of strong feeling and direct language, and his focus on nature and rustic life.

Bialostosky was drawn to Wordsworth's poetry before the charges of "anti-historical aestheticization" or "sheer language" (xviii) were heard. No friend of critical ideologies of right or left, he finds in Bakhtin's idea of dialogue a useful approach at a time when there seems to be a dominant critique of the poet. In a way he seems to echo Gerald Graff's "teaching the conflicts" approach, as he summons critics such as Gene Ruoff, Paul Magnuson, James Chandler, Alan Liu, Clifford Siskin, Marjorie Levinson, Judith Page, J. Hillis Miller and others, and he urges a genuine exchange of ideas. In an odd turn he cites Allan Bloom and his — at the time — enormously popular book *The Closing of the American Mind* as his prime example of rigid ideological critique and Wordsworth as closer to his ideal. Teachers, he writes, must facilitate "that emotional and intellectual exercise so central to Wordsworth's argument in the 'Preface'" (275).

Bialostosky, attending to poems like "Westminster Bridge," "It is a beauteous evening," "The Solitary Reaper," and "Lines Written in Early Spring," finds in Wordsworth "a decided continuity between 'ordinary' and 'aesthetic' experience, an ambivalence rather than a Coleridgean contempt toward popular culture" (28). The Bakhtinian ideal of voices in conversation is now, more than ever, a needed goal. Wordsworth's "savage torpor" is, he says, "as much the enemy now as it was in 1800" (275).

Religion and Religious Experience

J. R. Watson is one of a number of late twentieth-century critics who address the large question of religious experience in Wordsworth, the key focus being the poetry of the first half of his career before he became fully aligned with the Church of England. Hence the word "experience" rather than "doctrine" or "dogma" or "institution" is central.

Watson thinks of his book as among the first to use an anthropological approach, evoking primitive and mythic motifs in religion. Wordsworth emerges as a prophetic type holding out the ideal of a true community. His goal, he says, is to demonstrate the power of the poet's "early religious apprehensions, the weight of coherence and authority which comes from Wordsworth's individual experience of simple yet profound patterns of belief." Further, he would point up the centrality in the poetry of "fundamental, even primitive, ideas of the sacred," and, "above all, the relationship which exists between man and man and man and God, bound together in a natural love within the mind of man" (247).

Watson's method is analytical rather than historical, his chief concern is subject-matter. He chooses to call Wordsworth a "liminal" poet, someone at the edge of the beyond, experiencing "a private apprehension of the sacred," "close to the structure of primitive religious experience" (12). *The Prelude* links the child with the primitive, and is concerned with what Levi-Strauss called "'the central problem of anthropology, viz., the passage from nature to culture'" (21). The man-nature link, like the I-Thou of Martin Buber, is central to an understanding of Wordsworth's poetry. In the process of this linking the "experiencing imagination is the key" (36).

The Salisbury Plain trip and the "Guilt and Sorrow" poem that records it dramatized for Wordsworth a "separation from 'normal' society in its marginal figures," leading him to conclude that a "re-integration and death are better than perpetual isolation" (73). The *Lyrical Ballads* are poems of "becoming aware," standing at the "centre of Wordsworth's poetry because it involves dialogue and monologue, poet and external world" (102).

The *Immortality Ode* and *The Prelude* view a life obsessed with time and the physical as one which neglects "the spiritual values which give significance to man's existence" (139). But, argues Watson, there are "moments or experiences" beyond time when we can "draw near to God" and again "experience the oneness of the unfallen world we once knew" (140). The return to Grasmere is a return to the "primordial sacred time" (219), and *The Excursion* captures the regained Eden of home (247).

John A. Hodgson's *Wordsworth's Philosophical Poetry, 1797–1814* describes Wordsworth as a religious poet although the plot of his study is the history of the poet's "metaphysical beliefs from *The Borderers* to *The Excursion*" and its counterplot "the correlative history" of his "emblematizing vision." Hodgson sees Wordsworth passing through four poetic stages (1797–1798, 1798–1804, 1804–1805, post-1805) in a journey toward conservatism and orthodoxy. "God is Everywhere!", the title of Chapter 1, moves from *The Borderers* to *The Ruined Cottage*, a phase in which the theme of the "one life" develops and slowly fades. The vision described in the second chapter, "We See into the Life of Things," that of *Tintern Abbey* and the early *Prelude,* is one that fades more sharply as the poet recognizes a "peculiarly human nature" with its concomitant sense of human loss and sadness. In Chapter 3 Hodgson studies the *Immortality Ode* and the earlier books of *The Prelude,* arguing for the "Ode" as a connecting link between 1799 and 1805 *Prelude.* The celebrated Mount Snowdon passage, recording an earlier visionary Wordsworthian experience, but serving in the poem as a climactic religious moment, "guides and organizes the argument of the entire poem" (112).

Reviewing the book, Peter Manning makes the telling point that "Hodgson deftly shows the change between the Wordsworth of 1800, 'concerned for the survival or continuation in some form of the individual's *life,*' and the Wordsworth of 1804, 'concerned instead for the survival or continuation in some form of the individual's *mind*' (150), who having come to see in nature a God who is a type of Mind, strives to create works that 'might become/A power like one of Nature's' (1805 *Prelude,* 12.311–12)" (153).

Anne Rylstone, a student of the *Ecclesiastical Sonnets,* feels that even though Wordsworth never took "formal religious vows," he "is one of the most religious poets in English literature" (17). Choosing these late sonnets that follow the history of Christianity in England from primitive beginnings to the present, she argues that they provide "a valuable perspective on the extensive landscape that evolves over the course of the poet's many works." The Church, albeit an institution in its most obvious manifestation, nevertheless reveals "Christianity manifested in private suffering, endeavor, and spiritual triumph, a theme familiar to the reader of Wordsworth" (1).

The sonnets, the sheer number of which represent a major poetic accomplishment, capture for Rylstone the rhythms of Wordsworth's poetry from youthful early questioning and uncertainty to "affirmation and philosophical synthesis" (3). Nature and the Church come together in the "symbol of the Holy River, whose course represents the history of Christianity." Such an image "naturalizes the Church" as the divine element is humanized and the human is divinized (4).

Two very recent books address impressively the subject of "Romantic religion" in general and of several of the major Romantic poets in particular. Nancy Easterlin focuses on one in *Wordsworth and the Question of "Romantic Religion."* Avoiding the pieties and the appreciative tone that characterized so much writing about religion and literature in the past, she draws on "research in the psychology and sociology of religion to offer an interpretation of transcendent experiences, metaphysical concerns, and conflicting beliefs" (9) in developing her sense of "religious experience." Beyond structure, hierarchy, and a body of beliefs, she is partial to "a unique kind of emotional experience," to what she understands as William James's conception of religion as "man's passionate and comprehensive embrace of experience, one that includes perception of metaphysical presence" (35).

With a great deal of spade work deftly handled, she argues for a special religious dimension in Wordsworth, concentrating on three episodes in his career and reading them with a good deal of rigor. Thus, for example, *Tintern Abbey* is religious "in a particularly modern sense" because "it dramatically asserts authentic religious experience while simultaneously raising doubts" about that experience (37). There is a faith in the mystical "serene and blessed mood," but it is a questioning faith (71).

The Prelude, however, according to Easterlin, attempts no "pure renderings of spiritual states" as in *Tintern Abbey* (47). Instead we have passages grounded in the physical scene itself— Gondo Gorge, Simplon Pass, Snowdon — underscoring the poet's "belief that extraordinary experience is a dimension of ordinary experience" (86). Unlike the mystical experience of *Tintern Abbey, The Prelude* offers "a much briefer description of the experience"; an element of disappointment that nuances the description; and a direct linking with "imaginative experience" (90).

A significantly entitled final chapter, "Too Much Recompense: The Recompense of Institutions" uses *The Excursion* and *Ecclesiastical Sonnets* as key documents in Wordsworth's movement toward orthodoxy as the institutional tempers the poet's spiritual subjectivism. Easterlin's book offers a religious Wordsworth, but a modern conflicted poet whose work has the ring of reality.

Robert Ryan's *The Romantic Reformation: Religious Politics in English Literature 1789–1824* is another significant new contribution to this growing body of scholarship on religion and literature. Here, some twenty years after his *Keats: The Religious Sense*, Ryan focuses not on a single figure, but on the major Romantic writers from the French Revolution to shortly after the death of Keats. Noting, in the midst of a number of competing critical discourses, the relative absence of a discourse relating to religious experience, he works hard to avoid a narrow historicism on the one hand and a pious formalism on the other. His methodology is to establish connections between politics and religion first, viewing Romantic poetry "as more profitably considered as acts of Miltonic engagement in the religious culture of the time than as meditations in retirement from social realities" (5).

Wordsworth is, of course, a main player in Ryan's cast of characters, a poet who called on the spirit of Milton for an England "in need." Ryan is struck by the range of admiration for the religious dimension in the poetry — from John Keble, Newman's Oxford Movement colleague, to the Christian Socialist Charles Kingsley and his tribute to *The Excursion* as the work of "a man raised up as a light in a dark time" and to the "simple faith in man and God with which he delivered his message" (80). And he follows carefully the poet's political and religious evolution from the early radical enthusiast for the French Revolution, the author of the remarkable letter to the Bishop of Llandoff, to the later poet articulating his religious mission in the "Preface" to *The Excursion*.

A series of four articles during the 1990s by J. Robert Barth, S.J. studies aspects of Wordsworth's religious thought and experience. "The Temporal Imagination in Wordsworth's *Prelude*: Time and the Timeless" explores the poet's use of both natural and cyclical time, "two dimensions of time: his own personal linear time and the quasi-eternal time represented by the spots of time" (148), concluding that it is through his very time-bound faculty of imagination that the poet glimpses "intimations" of eternity. In "The Role of Humankind in the Poetry of Wordsworth and Coleridge," Barth contrasts the use of humanity by the two poets, arguing that "Wordsworth's primary subject is the relationship between himself and Nature, or Nature seen through the prism of the self; Coleridge's subject, even in the face of Nature, is relationship between persons, especially love." The difference between the two stems from "a difference in their conceptions of God, or at least in how each one discovers the divine" (164–65).

Barth continues his exploration of Wordsworth's religious thought by comparing his "search for transcendence" with that of the Jesuit poet Gerard Manley Hopkins. He discusses Wordsworth's *Immortality Ode*, a poem much admired by Hopkins, along with Hopkins's "The Leaden Echo and the Golden Echo." Both poems, Barth contends, see into Nature and thus see beyond Nature to a transcendent reality. "Both of them, in images of incomparable beauty, express the human yearning for life and beauty that will not fade and die." Wordsworth trusts reality more than Hopkins, but both dramatize "the tension between the incarnational and eschatological poles, the immanent and the transcendent, that marks the central tradition of Christianity" (188).

Barth, in a paper given at the 1999 Wordsworth Conference in Grasmere, just published in *The Wordsworth Circle*, traces Wordsworth's use of imagination in *The Prelude*, especially the deepening relationship between imagination and the "spiritual love" of Book XIV. He concludes that Wordsworth's is "a profoundly incarnational view of the imaginative faculty," so that "the transcendent is mediated in and through sense reality." The "higher love" of the concluding lines of the poem is not only an end in itself but also a means by which all other loves are "hallowed," and imagination is the power that "makes this vision of the world possible."

The Prelude and Wordsworth's Epic Impulse

Brian Wilkie's *Romantic Poets and the Epic Tradition* finds that tradition "alive in the English Romantic age" (vii) while recognizing that some have been skeptical. In a section on characteristics of classical epics, he singles out "a significant degree of imitativeness," "the ordeal-journey," a code of "heroism," the "purposefulness of the action," "the presence of supernatural agencies," and others (15). And in chapters on neglected exemplars like Southey and Landor and major poets like Shelley, Byron, Keats, and Wordsworth, he examines themes, characters, techniques, and style.

For our purpose, Wilkie's chapter on *The Prelude* is most important. Even when some contend that the epic tradition ended with Milton, he argues that "*The Prelude* does not, for example, differ from *Paradise Lost* more radically than *Paradise Lost* differs from the *Aeneid*" (viii). *The Prelude* is an epic of its age, Wordsworth's great attempt at epic expression pointing toward the past. For Wordsworth, Wilkie says, the time had come "to celebrate the loftiest subject of all, the mind of man," "his own" (65). And he does so in "messianic language" that is "applicable to the charismatic epic hero" (79). In an eloquent summary statement Wilkie concludes: "The more one reads *The Prelude* the clearer it becomes that in its intellectual and emotional grasp of human life and in the central relevance of its message the poem has the inevitability of the great epic visions" (111).

Kenneth Johnston offers a history of Wordsworth's master project in his *Wordsworth and "The Recluse."* Arguing that it is a living work, he traces the evolutionary process from "fragmented failure," to a turning away "in direct reaction to his perceived failure," to autobiographical poetry like that of *The Prelude*. These recoils, he continues, brought a restorative effect, and Wordsworth returned "to complete some larger or smaller portion of *The Recluse*." In three sections of his book, Johnston follows this pattern: "the First *Recluse* and the First *Prelude*, 1797–1799; *The Recluse* and *The Prelude*, 1800–1806; *The Recluse* and *The Excursion*, 1808–1814." (xiv).

Johnston views *The Recluse* as a philosophical poem, but with a peculiarly moral, psychological, and political ring. "Its philosophical assertions are everywhere crossed by its author's self-consciousness, a fact that seems much less unphilosophical in the late twentieth century than it did in the late eighteenth century." He counsels us to read *The Prelude* with a full awareness of its larger context, and, as we do, we note that its intense self-consciousness "arises from and occurs within a framework of accommodating Imagination to the residence of Human Life" (xvi).

Ronald Gaskell's *Wordsworth's Poem of the Mind: An Essay on "The Prelude"* is a relatively recent treatment of the poet's epic, a detailed close reading that looks back to the early work and ahead to the poetry of the later years. Obviously an admirer of the work, Gaskell describes it as "one of the great voyages of discovery, not just a first-hand account (though it is that too, and an incomparably vivid one) of the boyhood and coming of age of a great poet." He constructs his argument around three major Wordsworthian concerns — "nature and the One Life within us and abroad," "the mind's relationship with the world," and "the imagination." Interestingly in the three chapters devoted to these concerns, he is able to move beyond mere mechanical organization and summary and to show how they "overlap and interact" (vi).

Gaskell's opening chapter juxtaposes *Tintern Abbey* with *The Prelude*, arguing that in the former one can see the emergence of a more philosophical sense of nature as "one life," a sense that at times approaches the pantheistic. The feeling expressed, however, is "certainly religious" (19), richer and deeper than that of earlier poems like *An Evening Walk* and *Descriptive Sketches*. In the 1799 *Prelude* "it seems that the animism of boyhood and later . . . merged imperceptibly into a larger awareness, often rapturous, of the One Life" (19).

In his second chapter Gaskell poses and deals with the questions of how the mind encounters nature and whether there is a right relationship between the two. Early on he explains that when Wordsworth speaks of "mind, especially in the early books of *The Prelude*, he is usually thinking not of the intellect, but of the life of feeling." And it was his love of nature, rooted in childhood, "both in itself and in the renewed conviction it gave him of the value of feeling, that was decisive in his recovery from the crisis years of 1793–96" on which he focuses in Books X to XIII (31).

Gaskell regards *The Prelude* as "a sustained meditation of the mind on its own nature, its origin and powers" (42). This self-consciousness is notably missing in the earlier poems of the 1790s. At no point in *The Ruined Cottage,* for example, "is there any suggestion that nature 'liveth to the heart' or that there is One Life within us and abroad" (51). On the other hand, Wordsworth in the great Simplon Pass episode (*Prelude*, VI, 553–72), "is identifying imaginatively with the scene" and also "projecting onto it the turmoil of his feelings" (53).

Gaskell's final chapter addresses Wordsworth's refinement of the idea of mind in his concept of the imagination, thinking of it in three ways: "a creative response to landscape, . . . an intuitive sympathy with men and women, and as one of the powers requisite for the writing of poetry" (61). Imagination, he argues, "is a kind of intensified perception: perception energized by feeling," the rare gift celebrated in the spots of time section of *The Prelude*, among the "most moving" Wordsworth ever wrote (76). And the imagination of the more mature poet "differs from the excited imagination of the boy not only in the range of his human sympathies." Again and again after 1798 "is a tendency to look back, to rely on memory to reawaken feeling and generate poems" (93).

The climax of *The Prelude* is for Gaskell the Mount Snowdon passage with its "struggle to understand the imagination" (93). By the time readers reach Book XIII "the conception of the imagination is being stretched to cover everything Wordsworth values in the human mind" (100). Despite a sense of anti-climax in the closing lines of the poem, the great gift is a "poetry of experience — mostly, not quite all, boyhood experience" (101). Gaskell's highest tribute sees "Wordsworth rather than Blake who stands at the beginning of modern (or modernist) poetry, for if ever there were a poem of the act of mind it is *The Prelude*" (67).

Willard Spiegelman ventures into Wordsworth's heroic world in very special ways, ranging beyond the obvious Romantic epic *The Prelude*, with a look backward to the characters of the *Lyrical Ballads* and a look forward to *The White Doe of Rylstone* and *The Excursion*. For Spiegelman the Wordsworthian hero "is assuredly not 'the exceptional monster,' but an ever-present reality" (6). His heroes "are, paradoxically, ourselves" (6), and, in reading about them, we learn more fully about how to live (41).

In his children, the fathers of his men, we find the "first heroic figures," invested with "the heaviest symbolic trappings." Then there are the old men, noble figures — beggars, Simon Lee, others — who possess a "rugged" physical and emotional strength that gains a kind of ripeness in age (51).

The Prelude is, of course, the most overtly epic and heroic in the classical sense, and yet it does represent a new Romantic modernity. Spiegelman, calling attention to Wordsworth's plan for an even longer poem, "a great work never achieved," argues that "the poem is most fruitfully analyzed as the effort of a man attempting to make of himself an epic hero" (112), with Book VIII "Love of Nature Leading to Love of Man" as "the theoretical justification for the self-representation of the poet throughout the poem" (125).

Spiegelman's closing chapters are attentive to *The White Doe* and *The Excursion*. In the former he catches the full dimensions of heroism. It is a poem of difficult to reconcile oppositions that suggest life struggles that widen human awareness. And he chides readers who have been too quick to parody or poke fun at *The Excursion*, a poem that engaged Wordsworth for almost twenty years. This longest poem, he says, "ends with a formulaic reminder of the scope of his inevitable, natural heroism" and, returning to his earlier point about readers and audience, "the gentle Hearts and lofty Minds which he salutes are those of all of us" (221).

Wallace W. Douglas in *Wordsworth: The Construction of a Personality* follows a psychological route in *The Prelude* working from Wordsworth's earliest poems "to get a little closer to the pattern of Wordsworth's responses to the exigencies of living" (10). Moving from the not terribly encouraging critical responses to *An Evening Walk* and *Descriptive Sketches* to the Shakespearean ambitions of *The Borderers* and the experimental modes of the *Lyrical Ballads*, his goal is to "interpret the interpreters" in constructing a theory about Wordsworth's personality (13).

In *The Prelude* Douglas sees something "very close to a ritual or magical act," the "capturing of memories" and "the very act of writing them up" (19). In Goslar, away from Coleridge and with little poetic reputation to speak of, he turned to his own fundamental experience even though autobiography was "a second best thing" (53–54). In the midst of frustration — familial, political, professional — the guilt he felt for his father's death, the traumatic loss of his mother, Dorothy becomes a surrogate mother along with Nature. Grasmere is "the ultimate environment where the heart was dissolved, the mind soothed by fair trains of imagery and the presence of those affecting thoughts and remembrances which could be the means to rest" (168–69). Dorothy and Mary "could provide satisfaction of his primary narcissistic needs, and, hence, control of the conflict deriving therefrom. The energy thus freed would become available for investment in activities of the outer world, such as, to be quite simple about it, marriage, rearing a family, and writing poems" (177–78).

Frank D. McConnell in *The Confessional Imagination: A Reading of Wordsworth's "Prelude"* focuses, as its title suggests, on the poem's distinctively "confessional" dimension and its sense of an audience as necessary not only for the "rhetorical decorum" of the poem, but indeed for "the poem's very existence" (16). This poet-audience relationship has, McConnell argues, a Protestant touch, with Coleridge, the listener of the poem, "surely being absorbed into the Wordsworthian personality and the poet becoming his own audience" (24).

McConnell respects Hartman's view on "varieties of mediation as Wordsworth's impulse toward evasion of direct confrontation with the immortal spirit," but offers his own revision in his idea of the confessional poem. For him the "drive of *The Prelude* toward mediation is not an evasion or refusal of visionary power but a means to that power" (35). Interestingly, he continues, the power of the poem comes from "its transformation of allegorical or daemonic forms of consciousness" (61), the Simplon Pass passage, for example, using "narrative and time sense to discipline the daemonic tendencies of his experience" (87).

Returning again to the key word of his title, McConnell argues that the observer's confessional voice "effects the final liberation of the image from sight into vision" (108). As we finish the poem, we have witnessed the poet move from "a confessional unification of past and present into a new, Edenic language which acts out as well as asserts the power and blessedness he has earned through memory" (183). *The Prelude* is no less than "one of the great revelations of the human spirit" (190).

Thomas Weiskel's wide-ranging *The Romantic Sublime: Studies in the Structure and Psychology of Transcendence* uses as its working definition "that moment when the relation between the signifier and the signified breaks down and is replaced by an indeterminate relation." It also, quite eloquently in its "Personal Introduction," written by Weiskel's wife Patricia after his tragic accidental death at an early age, uses a journal entry that states "the problem of my life and the problem of my book are the same: to find either a mode of sublimation which does not attenuate what the sublime pretends to be or a mode of desublimation that is not merely natural" (xiii).

Wordsworth receives important attention as a pioneering force in thinking and writing about a new kind of sublime. Echoing McConnell, Weiskel regards the poet's external conversation with Coleridge as really a conversation with himself, "an agent or element in Wordsworth himself that would judge harshly the enterprise now in view" (168). And he regards highly the multi-faceted originality of Wordsworth — in elevating the everyday and in so doing destroying "the poem-which-is-about-something by taking the subject out of poetry"; and in naturalizing "the archaic, daemonic, and divine sources of power" (169).

For Weiskel, Wordsworth's gift with language defies analysis. Drawing on the oft-quoted passage in Book V of *The Prelude*, he argues that power "attends motion of winds which are embodied in a mystery . . . . The passage is evoking the penumbra of words, the power inherent not in what they mean but in that they mean; or in what they are, independent of their meaning — the *how* and not the *what* of sublimity" (181). The spots of time in the poem revive and renovate the mind because through them the self returns to the "liminal place where 'some working of the spirit/Some inward agitations' still are active" (185).

Weiskel finds two key quest movements in *The Prelude* — one toward "power, from image to symbol, from ordinary seeing, through self-consciousness (ambition), to the locus or spot of power, manifested in a symbol of sacrifice and guilt." And then there is that second movement away from power, "from symbol back to image," the humanizing direction Wordsworth celebrates in describing the imagination as redemptive (194). Once again the Simplon Pass passage is cited, this time for Weiskel as "a paradigm of the Wordsworthian threshold and hence the very type of Romantic transcendence" (195), "Eternity without types and symbols, apocalypse without the characters" (204).

Psychoanalysis

Wordsworth has also been the subject of a good deal of psychoanalytic criticism, especially over the last twenty years. Douglas Wilson's *The Romantic Dream: Wordsworth and the Poetics of the Unconscious* situates his "reading of the Wordsworthian dream between ancient and Freudian dream interpretation in order to gain a perspective on the oneiric moment of Romanticism" (xiii). His study traces the phenomenon of the dream in the Middle Ages and Renaissance, eighteenth-century dream theory and onward into theorizing about dreams and dramatic illusion in Coleridge and Nietzsche.

Wordsworth, he writes, "rarely deploys myth in a systematic form," but he does exemplify "the creative function of the Romantic dream" even though his approach remains "secular" (xiii). His opening chapter reveals his deep commitment to Freud's "The Uncanny," "a royal road to the unconscious which serves to empower the process of narrativity in Wordsworth's strategy of memory" and a way of exploring the poet's notable tendency to locate within the ordinary "moments of self-disruption that paradoxically remain 'hiding places of power'" (xiii–xiv).

Wilson uses dreams to deal with Wordsworth's sense of the loss of sensory power; "the childhood dream in the *Immortality Ode* is viewed as a myth of the fall from preexistence" (xv), and the discussion continues in his treatment of the "Elegiac Stanzas" and *Resolution and Independence*. Another chapter explores the connection between ventriloquism and dreaming and includes a discussion of *The Excursion*.

Wilson's treatment of *The Prelude* is provocative and engaging. Calling on "darkness and the language of power," he contends, "Wordsworth summons his reverie." But the fancy's intrusion on the imagination creates confusion and leads to "moral collapse." The violence in France and the power politics in England bring nightmare, to be conquered only by the return "to a state of mind analogous to dreaming" (xv).

The final chapter focuses on the dream of the Arab in Book Five of *The Prelude* as Wilson sees Wordsworth revitalizing his creativity in this episode as well as in those of the Drowned Man and the Boy of Winander. Yet as the poet finds a degree of consolation in his interpretation of the Arab dream, "its apocalyptic deluge recalls the revolutionary bloodbath and the fracturing of the political hopes" (xvii).

Richard McGhee in *Guilty Pleasures: William Wordsworth's Poetry of Psychoanalysis* offers a psychoanalytic reading of a large body of Wordsworth's poetry, building on the premise that "his super-ego had assumed the authority of his dead father," for most of his life "punishing his ego for having harbored feelings of hate for his beloved father" and suffering "guilt" and revealing "symptoms of endless mourning" (105). Freud's "Mourning and Melancholia" is used to illuminate the poet's state of mind in *The Prelude* and *The Excursion*, with the theme of melancholia overshadowing the Wanderer, the Solitary, Margaret, and "by implication, Wordsworth himself" (187).

Mentioned briefly earlier, Richard Onorato offers an early psychoanalytic reading of *The Prelude*. Beginning with his sense of novel metaphors and recurring experiences as he reads the poem, he argues that Wordsworth's loss of both parents by the time he was thirteen was traumatic and "deeply significant" to the poet's portrayal of himself and his growth (viii). For him *The Prelude* is "our only great example of poetic autobiography in English" (5), and the poet's "personal habit of observing of himself and of accounting for himself to himself . . . served psychic needs" (11). His epic came between the poet and his "great work and extended itself until it became the expression of a dominant intention to get hold of oneself" (14).

The epic motif of the journey dominates the poem with the mind half-creating what it perceives in tracing the "poetic growth to consciousness" (126). The poet's desire to describe poetry as the highest human activity and "to make the poet's mind comparable to God's mind," argues Onorato, "makes in fact the same connection between the Poet and God in point of Nature that the child once made between the child and the father in point of the mother" (175). Wordsworth is unconsciously approaching the subject of "freedom from the mother" as well as "the repressed experience of Oedipal conflict with the father" (178). What might be called the poet's "fatherless freedom" helps to explain his need to "invent himself" and to make a new commitment to "seeing revolutionary man in his own image" (343).

Summing up, Onorato regards *The Prelude* as "the record of an attempt to live with a high estimate of human worth." While attempting to deal with a severe individual human trauma as well as the larger trauma of human self-consciousness, the process becomes more important than the person. Wordsworth's personality, however important, is subordinate to "the account he wished to give of his Imagination. What may be imagined in the sublime egotism of his poetry confers a dignity on the mind attempting to imagine of itself something worthy of the power by which it is possessed" (403–4).

In the summer of 1984 a remarkable event took place at the annual Wordsworth Conference in Grasmere — a five-hour debate on a familiar point of contention among Wordsworthians, the relative merits of the 1805 and 1850 versions of *The Prelude*. The Moderator of the debate was Jonathan Wordsworth, who was — and continues to be — the Academic Director of the Conference. Herbert Lindenberger was cap-

tain of the 1805 team, with colleague Norman Fruman; J. Robert
Barth, S.J. led the 1850 team, assisted by Jeffrey Baker.

The debate followed a traditional format, with main speakers for
each side, opportunities for cross-examination and rebuttal, and ample
opportunity for audience participation. Arguments ranged from the
stylistic to the biographical to the theological. Interestingly enough,
Americans tended to prefer the 1850 version (the one to which they
were first introduced), while scholars from Great Britain often preferred
the 1805 version for the same reason. Discussions of Wordsworth in his
later years, as poet and critic of his own work, stirred strong feeling;
and differences of view over what some called Wordsworth's decline
into orthodoxy were sharp. By advance agreement, no vote was taken,
but each side had ample reason to believe that it had won the debate.

Wordsworth and Coleridge

Paul Magnuson's work on the Wordsworth-Coleridge connection continues earlier critical concern with this subject in a work of major importance.
Fresh and original in almost every way, it eschews generalizations about a
"moving spirit in their poetic dialogue." Magnuson perceptively pleads
the case that "Coleridge's poetry was the prime influence on Wordsworth's from the first days of their association until the winter of 1799–
1800, when Wordsworth began to describe himself as a self-generated
poet" (10). And he vigorously pursues the idea of a poetic dialogue,
seeing their poems as part of one work.

Magnuson uses specific examples: *The Ancient Mariner* and "The
Discharged Soldier" offer a complex dialogue on how these figures
connect to their places in the landscape. "These figures and their settings mirror the position of figures of speech in their lyric contexts and
of lyric passages in the context of the dialogue" (96). The isolated figure is an "enigmatic terror" in both settings and poems because there is
no clear meaning, no motivation. "'Christabel' is the unfinished narrative of the isolated figure" (96). When Wordsworth sought to offer sol-
ace and meaning for Margaret's life in *The Ruined Cottage*, argues
Magnuson, he turned to Coleridge's poetry — the earlier "This Lime-
Tree Bower" and his current works *The Ancient Mariner* and "Frost at
Midnight" (97).

And the Wordsworth-Coleridge dialogue continues. *Tintern Abbey*
responds to "Frost at Midnight" "and leads to a deeper pondering of
the issues in the early work on *The Prelude*" (164–165). Also, *Resolu-*

tion and Independence is a response to Coleridge's verse letter *Dejection: An Ode* and "the moods of that poem can be traced directly to their poetic dialogue in the end of March and beginning of April" (308).

Magnuson's earlier summing up statement is brave and provocative: "Coleridge writes to give Wordsworth a voice, so that Wordsworth can echo Coleridge's" (163).

Language, Meter, Poetic Technique

Theory is, of course, still a dominant force in contemporary Wordsworth criticism, but matters of technique still attract critics. In *Wordsworth: Language as Counter Spirit* Frances Ferguson takes the poet's language, or rather its textuality, as her main concern. For her, however, this textuality is something that cannot be escaped; Wordsworth saw language as a "gesture" toward an absence, something or someone lost. Hence the importance of epitaphs, attempts to replace a loss. As Lawrence Kramer comments in his review of Ferguson's book, "With the imagination and its incarnation, poetic language, are thereby memorial forms or epitaphs that Wordsworth took as the paradigms of language." For Wordsworth "the language of epitaph (or language *as* epitaph) is always more true to its object when the object is absent, as if presence and language were compatible" (227). '

Ferguson has none of the impatience with the poet's classifications — poems "founded on the affections," "of the Fancy," "of the Imagination," "of Sentiment and Reflection" — that many critics express. She believes that great poets are conscious of their artistry, and she follows these classifications in her discussion of *The Excursion*, sections of *The Prelude*, and especially the Lucy poems, with Lucy not so much "a remembered presence," as Kramer puts it, as a "remembered absence" (229).

In a review of David Haney's *William Wordsworth and the Hermeneutics of Incarnation* Don Bialostosky connects the book with a tradition of Wordsworth criticism going back to Coleridge's *Biographia Literaria* that regards Wordsworth as a philosophical poet and considers his work "in the philosophical and theological vocabulary of Continental idealist thought" (183). Haney, alluding to the poet's statement in his third "Essay Upon Epitaphs" that language should be an "incarnation" of thought, argues that Wordsworth treats words as living things rather than mere signs, taking issue with deconstructive critics who have used the statement to support their view of language as "counterspirit."

Operating from this central premise, Haney reads the Lucy poems, *The Prelude,* and *The Excursion* with a deeper sense of their philosophical and theological implications, and offers a critical posture at odds with the "impasse of deconstruction" (183).

Angela Esterhammer does double duty in an interesting essay on Wordsworth's "Ode to Duty," combining the familiar case for Milton's influence with a particular linguistic approach to the poetry. She stresses especially the performative aspect of language in Wordsworth, "texts as utterances that re-define the relationship between subject and object or individual and society." The "Ode to Duty," for example, performs an articulation of experience that is, in the broadest sense, *political,* since it involves the acknowledgment of power relations and the institution of duty and hierarchy (34).

In all of this language discussion Milton needs to be considered. There is, for example, Milton's influence on "rhetorical structure" as seen in the naming problem of the celebrated opening lines — "Stern Daughter of the Voice of God." Then there is the shadow of *Paradise Lost* in the "epistemology of seeing and hearing" in the *Ode* (35). Esterhammer's key point is summed up in her reminder that the foregrounding of the performative in Wordsworth's poetry goes hand in hand with Miltonic influence, Milton being a writer who is "intensely concerned with the performative power of divine, poetic, and politically authoritative language" (36).

Wordsworth criticism continues to be rich and varied in its particular topics. Edwin Stein addresses the familiar topic of allusion in a poet's work, but brings to the topic a history of the tradition, the ideas of "echo" and "mediation" in Wordsworth's poetic thought, and the poet's response to the Renaissance heritage of imitation. In addition, Stein studies the art of borrowings, the kinds of allusions that reveal a particular Wordsworthian artistry at work.

Stein uses no less than one thousand intertextual examples "to establish the factors which created Wordsworth's allusive habits, to theorize about the various forms of his intertextuality and to provide a taxonomy of the borrowings" (vii). Milton and Shakespeare are the most echoed poets and after these formidable predecessors come Gray, Spenser, the Bible, Thomson, Coleridge, and the ballads collected by Thomas Percy and others.

Wordsworth, Stein argues, was one of the first major English poets to see the nation's poetry as a long and worthy tradition, in many ways more important to capture than the classical tradition, and to incorporate into his own work, by quotation, echo, and allusion, the richness of its stories. And for Stein the poet's habit of borrowing "is one of the enabling acts of poetic expression" enacting and symbolizing "the process of interchange he believed took place between man and nature" (211). Wordsworth, he says, "tried to find in nature-molded feeling the ground of human redemption, not by abruptly casting out the old but by revaluing and reorienting it, giving it new birth" (213).

Brennan O'Donnell calls attention to the need for more careful attention to Wordsworth's versification than has been the case in the main lines of the critical tradition. Such attention, he feels, is necessary for "a proper understanding both of . . . individual poems and of overall achievement as a poet." After providing historical and critical contexts, he describes, with examples, Wordsworth's metrical practice in a variety of verse forms, contending that the poems "demonstrate that he habitually regarded the complex patterning of rhythmic and sonic elements within the context of conventional use to be a deeply vital and constitutive element of meaning" (6). O'Donnell is interested in connecting what the poet does metrically with the larger concerns of the poetry.

Part One of his study has two chapters that focus on Wordsworth's ideas about meter in the great prefaces as well as in his letters, notes, and conversations, ideas that were a part of his thinking from schooldays forward. He sees the celebrated definition of poetry — "spontaneous overflow of powerful feeling" — as committing him to a language governed by strong passion. Such language may be engagingly rhythmic but still without conventional metrical forms. Wordsworth challenges readers to attend "to the minutiae of metrical forms, to relationships between forms and subjects and among various forms and to the poet's management of rhythm, rhyme, assonance and alliteration" (8).

Part Two studies the early verse, particularly *An Evening Walk* and *Descriptive Sketches* and their focuses on stanzaic verse in a chapter on the *Lyrical Ballads* and the blank verse poems. O'Donnell's conclusion underlines again "the pervasive importance of his metrical art" (9). His summing up is terse and perceptive: "The creative 'voice' of Wordsworth's verse exists in the active tension between the syntax of passion and the passion of meter" (248).

Epilogue

The recent important work of Johnston and Bromwitch represents not a conclusion to a study such as this one, but rather the latest episode in a work in progress. Wordsworth continues and will continue to be an important poet in secondary school, undergraduate and graduate college and university curricula; in the current revival of reading and reading aloud fostered by the current American Poet Laureate Robert Pinsky; and in the research and writing of scholars and theorists of Romanticism and of the work of Wordsworth.

As it has been from its somewhat primitive beginnings in the periodical literature of the late eighteenth and early nineteenth centuries, so, it is safe to predict, it will continue in a new century. There will be ups and downs, disciples and adversaries, fashions and trends. Indeed the current literary culture wars promise to lead Wordsworth — perhaps poetry criticism and theorizing — in even more innovative and exciting directions. They may even stir a return to some of the older methodologies to the extent that they are found useful. As we conclude this study, one thing seems clear and that is the power of Wordsworth's poetry to engage, provoke, even entertain as it continues to have a major place in the literary canon. Maybe even more readers, inside and far beyond the Academy, will echo Matthew Arnold's lines, "Others will strengthen us how to bear/But who, ah! who, will make us feel?"

Works Consulted

Averill, James. *Wordsworth and the Poetry of Human Suffering.* Ithaca and London: Cornell UP, 1980.

Barth, J. Robert, S. J. "The Temporal Imagination in Wordsworth's *Prelude*: Time and the Timeless." *Thought.* 66 (1991): 139–50.

——. "The Role of Humankind in the Poetry of Wordsworth and Coleridge." *The Wordsworth Circle.* 22 (1991): 160–65.

——. "Wordsworth and Hopkins: In Pursuit of Transcendence." *Renascence.* 47 (1996): 175–89.

——. "'The Feeling Source': Imagination and Transcendance in *The Prelude*." *The Wordsworth Circle.* 30. 1 (Winter 2000): 26–36.

Bate, Jonathan. *Romantic Ecology: Wordsworth and the Environmental Tradition.* London and New York: Routledge, 1991.

Beer, John. *Wordsworth and the Human Heart*. New York: Columbia UP, 1978.

Bewell, Alan. *Wordsworth and the Enlightenment: Nature, Man, and Society in the Experimental Poetry*. New Haven and London: Yale UP, 1989.

Bialostosky, Don. *Wordsworth, Dialogics, and the Practice of Criticism*. New York and Cambridge: Cambridge UP, 1992.

——. Review of David Haney. *William Wordsworth and the Hermeneutics of Incarnation*. University Park: Pennsylvania State UP, 1993. *The Wordsworth Circle*. 26.4 (Autumn 1995): 183–84.

Byatt, A. S. *Wordsworth and Coleridge in Their Time*. London: Nelson, 1970.

Devlin, D. D. *Wordsworth and the Poetry of Epitaphs*. Totowa, New Jersey: Barnes and Noble Books, 1981.

Douglas, Wallace W. *Wordsworth: The Construction of a Personality*. Kent, OH: Kent State UP, 1968.

Easterlin, Nancy. *Wordsworth and the Question of "Romantic Religion."* Cranbury, NJ: Associated UP, 1996.

Esterhammer, Angela. "Wordsworth's 'Ode to Duty': Miltonic Influences and Verbal Performance." *The Wordsworth Circle*. 24.1 (Winter 1993): 34–37.

Fay, Elizabeth. *Becoming Wordsworthian: A Performative Aesthetics*. Amherst: U of Massachusetts P, 1995.

Ferguson, Frances. *Wordsworth: Language as Counter Spirit*. New Haven: Yale UP, 1977.

Friedman, Michael. *The Making of a Tory Humanist: William Wordsworth and the Idea of Community*. New York: Columbia UP, 1979.

Gaskell, Ronald. *Wordsworth's Poem of the Mind: An Essay on "The Prelude."* Edinburgh: Edinburgh UP, 1991.

Goldstein, Laurence. *Ruins and Empire: The Evolution of a Theme in Augustan and Romantic Literature*. Pittsburgh: U of Pittsburgh P, 1977.

Griffin, Robert. *Wordsworth's Pope: A Study in Literary Historiography*. Cambridge: Cambridge UP, 1995.

Haney, David. *William Wordsworth and the Hermeneutics of Incarnation*. University Park: Pennsylvania State UP, 1993.

Heffernan, James A. "History and Autobiography: The French Revolution in Wordsworth's *Prelude*." In *Representing the French Revolution: Literature, Historiography, and Art*. Dartmouth College; Hanover and London: UP of New England, 1992. 41–62.

Hodgson, John A. *Wordsworth's Philosophical Poetry, 1797–1814.* Lincoln: U of Nebraska P, 1980.

Johnston, Kenneth R. *Wordsworth and "The Recluse."* New Haven and London: Yale UP, 1984.

Jones, John. *The Egotistical Sublime: A History of Wordsworth's Imagination.* London: Chatto & Windus, 1954.

Kelley, Theresa M. *Wordsworth's Revolutionary Aesthetics.* Cambridge: Cambridge UP, 1988.

Kramer, Lawrence. Review of Frances Ferguson. *Wordsworth: Language as Counter-Spirit.* New Haven: Yale UP, 1977. *The Wordsworth Circle.* 9.3 (Summer 1978): 226–29.

Kroeber, Karl. "The Presence of Absences: Were the Other Two Wedding Guests William Wordsworth and Fletcher Christian?" *The Wordsworth Circle.* 29.1(Winter 1998): 3–9.

Lyon, Judson. *The Excursion: A Study.* New Haven: Yale UP, 1950; rpt. Archon Books, 1970.

Magnuson, Paul. *Coleridge and Wordsworth: A Lyrical Dialogue.* Princeton: Princeton UP, 1988.

Manning, Peter. "Review of John Hodgson, *Wordsworth's Philosophical Poetry, 1797–1814.*" *The Wordsworth Circle.* 12.3 (Summer 1981): 151–53.

——. "Wordsworth at St. Bees: Scandals, Sisterhood, and Wordsworth's Later Poetry." In *Reading Romantics: Texts and Contexts.* New York, Oxford: Oxford UP, 1990.

McConnell, Frank D. *The Confessional Imagination: A Reading of Wordsworth's "Prelude."* Baltimore: Johns Hopkins UP, 1974.

McGhee, Richard. *Guilty Pleasures: William Wordsworth's Poetry of Psychoanalysis.* New York: The Whiston Publishing Company, 1993.

——. "'And Earth and Stars Composed a Universal Heaven': A View of Wordsworth's Later Poetry." *Studies in English Literature.* 11.4 (Autumn, 1971): 641–57.

McKusick, James. "Romanticism and Ecology." *The Wordsworth Circle.* 28.3 (Summer 1997): 123–124.

Meisenhelder, Susan Edwards. *Wordsworth's Informed Reader: Structures of Experience.* Nashville, TN: Vanderbilt UP, 1988.

O'Donnell, Brennan. *The Passion of Meter: A Study of Wordsworth's Metrical Art.* Kent, OH: Kent State UP, 1995.

Onorato, Richard. *The Character of the Poet: Wordsworth in "The Prelude."* Princeton: Princeton UP, 1971.

Owen, W. J. B. "Wordsworth's Aesthetics of Landscape." *The Wordsworth Circle*. 7.2 (Spring 1976): 70–82.

——. *Wordsworth as Critic*. Toronto: U of Toronto P, 1969.

Rieder, John. *Wordsworth's Counterrevolutionary Turn: Community, Virtue, and Vision in the 1790s*. Newark: U of Delaware P, 1997.

Rountree, Thomas J. *This Mighty Sum of Things: Wordsworth's Theme of Benevolent Necessity*. Tuscaloosa, University of Alabama P, 1965.

Ryan, Robert. *The Romantic Reformation: Religious Politics in English Literature, 1789–1824*. Cambridge: Cambridge UP, 1998.

Rylstone, Anne. *Prophetic Memory in Wordsworth's "Ecclesiastical Sonnets."* Carbondale and Edwardsville: Southern Illinois UP, 1991.

Spiegelman, Willard. *Wordsworth's Heroes*. Berkeley and Los Angeles: U of California P, 1985.

Stein, Edwin. *Wordsworth's Art of Allusion*. University Park: Pennsylvania State UP, 1988.

Talbot, John H. *The Nature of Aesthetic Experience in Wordsworth*. New York: Peter Lang, 1989.

Thomas, Gordon K. "'Glorious Renovation': Wordsworth, Terror, and Paine." *The Wordsworth Circle*. 21.1 (Winter 1990): 3–9.

Watson, J. R. *Wordsworth's Vital Soul: The Sacred and Profane in Wordsworth's Poetry*. London: Macmillan, 1982.

Weiskel, Thomas. *The Romantic Sublime: Studies in the Structure and Psychology of Transcendence*. Baltimore: Johns Hopkins UP, 1986.

Wilkie, Brian. *Romantic Poets and the Epic Tradition*. Madison and Milwaukee: U of Wisconsin P, 1965.

Williams, John. *Wordsworth: Romantic Poetry and Revolution Politics*. Manchester and New York: Manchester UP, 1989.

Wilson, Douglas. *The Romantic Dream: Wordsworth and the Poetics of the Unconscious*. Lincoln: U of Nebraska P, 1993.

Chronological List of Works Consulted

Holcroft, Thomas. 1793. Review of *An Evening Walk*. *Monthly Review*. NS 12 (October): 216–18.

Review of *Descriptive Sketches*. 1793. *Analytical Review*. (March): 294–299.

Review of *An Evening Walk*. 1793. *Critical Review*. NS 8 (July): 347–48.

Review of *Descriptive Sketches*. 1793. *Critical Review*. NS 8 (July): 472–74.

Review of *An Evening Walk*. 1794. *Gentleman's Magazine*. (March): 252–53.

Southey, Robert. 1798. Review of *Lyrical Ballads* (1798). *Critical Review or Annals of Literature*. NS 24 (October): 197–204.

Burney, Charles. 1799. Review of *Lyrical Ballads* (1798). *Monthly Review*. NS. 29 (June): 202–10.

Stoddart, John. Review of *Lyrical Ballads*. 1799. *British Critic*. 17 (February): 125–31.

Byron, George Gordon, Lord. 1807. Review of 1807 *Poems*. *Monthly Literary Recreations*. 3 (July): 65–66.

Jeffrey, Francis. 1807. Review of *Poems* (1807). *Edinburgh Review*. 11 (October): 214–31.

Review of *Poems* (1807). 1807. *The Critical Review*. 3rd series. 11 (August): 399–403.

Review of *Poems in Two Volumes of 1807*. 1807. *Le Beau Monde*. 2 (October): 138–42.

"General View of Literature for 1808." *Edinburgh Annual Register*. 1–2. 1810: 417–30.

Montgomery, James. 1808. Review of *Poems* (1807). *Eclectic Review*. (January): 35–43.

Seward, Anna. 1811. *Letters of Anna Seward: Written Between the Years 1784 and 1807*. 6 vols. Printed for George Ramsay and Company, Edinburgh; and Longman, Hurst, Ries, Orme, and Brown, William Miller and John Murray, London. 6.258, 280.

Jeffrey, Francis. 1814. Review of *The Excursion*. *Edinburgh Review*. 24 (November): 1–30.

Lamb, Charles and William Gifford. 1814. Review of *The Excursion. Quarterly Review*. 12 (October): 100–11.

Review of *The Excursion*. 1814. *New Monthly Magazine*. 11 (September): 57.

Jeffrey, Francis. 1815. Review of *The White Doe of Rylstone. Edinburgh Review*. 25 (October): 355–63.

Lyall, William. 1815. Review of *Poems* (1815) and *The White Doe of Rylstone. Quarterly Review*. 14 (October): 201–225.

Montgomery, James. 1815. Review of *The Excursion. Eclectic Review*. 21 (January): 13–39.

Review of *The Excursion*. 1815. *British Critic*. 2nd Ser. 3 (May): 449–67.

Review of *The Excursion*. 1815. *British Review and London Critical Journal*. 6 (August): 50–64.

Review of the 1815 *Poems*. 1815. *Monthly Review*. NS. 78 (November): 225–34.

Review of *The White Doe of Rylstone*. 1815. *British Review*. 6 (November): 370–77.

Review of *The White Doe of Rylstone*. 1815. *Gentleman's Magazine*. 85–2 (December): 524–25.

Conder, Josiah. 1816. Review of *The White Doe of Rylstone. Eclectic Review*. NS. 5 (January): 33–45 and NS. 6 (July): 1–8.

Reynolds, John Hamilton. 1816. "Sonnet: To Wordsworth." *Champion*. 163 (February 18): 54.

Wilson, John. 1818. "Essay on the Lake School of Poetry, No. II, On the Habits of Thought, inculcated by Wordsworth." *Blackwood's Edinburgh Magazine*. 4 (December): 257–63.

Review of *The River Duddon*. 1820. *Literary Gazette*. 166 (March 25): 200–203.

Review of *The River Duddon*. 1820. *London Magazine; and Monthly Critical and Dramatic Review*. 1 (June): 618–27.

Review of *The River Duddon*. 1820. *Eclectic Review*. NS. 14 (August): 170–84.

Review of *The River Duddon*. 1820. *British Review*. 16 (September): 37–53.

Scott, John. 1820. "Living Authors." *London Magazine*. 1 (March): 275–85.

Talfourd, Thomas Noon. 1820. "On the Genius and Writings of Wordsworth." *New Monthly Magazine*. 14 (November): 498–506; (December): 648–55.

Bowring, John. 1822. Review of *Ecclesiastical Sketches* and *Memorials of a Tour on the Continent*. *Monthly Repository*. 17 (June): 360–65.

Jeffrey, Francis. 1822. Review of *Memorials of a Tour on the Continent*. *Edinburgh Review*. 37 (November): 449–56.

Review of *Ecclesiastical Sketches*. 1822. *Literary Gazette*. 271 (March 30): 191–92.

Review of *Memorials of a Tour on the Continent*. 1822. *Literary Gazette*. 272 (April 6): 210–12.

Review of *Ecclesiastical Sketches*. 1822. *General Weekly Register*. (May 5): 184–85.

Review of *Memorials of a Tour on the Continent*. 1822. *Literary Museum*. 4 (May 18): 52–53.

Wilson, John. 1822. Review of *Ecclesiastical Sonnets* and *Memorials*. *Blackwood's Edinburgh Magazine*. 12 (August): 175–91.

Review of *Memorials of a Tour on the Continent* and *Ecclesiastical Sketches*. 1823. *The Monthly Censor*. 2 (March): 324–35.

Clare, John. 1825. "Essay on Popularity." *European Magazine*. (November): 76–77.

Coleridge, Henry Nelson. 1835. Review of *Yarrow Revisited*. *Quarterly Review*. 54 (July): 181–85.

Review of *Yarrow Revisited*. 1835. *The Spectator*. 8 (May 23): 493–94.

Faber, Frederick William. 1842. *Sights and Thoughts in Foreign Churches and Among Foreign Peoples*. London: Rivington.

Review of *The Prelude*. 1850. *The Examiner*. 2217 (July 27): 478–79.

Review of *The Prelude*. 1850. *Athenaeum*. 1188 (August 3): 805–807.

Review of *The Prelude*. 1850. *The Spectator*. 23 (August 3): 738–39.

Review of *The Prelude*. 1850. *Critic: the London Literary Journal*. NS. 9 (August 15): 402–404.

Review of *The Prelude*. 1850. "The New Poem by Wordsworth." *Dublin University Magazine*. 36 (September): 329–37.

Review of *The Prelude*. 1850. *Tait's Edinburgh Magazine*. NS. 17 (September): 521–27.

Review of *The Prelude*. 1850. *Eclectic Review*. 4th Ser. 28 (November): 550–62.

Southey, Robert. 1850. *The Life and Correspondence of the Late Robert Southey*. 6 vols. Charles Southey, editor. London: Longman, Brown, Green.

Review of Wordsworth: *The Prelude*. 1851. *Prospective Review*. 7: 94–131.

Wordsworth, Christopher. 1851. *Memoirs of William Wordsworth*. 2 vols. London.

Hood, Edwin Paxton. 1856. *William Wordsworth: A Biography*. London, Edinburgh, Dublin: Cash.

Bowden, John Edward. 1869. *Life and Letters of Frederick William Faber*. Baltimore: John Murphy & Co.

Coleridge, John Taylor. 1869. *A Memoir of the Rev. John Keble*. Oxford: J. Parker.

Rossetti, Michael William, editor. 1870. "Prefatory Notice." *The Poetical Works of William Wordsworth*. London: Moxon: xv–xxiv.

Knight, William. 1878; 3rd edition, 1890. *The English Lake District as Interpreted in the Poems of William Wordsworth*. 3 vols. Edinburgh: D. Douglas.

Swinburne, Algernon Charles. 1884. "Wordsworth and Byron." *The Nineteenth Century*. London: Twentieth Century Limited. (April): 583–609; (May): 764–90.

Sutherland, James. 1887. *William Wordsworth: The Story of His Life with Critical Remarks on His Writings*. London: E. Stock.

Knight, William and Other Members of the Wordsworth Society, editors. 1888. *Selections from Wordsworth*. London: Moxon.

Knight, William. 1889. *Wordsworthiana: A Selection From Papers Read to the Wordsworth Society*. London and New York: Macmillan and Co.

——. 1889. *The Life of William Wordsworth*. 3 vols. Edinburgh.

Wordsworth, Elizabeth. 1889. *William Wordsworth*. London: Percival.

DeVere, Aubrey. 1897. *Recollections of Aubrey DeVere*. New York: Edward Arnold. London and New York: Macmillan.

Legouis, Emile. 1897. *The Early Life of William Wordsworth, 1770–1798: A Study of The Prelude*. Trans. J. W. Matthews, with a Prefatory Note by Leslie Stephen. London: J. M. Dent and Co.

Raleigh, Sir Walter Alexander. 1903. *Wordsworth*. London: E. Arnold.

Stephen, Leslie. 1904. "Wordsworth's Ethics." in *Hours in a Library*. 4 vols. New York: G. P. Putnam.

Arnold, Matthew. 1905. "Wordsworth." *Essays in Criticism, Second Series*. London and New York: Macmillan.

Robertson, Frederick M. 1906. *Lectures on the Influence of Poetry and Wordsworth*. London: H. R. Allenson.

Thoreau, Henry David. Torrey, Bradford and Francis H. Allen, editors. 1906, 1949. *The Journals of Henry D. Thoreau*. Boston: Houghton Mifflin Co.

Bradley, A. C. 1st ed., 1909, [reprint 1950]. *Oxford Lectures on Poetry*. London: Macmillan and Co., Ltd.

Keble, John. 1912. *Keble's Lectures on Poetry, 1932–1841*. 2 vols. Trans. Edward Kershaw Francis. Oxford: Clarendon.

Ruskin, John. 1903–1912. *The Works of John Ruskin*. 39 vols. E. T. Cook and Alexander Wedderburn, editors. London: George Allen; New York: Longmans, Green & Co.

Harper, George Maclean. 1916. *William Wordsworth: His Life, Work, and Influence*. 2 vols. New York: Charles Scribner's Sons.

Barstow, Marjorie L. 1917. *Wordsworth's Theory of Poetic Diction: A Study of the Historical and Personal Background of the "Lyrical Ballads."* New Haven: Yale UP.

Babbitt, Irving. 1919. *Rousseau and Romanticism*. New York: Houghton Mifflin.

Legouis, Emile. 1922. *Wordsworth and Annette Vallon*. New York: E. P. Dutton.

——. 1923. *Wordsworth in a New Light*. Cambridge, MA: Harvard UP.

Potts, Abbie Findlay. 1922. *The Ecclesiastical Sonnets of William Wordsworth*. New Haven: Yale UP.

Garrod, Heathcote W. 1923. *Wordsworth*. Oxford: Clarendon.

Hulme, T. E. 1924. *Speculations: Essays on Humanism and the Philosophy of Art*. Herbert Read, editor. New York: Harcourt, Brace, and Co.

Richards, I. A. 1929. *Practical Criticism: A Study of Literary Judgment*. New York: Harcourt, Brace, and Co..

Hazlitt, William. 1930–34. *The Complete Works of William Hazlitt*. P. P. Howe, editor. 21 vols. London: Dent.

Read, Herbert. 1930. *Wordsworth*. London: J. Cape.

Rader, Melvin. 1931. *Presiding Ideas in Wordsworth's Poetry*. U of Washington Publications in Language and Literature. 8.2. Seattle: U of Washington P. Rpt. New York: Gordian Press, 1968.

Babbitt, Irving. 1932. "The Primitivism of Wordsworth." *On Being Creative*. New York: Houghton Mifflin.

Smith, Elsie. 1932. *An Estimate of W. W. by His Contemporaries, 1793–1832*. Oxford: Blackwell.

Batho, Edith. 1933. *The Later Wordsworth*. Cambridge: Cambridge UP.

Willey, Basil. 1934. *The Seventeenth Century Background: Studies in the Thought of the Age in Relation to Poetry and Religion*. London: Chatto and Windus.

Patton, Cornelius Howard. 1935. *The Rediscovery of William Wordsworth*. Boston, MA: The Stratford Company Publishers.

Sperry, Willard. 1935. *Wordsworth's Anti-Climax*. Cambridge, MA: Harvard UP.

Coleridge, Hartley. 1936. *Letters of Hartley Coleridge*. Grace Evelyn Griggs and Earl Leslie Griggs, editors. London: Oxford UP.

Eaton, Horace Ainsworth. 1936. *Thomas DeQuincey: A Biography*. New York: Oxford UP.

Fairchild, Hoxie Neale. 1937–1968. *Religious Trends in English Poetry*. 3 vols. New York: Columbia UP.

James, D. G. 1937. *Skepticism and Poetry: An Essay on the Poetic Imagination*. London: George Allen and Unwin Ltd.

Robinson, Henry Crabb. 1938. *Henry Crabb Robinson on Books and Their Writers*. Edith Morley, editor. London: J. M. Dent and Sons, Ltd.

Havens, Raymond D. 1941. *The Mind of a Poet*. Baltimore: Johns Hopkins UP.

Burton, Mary. 1942. *The One Wordsworth*. Chapel Hill: U of N. Carolina P.

Meyer, George Wilber. 1943. *Wordsworth's Formative Years*. Ann Arbor: U of Michigan P.

Peek, Katherine Mary. 1943. *Wordsworth in England: Studies in the History of His Fame*. Bryn Mawr, PA.

Shackford, Martha. 1945. *Wordsworth's Interest in Painters and Pictures*. Wellesley, MA.

Stallknecht, Newton. 1945. *Strange Seas of Thought: Wordsworth's Philosophy of Man and Nature*. Durham: Duke UP.

Ward, William S. 1945. "Wordsworth, The 'Lake' Poets, and Their Contemporary Magazine Critics, 1798–1820." *Studies in Philology*. 42 (June): 87–113.

Brooks, Cleanth. 1947. *The Well Wrought Urn: Studies in the Structure of Poetry*. New York: Reynal and Hitchcock.

The Poetical Works of William Wordsworth. 1940–49. Ernest DeSelincourt and Helen Darbishire, editors. 5 vols. Oxford: Oxford UP.

Lyon, Judson. 1950. *The Excursion: A Study*. New Haven: Yale UP; [rpt. 1970, Archon Books].

Dunklin, Gilbert T., editor. 1951. *Wordsworth: Centenary Studies Presented at Cornell and Princeton Universities*. Princeton: Princeton UP.

Abrams, M. H. 1953. *The Mirror and the Lamp: Romantic Poetry and the Critical Tradition*. London, Oxford, New York: Oxford UP.

Potts, Abbie Findlay. 1953. *Wordsworth's Prelude: A Study of Its Literary Form*. Ithaca, NY: Cornell UP.

Jones, John. 1954. *The Egotistical Sublime: A History of Wordsworth's Imagination*. London: Chatto & Windus.

Beach, Joseph Warren. 1956. *The Concept of Nature in Nineteenth-Century English Poetry*. New York: Pageant Book Co.

Coleridge, Samuel Taylor. 1956. *Collected Letters of Samuel Taylor Coleridge*. 6 vols. Earl Leslie Griggs, editor. Oxford: Clarendon.

Moorman, Mary. 1957. *William Wordsworth: A Biography*. I. *The Early Years: 1770–1803*. Oxford: Clarendon.

Ferry, David. 1959. *The Limits of Mortality: An Essay on Wordsworth's Major Poems*. Middletown, CT: Wesleyan UP.

Mayo, Robert. 1959. "The Contemporaneity of the Lyrical Ballads." *PMLA* 69 (June): 486–522.

Perkins, David. 1959. *The Quest for Permanence: The Symbolism of Wordsworth, Shelley, Keats*. Cambridge, MA: Harvard UP.

Beatty, Arthur. 1960. *William Wordsworth: His Doctrine and Art in Their Historical Relations*. Madison: U of Wisconsin P.

Hirsch, E. D. 1960. *Wordsworth and Schelling: A Typological Study of Romanticism*. New Haven: Yale UP.

Woof, R. F. 1961. Review of David Perkins, *The Quest for Permanence: The Symbolism of Wordsworth, Shelley, Keats*. Cambridge, MA: Harvard UP, 1959. In *Dalhousie Review*. 41.1 (Spring): 93–95.

Eliot, T. S. 1961. *The Use of Poetry and the Use of Criticism: Studies in Relation of Criticism to Poetry in England*. Cambridge, MA: Harvard UP.

Benziger, James. 1962. *Images of Eternity: Studies in the Poetry of Religious Vision from Wordsworth to T. S. Eliot*. Carbondale and Edwardsville: Southern Illinois UP.

Brower, Reuben A. and Richard Poirier, editors. 1962. *In Defense of Reading: A Reader's Approach to Literary Criticism*. New York: E. P. Dutton & Co., Inc.

Lindenberger, Herbert. 1963. *On Wordsworth's "Prelude."* Princeton: Princeton UP.

Hartman, Geoffrey. 1964. *Wordsworth's Poetry, 1787–1814.* Cambridge, MA and London: Harvard UP.

Perkins, David. 1964. *Wordsworth and the Poetry of Sincerity.* Cambridge, MA: Harvard UP.

Whitehead, Alfred North. 1964. *Science and the Modern World.* New York: New American Library.

Moorman, Mary. 1965. *William Wordsworth: A Biography.* II. *The Later Years: 1803–1850.* Oxford: Clarendon.

Raysor, Thomas M. 1965. "The Establishment of Wordsworth's Reputation." *Journal of English and Germanic Philology.* 54: 61–71.

Rountree, Thomas J. 1965. *This Mighty Sum of Things: Wordsworth's Theme of Benevolent Necessity.* University of Alabama P.

Salvesen, Christopher. 1965. *The Landscape of Memory: A Study of Wordsworth's Poetry.* Lincoln: U of Nebraska P.

Wilkie, Brian. 1965. *Romantic Poets and the Epic Tradition.* Madison and Milwaukee: U of Wisconsin P.

Woodring, Carl. 1965. *Wordsworth.* Boston: Houghton Mifflin.

Scoggins, James. 1966. *Imagination and Fancy: Complementary Modes in the Poetry of Wordsworth.* Lincoln: U of Nebraska P.

Langbaum, Robert. 1967. "The Evolution of Soul in Wordsworth's Poetry." *PMLA.* 82.2: 265–272. Rpt. in *The Modern Spirit: Essays on the Continuity of Nineteenth and Twentiety Century Literature.* New York: W. W. Norton, 1970.

Newman, John Henry. 1967 [1864]. *Apologia Pro Vita Sua.* Martin J. Svaglic, editor. Oxford: Clarendon.

Rader, Melvin. 1967. *Wordsworth: A Philosophical Approach.* Oxford: Clarendon.

Reed, Mark. 1967. *Wordsworth: The Chronology of the Early Years, 1770–1799.* Cambridge, MA: Harvard UP.

Douglas, Wallace W. 1968. *Wordsworth: The Construction of a Personality.* Kent, OH: Kent State UP.

Hayden, John O. 1968. *The Romantic Reviewers, 1802–1824.* Chicago: U of Chicago P.

Heffernan, James A. 1969. *Wordsworth's Theory of Poetry: The Transforming Imagination.* Ithaca and London: Cornell UP.

Owen, W. J. B. 1969. *Wordsworth as Critic.* Toronto: U of Toronto P.

Wordsworth, William and Dorothy Wordsworth. 1969–1993. *The Letters of William and Dorothy Wordsworth.* Ernest DeSelincourt, editor. 7 vols. *The Middle Years,* Part I. *1806–1811.* Rev. Mary Moorman. Oxford: Clarendon.

Bate, W. J., editor. 1970. *Criticism: The Major Texts.* Enlarged Edition. New York: Harcourt Brace Jovanovich, Inc.

Byatt, A. S. 1970. *Wordsworth and Coleridge in Their Time.* London: Nelson.

Heath, William. 1970. *Wordsworth and Coleridge: A Study of Their Literary Relations in 1801–1802.* Oxford: Clarendon.

Hurd, Harold. 1970. *The March of Journalism: The Story of the British Press from 1622 to the Present Day.* Westport, CT: Greenwood Press Publishers.

Prickett, Stephen. 1970. *Coleridge and Wordsworth: The Poetry of Growth.* Cambridge: Cambridge UP.

Woodring, Carl. 1970. *Politics in English Romantic Poetry.* Cambridge, MA: Harvard UP.

Abrams, M. H. 1971. *Natural Supernaturalism: Tradition and Revolution in Romantic Literature.* New York: W. W. Norton and Co., Inc.

Adams, Hazard. 1971. *Critical Theory Since Plato.* New York: Harcourt Brace Jovanovich, Inc.

Bloom, Harold. 1971. *The Ringers in the Tower: Studies in the Romantic Tradition.* Chicago and London: U of Chicago P.

——. 1971. *The Visionary Company: A Reading of Romantic Poetry.* Revised and Enlarged Edition. Ithaca and London: Cornell UP.

McGhee, Richard. 1971. "'And Earth and Stars Composed a Universal Heaven': A View of Wordsworth's Later Poetry." *Studies in English Literature.* 11.4 (Autumn): 641–57.

Onorato, Richard. 1971. *The Character of the Poet: Wordsworth in The Prelude.* Princeton: Princeton UP.

Parrish, Stephen. 1971. *The Art of the Lyrical Ballads.* Cambridge, MA: Harvard UP.

Maclean, Catharine Macdonald. 1972. *Dorothy and William Wordsworth.* New York: Octagon Books.

Sheats, Paul. 1972. *The Making of Wordsworth's Poetry, 1785–1798.* Cambridge, MA: Harvard UP.

Emerson, Ralph Waldo. Gillman, William H., editor. 1973. 16 vols. *Journals and Miscellaneous Notebooks of Ralph Waldo Emerson.* Cambridge, MA: Belknap P of Harvard UP.

Kroeber, Karl. 1974. "Home at Grasmere: Ecological Holiness." *PMLA* 89.1 (1974): 132–41.

McConnell, Frank D. 1974. *The Confessional Imagination: A Reading of Wordsworth' "Prelude."* Baltimore: Johns Hopkins UP.

Newman, John Henry. 1974. *Letters and Diaries of John Henry Newman.* Charles Dessain and Thomas Gornall, editors. 31 vols. Oxford: Clarendon.

Wordsworth, William. 1974. *The Prose Works of William Wordsworth.* W. J. B. Owen and Jane Worthington Smyser, editors. 3 vols. Oxford: Clarendon.

Abrams, M. H. 1975. "Structure and Style in the Greater Romantic Lyric." *From Sensibility to Romanticism: Essays Presented to Frederick A. Pottle.* Frederick W. Hilles and Harold Bloom, editors. New York: Oxford UP. 527–60.

Abrams, M. H., editor. 1975. *English Romantic Poets: Modern Essays in Criticism.* 2nd edition. London, Oxford and New York: Oxford UP.

Bober, Natalie. 1975. *Wordsworth: The Wandering Poet.* New York: Thomas Nelson, Inc.

Reed, Mark. 1975. *Wordsworth: The Chronology of the Middle Years, 1800–1815.* Cambridge, MA: Harvard UP.

Brooks, Cleanth and Robert Penn Warren. 1976. *Understanding Poetry.* 4th edition. New York: Holt, Rinehart, and Winston.

Jordan, John. 1976. *Why the Lyrical Ballads: The Background, Writing, and Character of Wordsworth's 1798 Lyrical Ballads.* Berkeley: U of California P.

Owen, W. J. B. 1976. "Wordsworth's Aesthetics of Landscape." *The Wordsworth Circle.* 7.2 (Spring): 70–82.

Ferguson, Frances. 1977. *Wordsworth: Language as Counter Spirit.* New Haven: Yale UP.

Goldstein, Laurence. 1977. *Ruins and Empire: The Evolution of a Theme in Augustan and Romantic Literature.* Pittsburgh: U of Pittsburgh P.

Beer, John. 1978. *Wordsworth and the Human Heart.* New York: Columbia UP.

Christian, Robert Stone. 1978. *Eclipse and Resurgence: A Study of William Wordsworth's English and American Literary Reputation, 1822–1851.* U of South Carolina Ph.D. Dissertation.

Derrida, Jacques. 1978. "Structure, Sign and Play in the Discourse of the Human Sciences." In *Writing and Difference.* Tr. with Introduction and Additional Notes by Alan Bass. Chicago: U of Chicago P.

Kramer, Laurence. 1978. Review of Frances Ferguson, *Wordsworth: Language as Counter-Spirit*. Yale UP, 1977. *The Wordsworth Circle*. 9.3 (Summer): 226–29.

Roper, Derek. 1978. *Reviewing Before the Edinburgh, 1788–1802*. Newark: U of Delaware P.

Bloom, Harold, Paul DeMan, Jacques Derrida, Geoffrey H. Hartman, J. Hillis Miller. 1979. *Deconstruction and Criticism*. New York: Continuum.

Friedman, Michael. 1979. *The Making of a Tory Humanist: William Wordsworth and the Idea of Community*. New York: Columbia UP.

Gilbert, Sandra and Susan Gubar. 1979. *The Madwoman in the Attic: The Woman Writer and the Nineteenth Century Literary Imagination*. New Haven: Yale UP.

Wordsworth, William. 1979. *The Prelude, 1799, 1805, 1850: Authoritative Texts; Context and Reception; Recent Critical Essays*. Jonathan Wordsworth, M. H. Abrams, Stephen Gill, editors. New York and London: Norton.

Averill, James. 1980. *Wordsworth and the Poetry of Human Suffering*. Ithaca and London: Cornell UP.

Chandler, James. 1980. *Wordsworth's Second Nature: A Study of the Poetry and Politics*. Chicago and London: U of Chicago P.

Davies, Hunter. 1980. *Wordsworth: A Biography*. New York: Athenaeum.

Hodgson, John A. 1980. *Wordsworth's Philosophical Poetry, 1797–1814*. Lincoln: U of Nebraska P.

Devlin, D. D. 1981. *Wordsworth and the Poetry of Epitaphs*. Totowa, NJ: Barnes and Noble Books.

McFarland, Thomas. 1981. *Romanticism and the Forms of Ruin: Wordsworth, Coleridge, and Modalities of Fragmentation*. Princeton: Princeton UP.

Manning, Peter. 1981. Review of John Hodgson, *Wordsworth's Philosophical Poetry, 1797–1814*. Lincoln: U of Nebraska P, 1980. *The Wordsworth Circle*. 12.3 (Summer): 151–53.

Mill, John Stuart. 1981. *Autobiography and Literary Criticism of John Stuart Mill*. John M. Robson and Jack Stillinger, editors. Toronto: U of Toronto P.

Pater, Walter. 1981. "Preface." *Studies in the History of the Renaissance in Aesthetes and Decadents of the 1890's: An Anthology of British Prose and Poetry*. Karl Beckson, editor. Chicago: Academy Chicago Publishers. 280–85.

Simpson, David. 1982. *Wordsworth and the Figurings of the Real*. Atlantic Highlands, NJ: Humanities P.

Watson, J. R. 1982. *Wordsworth's Vital Soul: The Sacred and Profane in Wordsworth's Poetry*. London: Macmillan.

Coleridge, Samuel Taylor. 1983. *The Collected Works of Samuel Taylor Coleridge, Biographia Literaria or Biographical Sketches of My Literary Life and Opinions*. 2 vols. James Engell and W. Jackson Bate, editors. London: Routledge and Kegan Paul; Bollingen Series 75, Princeton UP.

McGann, Jerome. 1983. *The Romantic Ideology: A Critical Investigation*. Chicago and London: U of Chicago P.

De Man, Paul. 1984. "Symbolic Landscape in Wordsworth and Yeats." In *The Rhetoric of Romanticism*. New York: Columbia UP. 125–43.

Johnston, Kenneth R. 1984. *Wordsworth and "The Recluse."* New Haven and London: Yale UP.

Chandler, James. 1984. *Wordsworth's Second Nature: A Study of the Poetry and Politics*. Chicago: U of Chicago P.

Gittings, Robert and Jo Manton. 1985. *Dorothy Wordsworth*. Oxford: Clarendon.

Miller, J. Hillis. 1985. *The Linguistic Moment: From Wordsworth to Stevens*. Princeton: Princeton UP.

Showalter, Elaine, editor. 1985. *The New Feminist Criticism: Essays on Women, Literature, and Theory*. New York: Pantheon.

Spiegelman, Willard. 1985. *Wordsworth's Heroes*. Berkeley and Los Angeles: U of California P.

Adams, Hazard and Leroy Searle, editors. 1986. *Critical Theory Since 1965*. Tallahassee: Florida State UP.

Levinson, Marjorie. 1986. *Wordsworth Great Period Poems*. Cambridge: Cambridge UP.

Weiskel, Thomas. 1986. *The Romantic Sublime: Studies in the Structure and Psychology of Transcendence*. Baltimore: Johns Hopkins UP.

Simpson, David. 1987. *Wordsworth's Historical Imagination: The Poetry of Displacement*. New York: Methuen.

Wordsworth, Jonathan, Michael C. Jaye, Robert Woof, with the assistance of Peter Funnell. 1987. Foreword by M. H. Abrams. *William Wordsworth and the Age of English Romanticism*. New Brunswick and London: Rutgers UP and Grasmere, England: Wordsworth Trust, Dove Cottage.

Barrell, John. 1988. "The Uses of Dorothy: 'The Language of the Sense' in Tintern Abbey." *Poetry, Language, and Politics*. London: St. Martin's P. 137–67.

Gaull, Marilyn. 1988. *Romanticism: The Human Context*. New York and London: W. W. Norton.

Kelley, Theresa M. 1988. *Wordsworth's Revolutionary Aesthetics*. Cambridge: Cambridge UP.

Magnuson, Paul. 1988. *Coleridge and Wordsworth: A Lyrical Dialogue*. Princeton: Princeton UP.

Meisenhelder, Susan Edwards. 1988. *Wordsworth's Informed Reader: Structures of Experience*. Nashville, TN: Vanderbilt UP.

Mellor, Anne. 1988. *Romanticism and Feminism*. Bloomington and Indianapolis: Indiana UP.

Siskin, Clifford. 1988. *The Historicity of Romantic Discourse*. New York: Oxford UP.

Stein, Edwin. 1988. *Wordsworth's Art of Allusion*. University Park: Pennsylvania State UP.

Bewell, Alan. 1989. *Wordsworth and the Enlightenment: Nature, Man, and Society in the Experimental Poetry*. New Haven and London: Yale UP.

Gill, Stephen. 1989. *Wordsworth: A Life*. Oxford: Clarendon.

Levinson, Marjorie. 1989. "The New Historicism: Back to the Future." *Rethinking Historicism: Critical Reading in Romantic History*. Marjorie Levinson, editor. Oxford: Basil Blackwell. 18–63.

Liu, Alan. 1989. *Wordsworth: The Sense of History*. Stanford: Stanford UP.

Talbot, John H. 1989. *The Nature of Aesthetic Experience in Wordsworth*. New York: Peter Lang.

Williams, John. 1989. *Wordsworth: Romantic Poetry and Revolution Politics*. Manchester and New York: Manchester UP.

Coleridge, Samuel Taylor. 1990. *Poems on Various Subjects, 1796*. Oxford and New York: Woodstock Books.

Manning, Peter. 1990. "Wordsworth at St. Bees: Scandals, Sisterhood, and Wordsworth's Later Poetry." In *Reading Romantics: Texts and Contexts*. New York, Oxford: Oxford UP.

Thomas, Gordon K. 1990. "'Glorious Renovation': Wordsworth, Terror, and Paine." *The Wordsworth Circle*. 21.1 (Winter): 3–9.

Barth, J. Robert, S. J. 1991. "The Temporal Imagination in Wordsworth's *Prelude*: Time and the Timeless." *Thought*. 66: 139–50.

——. 1991. "The Role of Humankind in the Poetry of Wordsworth and Coleridge." *The Wordsworth Circle*. 22: 160–65.

Bate, Jonathan. 1991. *Romantic Ecology: Wordsworth and the Environmental Tradition*. London and New York: Routledge.

Gaskell, Ronald. 1991. *Wordsworth's Poem of the Mind: An Essay on "The Prelude."* Edinburgh: Edinburgh UP.

Rylstone, Anne. 1991. *Prophetic Memory in Wordsworth's "Ecclesiastical Sonnets."* Carbondale and Edwardsville: Southern Illinois UP.

Bialostosky, Don. 1992. *Wordsworth, Dialogics, and the Practics of Criticism.* New York and Cambridge: Cambridge UP.

Fry, Paul. 1992. "The Diligence of Desire: Critics On and Around Westminster Bridge." *The Wordsworth Circle.* 23.3 (Summer): 162–64.

Heffernan, James A. 1992. "History and Autobiography: The French Revolution in Wordsworth's *Prelude.*" In *Representing the French Revolution: Literature, Historiography, and Art.* Dartmouth College; Hanover and London: UP of New England: 41–62.

McFarland, Thomas. 1992. *William Wordsworth: Intensity and Achievement.* Oxford: Clarendon.

Downie, J. A. and Thomas N. Corns, editors. 1993. *Telling People What To Think: Early Eighteenth-Century Periodicals from "The Review" to "The Rambler."* London and Portland, OR: Frank Cass & Co., Ltd.

Esterhammer, Angela. 1993. "Wordsworth's 'Ode to Duty': Miltonic Influences and Verbal Performance." *The Wordsworth Circle.* 24.1 (Winter): 34–37.

Haney, David. 1993. *William Wordsworth and the Hermeneutics of Incarnation.* University Park: Penn State UP.

McGhee, Richard. 1993. *Guilty Pleasures: William Wordsworth's Poetry of Psychoanalysis.* New York: The Whiston Publishing Co.

Mellor, Anne. 1993. *Romanticism and Gender.* New York and London: Routledge.

Wilson, Douglas. 1993. *The Romantic Dream: Wordsworth and the Poetics of the Unconscious.* Lincoln: U of Nebraska P.

Page, Judith. 1994. *Wordsworth and the Cultivation of Women.* Berkeley and Los Angeles: U of California P.

Bialostosky, Don. 1995. Rev. of David Haney, *William Wordsworth and the Hermeneutics of Incarnation. The Wordsworth Circle.* 26.4 (Autumn): 183–84.

Fay, Elizabeth. 1995. *Becoming Wordsworthian: A Performative Aesthetics.* Amherst: U of Massachusetts P.

Griffin, Robert. 1995. *Wordsworth's Pope: A Study in Literary Historiography.* Cambridge: Cambridge UP.

O'Donnell, Brennan. 1995. *The Passion of Meter: A Study of Wordsworth's Metrical Art.* Kent, OH: Kent State UP.

Barth, J. Robert, S. J. 1996. "Wordsworth and Hopkins: In Pursuit of Transcendence." *Renascence.* 47: 175–89.

Easterlin, Nancy. 1996. *Wordsworth and the Question of "Romantic Religion."* Cranbury, NJ: Associated UP.

Williams, John. 1996. *William Wordsworth: A Literary Life.* New York: St. Martin's P.

Mahoney, John L. 1997. *William Wordsworth: A Poetic Life.* New York: Fordham UP.

McKusick, James. 1997. "Romanticism and Ecology." *The Wordsworth Circle.* 28.3 (Summer): 123–24.

Rieder, John. 1997. *Wordsworth's Counterrevolutionary Turn: Community, Virtue, and Vision in the 1790s.* Newark: U of Delaware P.

Bromwitch, David. 1998. *Disowned by Memory: Wordsworth's Poetry of the 1790s.* Chicago and London: U of Chicago P.

Gill, Stephen. 1998. *Wordsworth and the Victorians.* Oxford: Clarendon.

Grob, Alan. 1998. "William and Dorothy: A Case Study in the Hermeneutics of Disparagement." *Journal of English Literary History.* 65: 187–221.

Johnston, Kenneth R. 1998. *The Hidden Wordsworth: Poet, Lover, Rebel, Spy.* New York, London: W. W. Norton & Co.

Kroeber, Karl. 1998. "The Presence of Absences: Were the Other Two Wedding Guests William Wordsworth and Fletcher Christian?" *The Wordsworth Circle.* 29.1(Winter): 3–9.

Ryan, Robert. 1998. *The Romantic Reformation: Religious Politics in English Literature, 1789–1824.* Cambridge: Cambridge UP.

Lee, Hermione. 1999. Review of Kenneth Johnston, *The Hidden Wordsworth: Poet, Lover, Rebel, Spy.* New York: Norton, 1999. New York Times Book Review. (May 2): 14–15.

Barth, J. Robert, S.J. 2000. "'The Feeding Source': Imagination and Transcendence in *The Prelude.*" *The Wordsworth Circle.* 30.1 (Winter 2000): 26–31.

Index

French Revolution, 1–2, 9–10, 25, 84, 96, 98, 103, 108, 109, 125, 130
Freud, Sigmund, 132–33
Friedman, Michael, 106–107, 153
Fruman, Norman, 134
Fry, Paul, 95, 156
Frye, Northrop, 90

Garrod, H. W., 46, 77, 147
Gaskell, Ronald, 127–28, 155
Gaull, Marilyn, xv, xvi, 85, 88, 154
Gifford, William, xv, 18–19, 148
Gilbert, Sandra, 91, 153
Gill, Stephen, xvii, 31, 35, 36, 37, 49, 50, 155, 157, 161
Gilpin, William, 83
Gittings, Robert, 48, 154
Godwin, William, 109, 120
Goethe, Johann Wolfgang von, 80
Goldsmith, Oliver, xiv, 18
Golden Decade (1797–1807): regarded by many as Wordsworth's best years, 109–112
Goldstein, Laurence, 113, 152
Graff, Gerald, 121
Gravil, Richard, 85
Gray, Thomas, 136
Griffin, Robert, 119, 156
Griffiths, Ralph, xiv, 12
Griggs, Earl Leslie, 61
Grob, Alan, 90, 103–105, 157
Gubar, Susan, 91, 153

Haney, David, 135–36, 156
Harper, George, 46, 47, 75, 147
Harshbarger, Scott, 85
Hartley, David, 109
Hartman, Geoffrey, 60, 64, 67, 79, 81–82, 85, 92, 95, 98, 130, 149
Haven, Richard, 85
Havens, Raymond, 56, 82, 148
Hayden, John, xv-xvi, 150

Hazlitt, William, xvi; the Lake poets and the French Revolution, 9–10; the *Lyrical Ballads* and the spirit of the age, Wordsworth's egotism, praise and criticism of *The Excursion*, 19–21, 75, 147
Heath, William, 73–74, 151
Heffernan, James, 82–83, 100, 103, 150, 156
High Romantic Criticism and Theory, 79–83, 95, 98
Hilles, Frederick, 65, 156
Hirsch, E. D., Jr., 65–66, 116, 149
Hodgson, John, 123, 153
Holderlin, Friedrich, 80
Holcroft, Thomas, 2, 143
Home, Henry (Lord Kames), 116
Hopkins, Gerard Manley, 125–26
Hood, Edwin Paxton, 45, 146
Hulme, T. E., 57, 147
Hunt, Bishop, 85
Hunt, John, xvi
Hunt, Leigh, xvi
Hutcheson, Francis, 116
Hurd, Harold, xiv, 151
Hutchinson, Mary, 26, 49, 103, 120, 130
Hutchinson, Thomas, 46

James, D. G., 56–57, 148
James, William, 124
Jaye, Michael, 83, 158
Jeffrey, Francis, xv, 10, 11, 13–14, 17, 19, 23–24, 143, 144, 145
Johnson, Samuel, xiv
Johnston, Kenneth, 1, 4, 40, 49, 85, 127, 138, 154, 157
Jones, Robert, 1
Jones, John, 109–110, 149
Jordan, John, 4, 76, 152

Keats, John, xiv, 40, 114